# Family and Succession Law
# in England and Wales

# Family and Succession Law in England and Wales

### Six Edition

**Rebecca Probert**
**Maebh Harding**

This book was originally published as a monograph in the International Encyclopaedia of Laws/Family and Succession Law.

Founding Editor: Roger Blanpain
General Editor: Frank Hendrickx
Volume Editor: Walter Pintens

*Published by:*
Kluwer Law International B.V.
PO Box 316
2400 AH Alphen aan den Rijn
The Netherlands
E-mail: international-sales@wolterskluwer.com
Website: lrus.wolterskluwer.com

*Sold and distributed in North, Central and South America by:*
Wolters Kluwer Legal & Regulatory U.S.
7201 McKinney Circle
Frederick, MD 21704
United States of America
Email: customer.service@wolterskluwer.com

*Sold and distributed in all other countries by:*
Air Business Subscriptions
Rockwood House
Haywards Heath
West Sussex
RH16 3DH
United Kingdom
Email: international-customerservice@wolterskluwer.com

ISBN 978-94-035-0513-8

e-Book: ISBN 978-94-035-0514-5
web-PDF: ISBN 978-94-035-0515-2

# The Authors

Rebecca Probert was born in England in 1973. She studied law at St Anne's College Oxford, graduating in 1994. She then worked in the Family Law and Property Law teams at the Law Commission for England and Wales, and in 1997, gained a master's degree in law from University College, London. Since then she has taught family law and property law at a number of institutions, including the University of Wales, Aberystwyth, the University of Sussex and the University of Warwick. She is currently a Professor in Law at the University of Exeter.

Maebh Harding was born in Ireland in 1983. She obtained a BCL (Law and French Law) from University College, Dublin, in 2005. She held the NUI EJ Phelan Fellowship in International Law at University College, Dublin, from 2006 to 2008. Upon completing her PhD in 2008, she lectured in family and child law at the University of Portsmouth until 2013. She is currently an Associate Professor at the University of Warwick.

**The Authors**

# Table of Contents

**Table of Contents**

**Table of Contents**

**Table of Contents**

## Chapter 6. Parental Responsibility ..... 133

## Chapter 7. Adoption and Its Alternatives ..... 145

## Chapter 8. Child Arrangements Orders   155

**Table of Contents**

**Table of Contents**

**Table of Contents**

# List of Abbreviations

| | |
|---|---|
| A.C. | Law Reports, Appeal Cases |
| A-G | Attorney General |
| All E.R. | All England Reports |
| Art./Arts | Article/Articles |
| C.L. | Current Law Monthly Digest |
| cf. | compare with |
| Ch. | Chapter |
| Co | Company |
| C.N. (N.S.) | Common Bench Reports (New Series) |
| e.g. | for example |
| E.G. | Estates Gazette |
| E.H.R.R. | European Human Rights Reports |
| E.R. | English Reports |
| ed. | Edition |
| etc. | *et cetera* |
| EWCA Civ | Court of Appeal (Civil Division) |
| EWHC (Ch) | England and Wales High Court (Chancery Division) |
| EWHC (COP) | England and Wales High Court (Court of Protection) |
| EWHC (Fam) | England and Wales High Court (Family Division) |
| F.C.R. | Family Court Reporter |
| F.L.R. | Family Law Reports |
| Fam. | *Family Law* |
| H.L.C. | Clark & Finnelly's House of Lords' Reports |
| H.L.R. | Housing Law Reports |
| i.e. | *id est* |
| I.R. | Irish Reports |
| *ibid.* | *Ibidem* |
| J. | Justice (High Court) |
| K.B. | Law Reports, King's Bench |
| L.J. | Lord (or Lady) Justice |

## List of Abbreviations

| | |
|---|---|
| L.J. | Law Journal Newspaper |
| L.J.P. | Law Journal Reports, Probate, Divorce and Admiralty Division |
| L.R.H.L. | Law Reports, English and Irish Appeals |
| L.S.G. | Law Society Gazette |
| L.T. | Law Times |
| M.R. | Master of the Rolls |
| n. | Note |
| No. | Number |
| P. | President |
| P. | Law Reports, Probate |
| P.D. | Law Reports, Probate, Divorce and Admiralty Division |
| para./paras | paragraph/paragraphs |
| Q.B. | Law Reports, Queen's Bench |
| R | *Rex or Regina* |
| r. | Rule |
| s./ss | section/sections |
| S.I. | Statutory Instrument |
| S.J. | Solicitors' Journal |
| Sch. | Schedule |
| T.L.R. | Times Law Reports |
| UKFTT (TC) | United Kingdom First-tier Tribunal (Tax Chamber) |
| UKHL | United Kingdom House of Lords |
| UKSC | United Kingdom Supreme Court |
| W.L.R. | Weekly Law Reports |
| W.N. | Weekly Notes of Cases |
| W.T.L.R. | Wills & Trusts Law Reports |

# General Introduction

§1. General Background of the Country (Demographic Data)

## I.  Introduction

*1.* Geographically, England and Wales together form the greater part of Great Britain. England is larger and more populous than its western neighbour, covering an area of 130,281 square kilometres with a population density of 424 persons per square kilometre; Wales, by contrast, covers only 20,732 square kilometres and has a much smaller population density of 150 persons per square kilometre.[1]

*2.* Politically, England and Wales form part of the larger political unit of the United Kingdom of Great Britain and Northern Island. Its other constituent parts – Scotland and Northern Ireland – have their own distinct legal systems and therefore merit separate treatment. By contrast, from the early sixteenth century to the end of the twentieth, England and Wales existed as a single legal jurisdiction. Since 1998, Wales has had its own elected law-making body, the National Assembly for Wales. Initially, the Assembly did not have the power to pass primary legislation, but the Government of Wales Act 2006 allows it to pass legislation on a wide range of matters, including housing, health and education.[2] There is as yet no legislative body exclusive to England.

For the moment, the United Kingdom (UK) is also part of the European Union (EU), but its decision to leave is posing new and difficult questions for the management of cross-border family issues.

## II.  Demography

*3.* In 2016, the population of England comprised of over 55 million persons.[3] The southeast of the country is the most heavily populated, with around one-quarter

---

1. Calculated from the population estimates provided by the Office for National Statistics (ONS): *Population Estimates for UK, England and Wales, Scotland and Northern Ireland: mid 2016* (ONS, June 2017).
2. *Government of Wales Act* 2006, Pt. 4 and Sch. 7, as amended by The National Assembly for Wales (Legislative Competence) (Amendment of Sch. 7 to the Government of Wales Act 2006) Order 2010, S.I. 2010/2968).
3. ONS, *Population Estimates for UK, England and Wales, Scotland and Northern Ireland: mid 2016* (ONS, June 2017).

of the population occupying less than one-tenth of the land area. Within Wales, the population of just over 3 million persons is concentrated in the southern part of the country, where the major cities – including its capital, Cardiff – are located.

*4.* According to the 2011 census, the majority of those living in England and Wales can be described as White British (83% in England and 93% in Wales). There is, however, a growing ethnic minority community. Of the total population, almost 6% is of Asian origin, and just under 3% is Black Caribbean or Black African, and 0.8% Chinese. Those of mixed ethnic origin account for a small but growing proportion, currently just under 2%.[4] These different ethnic minority communities are not evenly spread across England and Wales but tend to concentrate in large cities, particularly London and conurbations in the East and West Midlands. To illustrate this disparity, in three local authorities within London (Brent, Westminster, and Newham), the proportion of the population born outside the UK is over 50%, while in Blaenau Gwent in Wales, it is only 1.5%.

*5.* The same pattern is echoed in the statistics relating to religious belief. The majority of the population (59.3%) identified themselves as Christian in the 2011 census, although it should be noted that this bears little correlation to the figures for regular church attendance. A total of 25% described themselves as having no religion, and 7% chose not to answer the question. A further 4.8% identified as Muslim, 1.5% as Hindu, 0.5% as Jewish and 0.4% as Buddhist. Again, religious affiliation varied by location, with over a fifth of the population of London identifying with a non-Christian religion.[5]

*6.* England and Wales both have ageing populations: in the 2011 census the proportion of persons recorded as being over the age of 65 had reached an unprecedented 16.4%, with 430,000 individuals having passed their ninetieth birthday.[6] This was due to both increasing life expectancy and a fall in the birth rate, and these trends are projected to continue. Today, a boy born in England can expect to live to the age of 79.5 (78.5 in Wales); the life expectancy rate for girls is still higher, being over 83 years for those in England and 82 for those in Wales; these averages do, however, mask considerable regional variations. Men who have reached the age of 65 can expect to live for another eighteen years, women for more than twenty.[7]

*7.* In the past few decades, the trend has been for women to have fewer children, and at a later age: in 2016, the average age of women giving birth was 30.4 years and the total fertility rate was just 1.81 children per woman.[8] There has, however, been a slight upturn in fertility rates in the past few years, largely due to the

---

4. ONS, *2011 Census: Key Statistics and Quick Statistics for Local Authorities in the United Kingdom* (July 2013).
5. ONS, 'Religion in England and Wales 2011' (December 2012).
6. ONS, '2011 Census – Population and Household Estimates for England and Wales, March 2011' (July 2012).
7. ONS, 'Life Expectancy at Birth and at Age 65 by Local Areas in England and Wales: 2012 to 2014' (November 2015).
8. ONS, 'Births in England and Wales, 2016' (July 2017).

increase of the number of women of childbearing age within the population, rather than an overall increase in the average number of children born to any one woman.

8. The family forms into which children are born have changed dramatically over the past few decades. In 2016, 48% of births occurred outside marriage or civil partnership.[9] The majority of these children were born to cohabiting couples, or at least one can infer so from the fact that most were jointly registered by a couple who gave the same address. But solo parenting, separation and divorce mean that almost one-quarter of children are living in a lone-parent household, usually with their mother. High rates of repartnering mean that many children acquire new parent-figures. Despite high rates of divorce and family breakdown, it is still the case that the majority of children live with both natural parents and will do so throughout their childhood.

9. Trends in divorce over the past few decades reflect both social change and the liberalization of divorce law. The number of divorces began to rise steeply in the 1960s, and increased still faster in the wake of the Divorce Reform Act 1969, which had widened the range of circumstances in which a divorce could be obtained and provided many who would otherwise have been unable to obtain a divorce with a means of legally terminating a marriage where the parties had already been separated for many years. The numbers resorting to divorce continued to rise through the 1970s and 1980s, peaking at just over 180,000 (for the UK as a whole) in 1993. Since then there has been a consistent fall in both the number and rate of divorces; in 2016, there were 107,221 divorces in England and Wales, 106,959 between opposite-sex couples and 112 between same-sex couples. This fall in the overall number of divorces is not simply attributable to a decline in the marital population, since the divorce rate – which is calculated by reference to the married population – has also fallen since 1993 and in 2016 stood at 8.9 divorcing persons per 1,000 married persons of the opposite sex. The average (mean) age at divorce has also risen, to 46.1 years for men and 43.7 years for women, reflecting both the rising age at first marriage (now over 30 years for both men and women) and the increasing duration of those marriages that do end in divorce (12 years in 2016, up from 10.5 years in 1999).[10]

10. A further significant change relates to the number of adults who are choosing not to marry at all. In 1979, 74% of women aged between 18 years and 49 years were married; by the beginning of the twenty-first century, this had fallen to under half, although there are still around 250,000 marriages celebrated in England and Wales each year.[11] The decline in the popularity of marriage is in part explained by the increasing popularity of cohabitation: it is now estimated that there are around 3.1 million opposite-sex cohabitants and 101,000 same-sex cohabitants.[12] For many, cohabitation is a short-term option while a couple decides whether or not they are

9. *Ibid.*
10. ONS, 'Divorces in England and Wales, 2016' (October 2017).
11. ONS, 'Marriages in England and Wales, 2014' (March 2017).
12. ONS, 'Families and Households, 2017' (November 2017).

suited. One study of those who were cohabiting in 1991 found that ten years later 39% had separated, 39% had married their partner and the remaining 22% were still cohabiting.[13] However, cohabiting couples are just as likely to have dependent children as their married counterparts – in 2017, 38% of families headed by married or cohabiting couples contained dependent children.[14]

*11.* A final significant change relates to the recognition of same-sex relationships. December 2005 saw the implementation of the Civil Partnership Act 2004,[15] which allowed same-sex couples to register a civil partnership and thereby acquire virtually the same rights and responsibilities as married couples. By the end of 2014, a total of 62,621 civil partnerships had been registered in England and Wales.[16] However, the number of new civil partnerships has fallen following the passage of the Marriage (Same Sex Couples) Act 2013: in 2016 there were just 890 new civil partnerships formed in England and Wales.[17] By contrast, 4,850 same-sex couples entered into marriages in England and Wales in 2014, after the 2013 Act came into force on 29 March 2014.[18] Those who were already in a civil partnership had to wait until 10 December 2014 to convert their partnership into a marriage, if they so wished, and 2,411 chose to do so in the final weeks of 2014.[19] There were slightly more marriages involving female couples than male couples,[20] and rather more civil partnerships involving male couples than female couples.[21]

§2. HISTORICAL BACKGROUND OF FAMILY AND SUCCESSION LAW[22]

**I. Family Law**

*12.* The year 1857 marks a key turning point in the history of family law: indeed, it has been seen as marking the beginning of family law in its modern sense.[23] Prior to that date, much of what we now consider 'family law' was under the jurisdiction of the ecclesiastical courts, apart from a brief period in the mid-seventeenth century when they were temporarily abolished during the English Commonwealth. The rules governing the celebration of marriage had been put on a statutory basis in 1753, but the ecclesiastical courts continued to enjoy the right to decide whether or not a marriage had been validly celebrated, and the issue of capacity to marry was also determined by the canon law. Divorce – in its modern sense of terminating an

---

13. B. Wilson & R. Stuchbury, *Do Partnerships Last? Comparing Marriage and Cohabitation Using Longitudinal Census Data*, 139 Population Trends 37, 46 (2010).
14. ONS, 'Families and Households, 2017' (November 2017).
15. *See* Part II, Ch. 2.
16. ONS, 'Civil Partnerships in the UK, 2012' (October 2013).
17. ONS, 'Civil Partnerships in England and Wales, 2016' (September 2017).
18. ONS, 'Marriages in England and Wales: 2014' (March 2017).
19. *Ibid.*
20. *Ibid.*
21. ONS, 'Civil Partnerships in England and Wales: 2016' (September 2017).
22. The most comprehensive account of the making of English family law is provided by S. Cretney, *Family Law in the Twentieth Century: A History* (Oxford U. Press 2003).
23. *See*, e.g., R.H. Graveson & F.R. Crane, *A Century of Family Law* (Sweet & Maxwell 1957).

existing marriage and freeing the parties to remarry – was not then available, save by the costly process of a private Act of Parliament.[24] The ecclesiastical courts could, however, grant a divorce *a mensa et thoro*, freeing a spouse from the obligation to cohabit with an adulterous or cruel spouse. In the absence of a good reason for separation, the obligation to cohabit would be enforced through a decree of restitution of conjugal rights. If a separation was granted, financial provision for the wife would be ordered, the amount depending on whether she was the innocent or guilty party.

*13.* In 1857, jurisdiction over such matters was transferred from the ecclesiastical courts to the new Court for Divorce and Matrimonial Causes.[25] It had the power to determine the validity of a marriage – although the principles on which such decisions were made remained substantially the same.[26] More fundamentally, this new court had the power to grant a divorce (or a judicial separation, the successor to the divorce *a mensa et thoro*). The actual principles on which a divorce or judicial separation could be granted were little altered by the new legislation. A husband had to show that his wife had committed adultery, as had been necessary for Parliament to pass an Act dissolving the marriage.[27] A wife, by contrast, had to prove not only that her husband had committed adultery but also that this had been 'aggravated' either by his cruelty, by the incestuous nature of the adultery, by his committing the crime of bigamy or rape, or by his deserting the wife for a period exceeding two years; alternatively, she could seek to establish that he had committed sodomy or bestiality.[28] Judicial separations could be granted to either party upon evidence of adultery, cruelty or desertion without cause for a period of two years or more.[29] But, despite such continuities in legal principle, the 1857 Act had a profound impact by making divorce available to a much wider range of persons.[30] It would be too much to say that it made divorce accessible to everyone – the cost was still out of the reach of many – and the few hundred petitions received by the court in the first year of its operation seem minimal by modern standards. Yet it was, and remains, the largest proportionate increase in divorce in England and Wales.

The granting of a divorce or judicial separation meant that other, ancillary matters had to be decided. The 1857 Act provided that a wife separated from her husband by virtue of a judicial separation should be considered a *feme sole* for the purpose of being able to acquire and own property in her own right.[31] It also gave the court the power to order the husband to provide maintenance for his former wife

---

24. S. Wolfram, *Divorce in England 1700–1857*, 5 Oxford J. Leg. Stud. 155 (1985).
25. *Matrimonial Causes Act* 1857, s. 6.
26. *Ibid.*, s. 22.
27. *Ibid.*, s. 27.
28. *Ibid.*, s. 27.
29. *Ibid.*, s. 16.
30. G. Savage, *The Operation of the 1857 Divorce Act, 1860–1910: A Research Note*, 16 J. Social History 103 (1982).
31. *Matrimonial Causes Act* 1857, s. 25.

(whether or not he was the party seeking the divorce), and to order that any property to which a guilty wife was entitled should be settled for the benefit of the husband or the children.[32] And, of course, there was also the question as to where the children should live. Prior to the 1857 Act, 'there were few circumstances in which any court would interfere with a father's custody of his infant children'.[33] The Custody of Infants Act 1839 had allowed a mother to petition for access to children under the age of 7 years – although a mother who had committed adultery was debarred from even this limited right. The 1857 Act allowed the court to make ancillary orders regulating the custody of the parties' children up to the age of 21 years, in such terms as it deemed 'just and proper'.[34]

*14.* Change came slowly and gradually. Wives acquired the right to divorce husbands on the ground of adultery alone under the Matrimonial Causes Act 1923, and new grounds for divorce and nullity were added by the Matrimonial Causes Act 1937. The rule that control and ownership of a wife's property vested in the husband upon marriage was whittled away. First, the Married Women's Property Act 1870 provided that a married woman's earnings, as well as certain investments and inheritances, would constitute her separate property. Then, twelve years later, the Married Women's Property Act 1882 provided that any property owned by a wife before marriage or acquired thereafter would be her separate property. Other aspects of the doctrine of unity were also abolished by legislation.[35] With regard to children, the Custody of Infants Act 1873 provided that a mother (adulterous or not) could be awarded custody of a child up to the age of 16 years (extended to 21 years by the Guardianship of Infants Act 1886); it was broader in scope than the 1857 Act as such orders could be made independently of proceedings for divorce, separation or nullity. The rights of a married mother were enhanced still further by the Guardianship of Infants Act 1925, although complete equality between spouses in relation to their children was not achieved until much later.

*15.* More substantial reforms did not occur until the late 1960s and early 1970s. The Divorce Reform Act 1969 made the irretrievable breakdown of marriage the sole ground for divorce, and allowed divorce by consent, and divorce after a period of separation, for the first time.[36] The Nullity of Marriage Act 1971 finally codified the law governing the circumstances in which a marriage would be void or voidable.[37] And the Matrimonial Proceedings and Property Act 1970 gave the courts far wider powers to reallocate assets when a marriage ended.[38] All three were subsequently consolidated in the Matrimonial Causes Act 1973. The Guardianship of Infants Act 1973 finally conferred equal rights and authority on mothers and

---

32. *Ibid.*, s. 45.
33. P.H. Pettit, *A Century of Family Law* 56–87 (R.H. Graveson & F.R. Crane eds, Sweet & Maxwell 1957).
34. *Matrimonial Causes Act* 1857, s. 35.
35. *See*, e.g., *Law Reform (Married Women and Tortfeasors) Act* 1935; *Law Reform (Husband and Wife) Act* 1962.
36. *See* Part II, Ch. 3.
37. *See* Part II, Ch. 1.
38. *See* Part III, Ch. 2.

fathers,[39] and the Law Reform (Miscellaneous Provisions) Act 1970 swept away a whole raft of legal actions – such as the right to claim damages for breach of a promise of marriage or for the adultery of a spouse – that had become increasingly ill-suited to the norms of a modern system of family law.

*16.* In recent years, family law has had to grapple with an increasingly diverse range of situations. The development of assisted reproductive techniques has required the Parliament to devise legal rules for the regulation and legal conse-quences of such methods (*see*, e.g., the Human Fertilization and Embryology Acts of 1990 and 2008).[40] The increasing recognition of gender identity dysphoria encouraged the passage of the Gender Recognition Act 2004.[41] The desire to afford legal recognition to same-sex couples led first to the Civil Partnerships Act 2004,[42] and then to the Marriage (Same-Sex Couples) Act 2013. The desire of opposite-sex couples for an alternative to marriage has led one couple to challenge the fact that a civil partnership is not available to them. Their case is currently before the Supreme Court.

## II. Succession Law

*17.* The year 1857 was also a key year in the history of succession law. Again, it marked a transfer of jurisdiction from the ecclesiastical court, this time to a new Court of Probate.[43] Previously the ecclesiastical courts had jurisdiction over the pro-bate of wills and the grant of letters of administration for the estates of those who died without making a will. The Court of Probate Act 1857 established a Principal Probate Registry and forty District Probate Registries for England and Wales. The histories of family law and succession law coincided once again in 1873, when the Judicature Act of that year reformed the existing court system and created a new court of Probate, Divorce, and Admiralty Division – a grouping summed up by one commentator as 'wills, wives, and wrecks'.

*18.* Some reforms had already been put into effect by 1857. The Wills Act 1837 required that all wills be made in writing,[44] thereby putting an end to the possibility of making a nuncupative will. But the transmission of property on death other than by will remained governed by a bewildering array of rules; the devolution of real property was determined by the common law rules of descent, with limited rights for any surviving husband or wife of the deceased, while personal property was sub-ject to an entirely different set of rules under the Statute of Distributions 1670. Leg-islation passed in 1925 provided a uniform set of rules for both real and personal

---

39. *See* further Part II, Ch. 6.
40. *See* Part II, Ch. 5.
41. *See* Part II, Ch. 1.
42. *See* Part II, Ch. 2.
43. *Court of Probate Act* 1857.
44. *See* Part IV, Ch. 2.

property,[45] and improved the position of the surviving spouse, who now stood to inherit the bulk of the estate upon intestacy.[46]

*19.* It is sometimes said that freedom of testation is a basic principle of English law. Yet it was only for a relatively brief period that individuals enjoyed the freedom to leave their property to whomsoever they chose without restriction or fear of later interference. It was not until 1833 that a husband was able to bar his wife's right to dower by will, and restrictions on the disposal of personal property remained in many parts of the country until 1856.[47] And in 1938, the Inheritance (Family Provision) Act was passed, which allowed a court to make provision for certain classes of persons on the basis that the testator had failed to make reasonable provision for them. The categories of those who could make an application for such provision were initially limited to the surviving spouse, an unmarried or disabled daughter, and a minor or disabled son. Changes in family form over the course of the century have led to new categories being added, including stepchildren who have been treated as children of the family, cohabitants and, most recently, civil partners.[48]

## §3. SOURCES OF FAMILY AND SUCCESSION LAW

### I. Constitution

*20.* England and Wales is unusual in having no written Constitution. The UK Parliament is competent to legislate on all aspects of family and succession law for both England and Wales.

### II. Legislation

#### A. *Family Law*

*21.* Family law in England and Wales is scattered through numerous statutes rather than being contained in a single code. This said, certain key pieces of legislation can be identified. The Matrimonial Causes Act 1973 sets out the law on eligibility to marry (and the circumstances in which a marriage may be void or voidable), divorce, and the reallocation of property upon divorce. The Children Act 1989 deals with such issues as parental responsibility, the resolution of disputes between parents upon divorce or separation, and the responsibilities and roles of local authorities when children are in need of protection. However, it falls far short of a comprehensive code dealing with all the law relating to children. Issues of legal

---

45. *Law of Property Act* 1925.
46. *Administration of Estates Act* 1925. *See* Part IV, Ch. 1.
47. *See* A.G. Guest, *Family Provision and the Legitima Portio*, 73 L. Q. Rev. 74 (1957).
48. *See* Part IV, Ch. 3.

parentage are dealt with either by common law rules or (in cases of assisted repro-duction) by the Human Fertilization and Embryology Act 2008; the payment of child support by absent parents is covered by the Child Support Act 1991, as amended by a number of subsequent statutes, most recently the Child Maintenance and Other Payments Act 2008; and adoption is regulated by the Adoption and Chil-dren Act 2002.

Other statutes deal with specific legal issues. The Marriage Act 1949 is devoted to the formalities necessary for a valid marriage (although additional provision is made for specific situations by the Marriage (Registrar General's License) Act 1970) while Part IV of the Family Law Act 1996 addresses the problem of domestic violence. The Gender Recognition Act 2004 provided a mechanism for a person with gender identity dysphoria to be recognized as a member of the opposite gen-der, while the Civil Partnership Act 2004 created a new form of relationship for same-sex couples and the Marriage (Same-Sex Couples) Act 2013 makes provision for same-sex couples to marry.

22. Some areas of family law are not governed by statute at all. Notable examples include the ownership of assets during marriage and the division of assets when a cohabiting relationship breaks down, both of which are governed by gen-erally applicable principles of property law. It should also be noted that much leg-islation in the area of family is discretionary in form; it does not dictate what the result in a particular situation should be, but sets out the basic principles or factors that should guide a judge in making a decision.

*B. Succession Law*

23. In the context of succession law, the three key pieces of legislation are the Wills Act 1837 (which sets out the conditions for making a will), the Administra-tion of Estates Act 1925 (which provides, *inter alia*, how the estate should be divided if the deceased died without making a will), and the Inheritance (Provision of Family and Dependants) Act 1975 (which allows certain categories of persons to claim provision from the estate of the deceased on the basis that the disposal of the estate did not make reasonable financial provision for them). The Inheritance and Trustees' Powers Act 2014 has made a number of changes to the latter two pieces of legislation.

### III. Treaties

24. The UK is a signatory to a number of international instruments. Three dif-ferent types of international instruments must be distinguished: those that are directly effective without the need for legislation, those that have been incorporated into the law of England and Wales by legislative action, and those that do not form part of domestic law and are of persuasive effect only.

25. The EU has had a significant impact on English domestic family law, enacting Regulations that are directly applicable in the domestic law of England and Wales subject to an opt-out to limit the application of EU measures relating to judicial cooperation in civil law matters.[49] The EU's first foray into the field of family law was Council Regulation (EC) No. 1347/2000 of 29 May 2000 on Jurisdiction and the Recognition and Enforcement of Judgments in Matrimonial Matters and in Matters of Parental responsibility for Children of Both Spouses (Brussels II), which introduced both uniform standards for jurisdiction in these areas among Member States and provided for the recognition and enforcement by Member States of judgments made in another Member State. It was replaced in 2005 by Council Regulation (EC) No. 2201/2003 of 27 November 2003 concerning Jurisdiction and the Recognition and Enforcement of Judgments in Matrimonial Matters and in Matters of Parental responsibility (Brussels II Revised), which went further than its predecessor in extending the scope of the regulation to all judgments relating to parental responsibility, and not just to those relating to children of married parents.

In 2005, the EU issued a Green Paper on the applicable law and jurisdiction in divorce matters which led to the adoption of Council Regulation (EU) No. 1259/2010 implementing enhanced cooperation in the area of the law applicable to divorce and legal separation (Rome III). This measure extended the scope of EU regulation from issues of jurisdiction and recognition of foreign judgments to determining the rules of applicable law to be applied by national courts. Under Article 15 of the Maintenance Regulation, which came into force in 2011, applicable law is determined by reference to the Hague Protocol on the Law Applicable to Maintenance Obligations. Since then Council Regulation (EU) 2016/1103 and Council Regulation (EU) 2016/1104 have implemented measures of enhanced cooperation relating to the property consequences of marriage and registered partnerships including provisions for applicable law.

The UK made a policy decision to opt out of all proposed EU regulations relating to applicable law in family matters. The Government was concerned that under such provisions the applicable law to determine sensitive family matters could be from any country or legal tradition.[50] The courts of England and Wales simply do not apply foreign law in family law cases as law, although the fact that a case has a connection to a foreign system of law may be given evidential weight when exercising judicial discretion. While the UK has implemented the Maintenance Regulation,[51] it has not adopted the Hague Protocol and so the applicable law aspects of this regulation outlined in Article 15 are not binding on the courts of England and Wales. The courts continue to apply domestic law as the *lex fori* when granting a divorce and when determining the financial and property consequences of divorce or dissolution of same-sex partnership in all cases heard in the jurisdiction.[52]

However, the UK is bound by the EU regulation on the mutual recognition of protection measures in civil matters (Regulation (EU) No. 606/2013). This regulation

---

49. Protocol No. 4 1997 annexed by the Treaty of Amsterdam to the EC Treaty. This protocol is maintained by Protocol No. 1 annexed to the Treaty of Lisbon [2007] C306/165.
50. European Scrutiny Committee *Twenty-Ninth Report* (HC 2010-12, 428-xxvii) [6.15].
51. Civil Jurisdiction and Judgments (Maintenance) Regulations 2011, S.I. 2011/1484.
52. *See*, e.g., *Radmacher v. Granatino* [2010] UKSC 42.

ensures that decisions protecting a person from physical or psychological harm from a named person causing risk made in one Member State are recognized and enforced in another Member State as well.[53]

The UK's decision to leave the European Union, 'Brexit', raises a number of complicated issues for the English courts when dealing with cross-border family law. While the various different Hague Conventions[54] provide an alternative framework for the recognition and enforcement of judgments relating to children, and mechanisms to return children following child abduction,[55] the legal infrastructure to deal with cross-border divorces is sorely lacking.[56] Whether or not a divorce or court decision relating to maintenance granted by an EU Member State will be recognized in the UK will be determined by English conflict of law rules. At the time of writing, it was proposed that existing EU regulations will become part of English law[57] upon 'Brexit', so the English courts may continue to use the rules laid out in Brussels II Revised and the Maintenance Regulation. However, if the UK leaves the EU without putting alternative legal provisions in place, the issue of whether or not English divorce decrees, orders relating to maintenance and protective orders will be recognized in other EU Member States will be left up to the individual national rules of each EU Member State.

The impact of the EU on the law of succession has been rather more limited to date. The 1968 Brussels Convention on Jurisdiction and Enforcement of Judgments in Civil and Commercial Matters expressly excluded wills and succession from its scope, as did Council Regulation (EC) No. 44/2001 of 22 December 2000 on Jurisdiction and the Recognition and Enforcement of Judgments in Civil and Commercial Matters that replaced it. In 2005, the EU issued a Green Paper on the conflict of laws in matters of succession, suggesting the need for harmonization,[58] and in 2015 the provision of Regulation (EU) No. 650/2012 (Brussels IV) came into effect. The UK government decided not to opt into the regulation[59] but UK nationals who hold assets in EU Member States who are signed up to the regulation may continue to be affected by the Regulation, even after 'Brexit'.

*26.* The European Convention for the Protection of Human Rights and Fundamental Freedoms falls into the second category of international instruments, having been incorporated into domestic law by the Human Rights Act 1998. Since the Act came into force in 2000 it has had a profound effect on all areas of law. Courts are

---

53. Denmark is not bound by the Regulation.
54. That is The Hague Convention on the Civil Aspects of International Child Abduction 1980, the Hague Convention on Protection of Children and Cooperation in Respect of Intercountry Adoption 1993, and the Hague Convention on the Protection of Children 1996.
55. *See*, P Beaumont, *Private International Law Concerning Children in the UK after Brexit: Comparing Hague Treaty Law with EU Regulations*, (2017) 29 Child and Family Law Quarterly 213–232.
56. *See*, J Carruthers and E Crawford, *Divorcing Europe: Reflections from a Scottish Perspective on the Implications of Brexit for Cross Border Divorce Proceedings'* (2017) 29 Child and Family Law Quarterly 233–252.
57. European Union (Withdrawal) Bill 2017–2019.
58. European Commission, *Green Paper – Succession and Wills*, COM (2005), 65.
59. Ireland and Denmark are not part of the regulation.

now required to interpret legislation in a way that is compatible with the Convention, even if this was not the original intention of Parliament.[60] If the change that would be required to ensure compatibility falls outside the legitimate scope of 'interpretation', the court is required to issue a declaration of incompatibility.[61]

Other examples of conventions that have been incorporated into domestic law include the Hague Convention on the Civil Aspects of International Child Abduction 1980 (incorporated by the Child Abduction and Custody Act 1985), the Hague Convention on Protection of Children and Cooperation in Respect of Intercountry Adoption) 1993 (incorporated by the Adoption (Intercountry Aspects) Act 1999), and the 1996 Hague Convention on the Protection of Children (introduced via secondary legislation[62]).[63] These conventions will become the primary legal framework for dealing with cross-border disputes relating to children following 'Brexit'. In the field of succession law, the Wills Act 1963 gave effect to the Hague Convention on the Conflict of Laws Relating to the Form of Testamentary Dispositions 1961.

27. Into the third category fall such international conventions as the United Nations Declaration of Human Rights 1948 and the United Nations Convention on the Rights of the Child (UNCRC) 1989. Such conventions may influence domestic law in two ways: first, there is a degree of political pressure to maintain the standards set out in such conventions – enhanced in the case of the UNCRC by the obligation to make regular reports on the extent to which UK law complies with the standards that it sets. As Baroness Hale has pointed out, 'the spirit [of Article 3 of the UNCRC], if not the precise language, has … been translated into our national law'.[64] The Welsh Assembly has made a stronger commitment to the UNCRC than Westminster creating an express duty for Welsh ministers to pay due regard to the convention when exercising any of their functions.[65] The Children and Young People (Scotland) Act 2014 introduced a similar duty for Scottish Government Ministers. Second, conventions may be used as an interpretive tool by the courts. If a particular legislative provision is capable of two interpretations, one of which would conform to the requirements of a convention and one of which would not, the courts will presume that Parliament intended to legislate in line with its international obligations and will choose the interpretation that best complies with the standards set by the convention.

---

60. *Human Rights Act* 1998, s. 3. *See*, e.g., *Ghaidan v. Godin-Mendoza* [2004] UKHL 30.
61. *Ibid.*, s. 4. *See*, e.g., *Bellinger v. Bellinger* [2003] UKHL 21.
62. Parental Responsibility and Measures for the Protection of Children (International Obligations (England and Wales and Northern Ireland) Regulations 2010, S.I. 2010/1898.
63. For an overview, *see* N. Lowe, *Keeping Pace with International Family Law: Safeguarding the UK Position* [2013] I.F.L. 114.
64. *ZH (Tanzania) v. Secretary of State for the Home Department* [2011] UKSC 4, para. 23.
65. Rights of Children and Young Persons (Wales) Measure 2011.

## IV. Jurisprudence (Case Law)

*28.* Case law plays an important role in England and Wales. As noted above, some areas of the law are not covered by statute and are left instead to the application of the common law. And since much legislation in the field of family law is discretionary in nature, the application of the law to a particular set of facts is left to be determined on a case-by-case basis. Even if a statute appears to lay down a clear rule, a judge will still need to decide how it should be interpreted and applied to the facts of a particular case – facts that may not have been foreseen at the time the legislation was drafted.[66]

*29.* It is a general rule that judicial decisions form precedents for subsequent cases. The hierarchy of courts is reflected in a hierarchy of precedent, with each court being obliged to follow the decisions of a higher court. Thus, the Court of Appeal is bound by decisions of the Supreme Court, as well as by earlier decisions of the House of Lords, and the High Court is bound by decisions of both. The Supreme Court is not bound by its own decisions, nor is the High Court; the Court of Appeal, by contrast, is bound by its own decisions unless the earlier decision was made *per incuriam*, or conflicts with another decision of the Court of Appeal or a later decision of the Supreme Court. In the sphere of family law, however, the fact that each case will turn on its own specific facts means that precedents are of more limited utility; they may offer guidance, but since they are unlikely to be based on identical facts they cannot be determinative.

The discretionary nature of much of family law is also reflected in the approach taken to appeals. It was recognized by the House of Lords in *G v. G (Minors: Custody Appeal)*[67] that two judges may come to different conclusions on the same set of facts without either being wrong. It was therefore held that an appellate court was only entitled to intervene 'where the decision exceeds the generous ambit within which reasonable disagreement is possible, and is, in fact, plainly wrong'.[68]

§4. THE COURTS ADMINISTERING FAMILY AND SUCCESSION LAW

## I. The Supreme Court

*30.* On 5 October 2009, the Supreme Court sat to hear its first case. It was established by the Constitutional Reform Act 2005 to take over the judicial functions of the House of Lords, and is thus the highest domestic appellate court for the whole of the UK. It consists of twelve Justices, presided over by a President (from 2 October 2017 Baroness Hale of Richmond), who are appointed from the senior ranks of the judiciary according to a procedure laid down by statute.[69] Three have expertise

---

66. *See*, e.g., *Leeds Teaching Hospital Trust v. A* [2003] EWHC 259 (mix-up at IVF clinic: *see* Part II, Ch. 5, para. 293).
67. [1985] 1 W.L.R. 647.
68. *See also Re D (Leave to Remove: Appeal)* [2010] EWCA Civ 50, para. 8; *Re B* [2013] UKSC 33.
69. *Constitutional Reform Act 2005*, ss 25–31.

in the field of family law: Baroness Hale, Lord Wilson of Culworth and Lady Black (the last of these being only the second woman to be appointed to the Supreme Court, taking office in October 2017).

Cases are usually heard by five Justices, but exceptionally seven or even nine may sit together.[70]

*31.* There is no automatic right of appeal to the Supreme Court. Leave to appeal must be granted before a case can be heard. The new court has delivered a number of decisions in the field of family law, including *In re B (A Child)*,[71] on the application of the welfare principle, *Radmacher v. Granatino*[72] on the issue of prenuptial agreements, *Prest v. Petrodel Resources Limited and others,*[73] on whether properties vested in companies could be treated in financial relief proceedings as beneficially belonging to the husband, *Vince v. Wyatt*,[74] on the striking out of a claim for financial relief many years after the divorce and *Sharland v. Sharland*[75] and *Gohil v. Gohil*[76] on whether the husbands' misrepresentations justified the financial orders being set aside.

## II. The Court of Appeal

*32.* The Civil Division of the Court of Appeal hears appeals from both the High Court and from decisions of circuit judges within the Family Court. Leave to appeal is required.[77] There are thirty-eight judges of the Court of Appeal; they are referred to as Lord Justice (or Lady Justice). Cases are normally heard by three judges sitting together, but the Master of the Rolls (who presides over the civil division of the Court of Appeal) may direct that a case may be heard by a sole judge.[78]

## III. The High Court

*33.* The High Court is divided into three Divisions: Queen's Bench, Chancery, and Family. For present purposes our concern is with the last two. The Family Division was created in 1970[79] to deal with all aspects of family law, but following the creation of the single family court its jurisdiction is now more limited. It shares jurisdiction over proceedings under the Inheritance (Provision for Family and Dependants) Act 1975 with the Chancery Division, and is responsible for dealing

---

70. *See*, e.g., *Radmacher v. Granatino* [2010] UKSC 42.
71. [2009] UKSC 5.
72. [2010] UKSC 42.
73. [2013] UKSC 34.
74. [2015] UKSC 14.
75. [2015] UKSC 60.
76. [2015] UKSC 61.
77. *Matrimonial and Family Proceedings Act* 1984, s. 31K; *Access to Justice Act (Destination of Appeals) (Family Proceedings) Order* 2014/602.
78. *Ibid.*, s. 59.
79. *Administration of Justice Act* 1970.

with all cases of non-contentious probate. It also has an inherent jurisdiction, which originates in the role of the Crown as *parens patriae* and which may be invoked to protect vulnerable adults[80] and children[81] in the absence of relevant statutory regulation. It also has jurisdiction to deal with international cases under the Hague Convention or Brussels IIA.

*34.* The Chancery Division is responsible for dealing with issues relating to property and trusts and with contentious probate matters (i.e., where the validity of a will is disputed). It is also required to decide upon some matters that might be thought to fall within the province of family law, namely the ownership of assets by married couples and civil partners (e.g., if there is a dispute with a third party or where one of the couple has died) or other family members (in all cases, there being no adjustive regimes for those who have not formalized a relationship).

## IV. The County Court

*35.* There is now formally one single county court system in England and Wales, although cases are heard at local county court centres across the country. County courts deal with civil cases and have jurisdiction to hear cases under the Inheritance (Provision for Family and Dependants) Act 1975.[82] Probate claims can now only be brought in the Central London County Court or a county court hearing centre that also has a Chancery district registry. The family law role of the county courts has now been subsumed within the single family court.

## V. The Single Family Court

*36.* In April 2014 a single family court came into existence.[83] Within each geographical area, there is now one Designated Family Centre led and managed by a Designated Family Judge; one central location where hearings will take place, with subsidiary hearing centres as appropriate; a 'single point of entry' for the issue of proceedings; and a centralized and unified administration.[84] Within each court, there are High Court judges, circuit judges, district judges and lay justices, and the Designated Family Judge will allocate all applications to the level of judge appropriate for the type of case.[85] The new regional Family, Drug and Alcohol Courts hear care proceedings where parents have substance abuse issues. These specialist courts take

---

80. *See*, e.g., *Re SK (Proposed Plaintiff) (An Adult by way of her Litigation Friend)* [2004] EWHC 3202; *M v. B, A and S (By the Official Solicitor)* [2005] EWHC 1681.
81. *See*, e.g., *Re C (A Minor) (Wardship: Medical Treatment) (No. 2)* [1990] Fam. 39; *Re K (Adoption and Wardship)* [1997] 2 F.L.R. 221; *Re A (Minors) (Conjoined Twins: Medical Treatment)* [2001] 1 F.L.R. 1.
82. *County Courts Act* 1984, s. 25.
83. *Crime and Courts Act* 2013, s. 17, inserting *Matrimonial and Family Proceedings Act* 1984, s. 31A.
84. *The Single Family Court in London: A Joint Statement by the President of the Family Division and HMCTS London Region* (April 2013).
85. *See* the *Family Court (Composition and Distribution of Business) Rules* 2014, S.I. 2014/840.

a problem-solving approach and support is provided by a multidisciplinary team. Provision is also made for a system of appeals from different levels of judges within the Family Court.[86] The system will not, however, be entirely self-contained, since the Gender Recognition Panel will continue to hear applications for a change of gender and appeals against calculations of child maintenance will still be made to a specialist tribunal.

## VI. Is the Matter Appropriate for Judicial Resolution?

*37.* Some family matters – e.g., the legal termination of a marriage by the grant of a divorce – require court action. Others – such as the division of assets on relationship breakdown, or decisions as to with whom any children should live – do not. There has been increasing emphasis in recent years on diverting cases away from the courts, by promoting private arrangements and alternatives such as mediation, arbitration or collaborative law. There are also serious issues about access to the courts in the wake of cuts to legal aid for family disputes.[87] Many family disputes will, therefore, never come before the courts.

---

86. For the routes of appeal *see Matrimonial and Family Proceedings Act* 1984, s. 31K; *Access to Justice Act (Destination of Appeals) (Family Proceedings) Order* 2014/602.
87. *See* E. Hitchings, Official, operative and outsider justice: the ties that (may not) bind in family financial disputes, 29 C.F.L.Q 359 (2017).

# Part I. Persons

## Chapter 1. The Status of a Person

### §1. Definition of a Person

*38.* The concept of a legal person encompasses both human beings and 'artificial' persons such as corporations.

*39.* Every human being has legal personality, although the exercise of legal rights may be limited during a child's minority or during periods of mental incapacity.

Legal personality is, however, only acquired at birth. It has been decided that a foetus 'cannot have a right of its own at least until it is born and has a separate existence from its mother'.[88] Thus a foetus is not a 'child' for the purposes of the Children Act 1989, and a local authority concerned about its welfare cannot apply for an order to protect it, although action may be taken as soon as the child is born. Nor can the inherent jurisdiction of the High Court be exercised to make a foetus a ward of court. The court in *Re F (in utero) (Wardship)*[89] noted that the rights of the unborn child might be in conflict with those of the mother: to intervene to protect the child would inevitably impose constraints on the mother. In addition, the concept of a 'child of the family' – which covers the situation where the new spouse of a parent treats that parent's children as his or her own – does not include an unborn child.[90]

*40.* Certain individuals may also have a separate legal personality as a corporation sole. A corporation sole is an entity that has legal personality independently of the individual who occupies a particular role or office for the time being. Examples include the Crown and ecclesiastical officers (from archbishops to vicars). Their classification as a corporation sole means that property may be held by the office, rather than by the individual who holds that office at any given time, and will pass automatically to the successor to that office.

---

88. *Paton v. The British Pregnancy Advisory Service Trustees* [1979] Q.B. 276, at 279; applied in *Re DM* [2014] EWHC 3119 (Fam).
89. [1988] 2 F.L.R. 307.
90. *A v. A (Family: Unborn Child)* [1974] Fam. 6.

*41.* Groups of people may also form a single legal person as a corporation aggregate. Such a corporation may be created by means of a royal charter of incorporation, by statute, or by registering as a company.[91] A company may be either public or private.[92] Its members must subscribe their names to a memorandum of association.[93] Upon registration, a certificate of incorporation will be issued, which must either be signed by the registrar or authenticated by the registrar's official seal.[94] The effect of registration is that all those who have subscribed to the memorandum form a body corporate.[95]

*42.* Other groups of persons – such as clubs and societies – who have not formed a corporation are referred to as unincorporated associations, and the law has struggled to devise a theory to accommodate the holding of property by such persons.[96]

*43.* A third form of non-human legal entity is the Limited Liability Partnership (LLP), a new form of legal entity introduced in 2000.[97] This has some features in common with the incorporated company – in that liability for any debts attached to the partnership as a whole, rather than to the individual partners – but may otherwise be organized as a partnership.[98] In order for an LLP to be incorporated, the requisite documentary and registration requirements must have been fulfilled.[99]

## §2. Capacity

*44.* The basic rule is that all adults who are sui juris have full legal capacity. The rules that deprived a married woman of full capacity have long since been abolished.[100] So have those depriving convicted prisoners of legal rights,[101] although a prisoner is not entitled to vote while serving a sentence,[102] a restriction that has generated some controversy in recent years and which has been found to breach the European Convention on Human Rights.[103] Persons may, however, lack full legal capacity as a result of mental incapacity.[104]

The legal capacity of minors is more complex, and requires a more detailed consideration.

---

91. *Companies Act* 2006, s. 7, s. 15.
92. *Ibid.*, s. 4.
93. *Ibid.*, s. 7(1)(a), s. 8.
94. *Ibid.*, s. 15(3).
95. *Ibid.*, s. 16(2).
96. *See*, e.g., *Re Recher's WT* [1972] 3 All E.R. 401; *Re Grant's WT* [1979] 3 All ER 359.
97. *Limited Liability Partnerships Act* 2000, s. 1(1).
98. *Ibid.*, s. 5, s. 15(c).
99. *Ibid.*, s. 2.
100. *See*, e.g., *Married Women's Property Act* 1882, *Law Reform (Married Women and Tortfeasors) Act* 1935.
101. *Criminal Justice Act* 1948; *Criminal Law Act* 1967.
102. *Representation of the People Act* 1983, s. 3.
103. *See* most recently *McHugh and others v. the UK* (2015), Application No. 51987/08.
104. *See* Part I, Ch. 7.

## I. Minors

*45.* The age of majority was previously set at 21 years, but this was changed to 18 years in 1969. The Family Law Reform Act 1969 provided that a person 'shall attain full age on attaining the age of eighteen',[105] and that in the absence of any contrary definition or intention the terms 'infant', 'infancy', 'minor', and 'minority' would be construed accordingly.[106] At the age of 18, therefore, a person acquires the capacity to own a legal estate in land,[107] make a will,[108] and vote.[109] 'Child' is similarly defined by the Children Act 1989 as a person under the age of 18.[110]

However, a child under 18 may acquire legal rights if a specific statute makes provision to this effect. In addition, the courts have held that a child of sufficient understanding may be competent to make certain decisions.

### A. Statute

*46.* There are a number of statutory provisions setting out the age at which a child may perform certain actions. In recent years there has been a degree of convergence around the legal age of majority. The age at which one could buy fireworks or tobacco, e.g., has been raised from 16 to 18,[111] and that for the purchase of a crossbow from 17 to 18,[112] while the age at which one could become a Member of Parliament has been reduced from 21 to 18.[113] More significantly, there is now a duty on those aged under 18 to participate in some form of education or training instead of or in addition to paid work.[114]

*47.* But there are also statutory provisions that allow certain rights to be exercised at a much younger age. A child may withdraw money from a savings account at the age of 7; however, the child will be held criminally responsible for his or her actions at the age of 10.[115] A child may undertake paid employment for a limited number of hours per week at 14;[116] he or she may enter the bar of a licensed premises at 14; he or she may have a shotgun without supervision at 15,[117] and he or she may buy a pet at the age of 16.[118] At 16, the child is on the cusp of adulthood and may consent to sexual intercourse (with a person of the same or opposite

---

105. *Family Law Reform Act 1969*, s. 1(1).
106. *Ibid.*, s. 1(2).
107. *Law of Property Act 1925*, s. 1(6).
108. *Wills Act 1837*, s. 7. Note that members of the armed forces may make a will at an earlier age.
109. *Representation of the People Act 1949*, s. 1(1)(c).
110. *Children Act 1989*, s. 105(1).
111. *Pyrotechnic Articles (Safety) Regulations 2015/1553 reg* 31; *Children and Young Persons Act 1933*, s. 7, as amended by the *Children and Young Persons (Sale of Tobacco etc.) Ord.* 2007/767.
112. *Crossbows Act 1987*, s. 2, as amended by the *Violent Crime Reduction Act 2006*, s. 44.
113. *Electoral Administration Act 2006*, s.17.
114. *Education and Skills Act 2008*, s. 2.
115. *Crime and Disorder Act 1998*, s. 34.
116. *Children and Young Persons Act 1933*, s. 18.
117. *Firearms Act 1968*, s. 22(3). An age limit of 18 applies to other firearms.
118. *Animal Welfare Act 2006*, s. 11.

sex),[119] or even marry,[120] although only with the consent of those with parental responsibility.[121] At 17, a child may hold a driving license.

*48.* These statutory provisions have developed in a rather piecemeal fashion and do not give the impression of a code that is carefully worked out with psychological evidence about the development of children in mind. It is clear that some important decisions with long-lasting consequences may be taken at a relatively young age, while others must be deferred until adulthood. Moreover, children are excluded from age discrimination protection relating to the provision of goods, facilities and services provided by the Equality Act 2010.

*49.* The legal position of the young adult aged 16 or 17 is particularly anomalous. The national minimum wage payable for such persons is lower than that which is payable to older workers. Those under the age of 18 cannot usually make a claim for universal credit in their own right,[122] unless they fit into one of five exceptional categories.[123] At the same time, the entitlement of their parents to child benefit and child tax credits will cease with the child reaching the age of 16 save where the child is in full-time education or in approved training courses[124] and a parent will not face criminal sanctions for failing to provide adequate food, clothing, medical aid, or lodging to a child who has attained the age of 16.

## B. *Common Law*

*50.* In the absence of a minimum age being prescribed by statute, the ability of a child to make a decision will depend on a court's assessment of that child's level of understanding. This is made explicit in certain contexts – for example, if a child is seeking leave to apply for a section 8 order under the Children Act 1989.[125] In other contexts, it is a matter of inference.

*51.* The leading case is still that of the House of Lords in *Gillick v. West Norfolk and Wisbech Area Health Authority and Department of Health and Social Security*.[126] In this case, Mrs Gillick, who had five daughters, challenged the guidance on family planning issued by the Department of Health and Social Security to area health authorities. She objected to the suggestion that in exceptional cases a doctor could, in the exercise of his or her clinical judgment, prescribe contraception for a girl under the age of 16 without the knowledge or consent of her parents, and also

---

119. *Sexual Offences (Amendment) Act* 2000.
120. *Matrimonial Causes Act* 1973, s. 11(a)(ii).
121. *Marriage Act* 1949, s. 2.
122. *Welfare Reform Act 2012*, s.4.
123. *Universal Credit Regulations 2013/376* reg. 8.
124. *See* N. Wikeley, *Family Law and Social Security*, in *Family Life and the Law: Under One Roof*, 97–113 (R. Probert ed., Ashgate 2007).
125. *Children Act* 1989, s. 10(8). *See, e.g., Re C (A Minor) (Leave to Seek section 8 Order)* [1994] 1 F.L.R. 26, and *see* further Part II, Ch. 8, para. 375.
126. [1986] A.C. 112.

sought an assurance from the area health authority that no contraceptive advice or treatment would be given to any of her daughters while under 16 years of age without her knowledge and consent. The area health authority refused to give such an assurance, and Mrs Gillick sought a declaration that the guidance itself was unlawful.

The House of Lords held – by a bare majority – that her application should have been dismissed. The key aspect of the decision for present purposes was the statement of Lord Scarman that a child has the right to make his or her own decisions 'when he reaches a sufficient understanding and intelligence to be capable of making up his mind on the matter requiring decision'.[127] This means that the age at which a child may take a particular decision will depend both on the maturity of the individual child and upon the seriousness of the decision to be taken. Any given child might be competent to take one type of decision but not another.

52. There was, however, a further division within the majority in *Gillick* as to the relationship between the rights of the child and the rights of the parent. Lord Fraser of Tullybelton envisaged that parental rights did not disappear until the child reached the age of 18 but would dwindle as the child grew in age and understanding; Lord Scarman, by contrast, suggested that a parent would lose the right to make a decision for a child who was competent to make that decision.

53. The importance of the distinction between parents and children enjoying parallel rights, and children enjoying exclusive rights, is illustrated by the issue of consent to medical treatment. A child who has attained the age of 16 is entitled to give a valid consent to any surgical, medical, or dental treatment 'which, in the absence of consent, would constitute a trespass to his person'.[128] The legislation specifically provides that if such a person consents it is not necessary to obtain consent from the child's parent or guardian. A child under the age of 16 who has sufficient understanding and intelligence to make the decision may also consent.[129] But if the child wishes to refuse medical treatment, then a person with parental responsibility may give a valid consent to the treatment being carried out, even if the child is competent and/or over the age of 16.[130] The fact that parents can consent does not, however, mean that their consent is required; if the medical treatment is needed to save the life of the child, the medical authorities may seek the authorization of the court. The court may declare the proposed treatment to be lawful, even if it is opposed by both parents and the child,[131] if this is deemed to be in the best interests of the child.[132] The courts have, perhaps understandably, been reluctant to allow minors to

---

127. *Ibid.*, at 186.
128. *Family Law Reform Act* 1969, s. 8(1).
129. *Gillick v. West Norfolk and Wisbech Area Health Authority and Department of Health and Social Security* [1986] A.C. 112 (consent to receiving contraceptive advice); *R (ota Axon) v. Secretary of State for Heath* [2006] EWHC 372 (Admin) (consent to abortion).
130. *Re W (A Minor) (Medical Treatment: Court's Jurisdiction)* [1993] 1 F.L.R. 1.
131. *Re E (A Minor) (Wardship: Medical Treatment)* [1993] 1 F.L.R. 386.
132. *Re P (Medical Treatment: Best Interests)* [2003] EWHC 2327.

make decisions that are likely to result in their death, although this stands in sharp contrast to the position of mentally competent adults, who may refuse treatment even if it will result in their death.[133]

54. These cases, with their explicit focus on the best interests of the child, cast a rather different light on the decision of the House of Lords in *Gillick*. It could be argued that their Lordships were influenced more by considerations of welfare than children's rights. It was recognized that the choice did not necessarily lie between the provision of contraceptive advice and treatment with parental knowledge and consent and the provision of such advice without such knowledge or consent, but rather between the provision of such advice on a confidential basis and the child embarking on sexual relations without any such advice. Lord Fraser, e.g., set out a number of conditions regarding which a doctor should satisfy himself or herself before providing contraceptive advice or treatment to a girl under the age of 16, including, in addition to the ability of the girl to understand the relevant advice, the likelihood that the girl would begin or continue to have sexual intercourse with or without such advice, the likelihood that the girl's mental and/or physical health would suffer if she did not receive such advice, and, most telling of all, 'that her best interests required him to give her contraceptive advice, treatment, or both without the parental consent'.[134] Providing contraceptive advice and treatment without parental knowledge or consent was clearly seen as a lesser evil than unwanted teenage pregnancies.

55. Despite these cases, there are indications that judges are increasingly sympathetic to the argument that children have autonomous rights. In *R (ota Axon) v. Secretary of State for Heath*,[135] the judge noted the 'keener appreciation of the autonomy of the child and the child's consequent right to participate in decision-making processes that fundamentally affect his family life'.[136] The case of *Re Roddy (A Child) (Identification: Restriction on Publication)*[137] sent a still stronger message regarding children's rights. In that case, a 16-year-old girl who had become pregnant at the age of 12 and whose baby had been taken into care and subsequently adopted was allowed to tell her story to the media. The judge held:

> In my judgment (and I wish to emphasize this) it is the responsibility – it is the duty – of the court not merely to recognize but ... to *defend* ... the right of the child who has sufficient understanding to make an informed decision, to make his or her own choice.[138]

More recently in *Re A*,[139] Mostyn J held that the question of whether or not the course of action was in the best interests of the child was simply not relevant where

---

133. *Re B (Adult: Refusal of Treatment)* [2002] EWHC 429.
134. [1986] A.C. 112, at 239.
135. [2006] EWHC 372 (Admin).
136. At para. 76.
137. [2003] EWHC 2927.
138. At para. 57.
139. [2014] EWFHC 1445 (Fam) [10].

a child under the age of 16 had sufficient understanding and intelligence to make a decision. In this case, a 13-year-old girl was determined to be capable of deciding whether or not she should terminate her pregnancy.

# Chapter 2. Registration of Civil Status

§1. REGISTRATION

*56.* Prior to 1837, registration of baptisms, marriages, and burials was a matter for the religious authorities, although the completeness of the Anglican parochial registers of marriage was enhanced by the fact that all marriages – save those of Quakers, Jews and members of the Royal Family – had to be celebrated in the Church of England.[140] A system for the civil registration of births, marriages and deaths has existed in England and Wales since that date,[141] and since then adoptions, parental orders, gender recognition and civil partnerships have been added to the list of registrable events.

## I. Births

*57.* A child must be registered within forty-two days of its birth. If the parents are married to each other, either of them may register the birth. If the parents are unmarried, then the name of the father can only be entered on the form in certain specified circumstances: either both the mother and the father must be present, or the person registering the birth must make a declaration in a prescribed form regarding the paternity of the child or have evidence of the other's consent (e.g., a statutory declaration by the other parent acknowledging the father's paternity or a parental responsibility agreement in the appropriate form), or alternatively, a court order.[142] It is of course unlikely that a father would be able to obtain a parental responsibility order in the forty-two-day period allowed for registration, but it is possible for the particulars to be amended at a later date through re-registration.[143] In 2009, legislation was passed with the professed intention of ensuring that the father's name was recorded wherever possible but was never implemented. The Welfare Reform Act 2009 would have required a mother who attended the register office alone to provide information about the father, who would then be contacted to confirm his paternity. However, the mother would not have been required to produce such information if the child had no legal father by virtue of section 41 Human Fertilization and Embryology Act 2008, or the father had died, or the mother did not know the father's identity or whereabouts, or the father lacked capacity (as defined by the Mental Capacity Act 2005) and so was unable to confirm whether he was the father, or the mother had reason to fear for her safety or that of the child if the father was contacted in relation to the registration of the birth. The breadth of these exemptions was criticized as diluting the initial aim of the legislation, and as yet, they have not been brought into force.[144]

---

140. *Clandestine Marriages Act* 1753.
141. *Births and Deaths Registration Act* 1836; *Marriage Act* 1836.
142. *Births and Deaths Registration Act* 1953, s. 10(1).
143. *Ibid.*, s. 10A.
144. On this, *see* the discussion in the House of Commons on 21 Oct. 2014: *Hansard* (HC), vol. 586, col. 177 et seq.

*58.* It should be noted that the register records legal status rather than biological fact. If a child is born as a result of assisted reproduction it is the legal parents who will appear on the birth certificate, not those who provided the genetic material (although in most cases these categories will overlap). It is even possible for a man who died before the child was even conceived to be registered as the child's legal father, not only if he was the biological father of the child[145] but also if he would have been treated as the father had he been alive.[146] The mother's deceased same-sex partner or wife may also be registered as the child's legal parent.[147] However, the conditions in which any post-mortem registration will be possible are tightly controlled; the deceased must have consented in writing to the treatment continuing after his or her death and to being named as the father or parent on the birth certificate. Moreover, if there is another individual who is deemed to be the legal father or parent at the time of the child's birth, then the later relationship takes priority over the earlier one. If it is later established that the man recorded on the birth register was not the child's father, the register must be amended expeditiously.[148]

## II. Gender

*59.* The register must record whether the child is male or female. At common law it was held that the sex of an individual was determined at birth by biological factors – chromosomal, gonadal and genital – and could not be altered by later events.[149] However, in the wake of a finding by the European Court of Human Rights that the UK's failure to recognize the reassigned sex of a transsexual was in breach of both Article 8 and Article 12 of the European Convention on Human Rights,[150] the Gender Recognition Act 2004 was passed. This allows an adult to obtain a 'gender recognition certificate' from a specially created body – the gender recognition panel – established to consider such applications. The applicant must satisfy three requirements. First, it is necessary to prove – by means of supporting medical evidence[151] – that he or she has gender dysphoria; second, it must be established that the applicant 'has lived in the acquired gender throughout the period of two years ending with the date on which the application is made'; third, the panel must be satisfied that the applicant intends to continue to live in the acquired gender until death.[152] If these conditions are satisfied, the panel must grant the gender recognition certificate.[153]

---

145. *Human Fertilization and Embryology Act* 2008, s. 39.
146. *Ibid.*, s. 40(1) and 40(2).
147. *Ibid.*, s. 46.
148. Family Procedure Rules 2010, r. 8.22; *see also F (Children)* [2011] EWCA Civ 1765, para. 23.
149. *Corbett v. Corbett* [1971] P. 83.
150. *Goodwin v. UK* [2002] 2 F.L.R. 487; *I v. UK* [2002] 2 F.L.R. 518.
151. *Gender Recognition Act* 2004, s. 3.
152. *Ibid.*, s. 2(1).
153. *Ibid.*, s. 2(2).

*60.* Prior to the Marriage (Same-Sex Couples) Act 2013, if the applicant was married or in a civil partnership, the panel could only grant an interim gender recognition certificate,[154] with the full certificate being granted only once the marriage or civil partnership had been annulled. With the advent of same-sex marriage, the need for a marriage to be annulled has been removed, although the legislation has been amended to require the consent of the other spouse to the continuation of the marriage after the grant of a full gender recognition certificate as a condition for it being granted.[155] Where such consent is not forthcoming, then it remains the case that only an interim gender recognition certificate can be granted and the marriage must be annulled before the full certificate can be granted.[156]

*61.* Where the person undergoing gender reassignment was in a civil partnership, however, a two-stage process is still in place, since opposite-sex couples cannot enter into such a relationship. In such cases the couple have the option of either converting their civil partnership into a marriage or, alternatively, obtaining an annulment on the basis of the interim gender recognition certificate. The legislation also makes provision for the (possible but somewhat unlikely) scenario in which both civil partners are simultaneously undergoing gender reassignment, in which case they may remain as civil partners.[157]

*62.* The effect of a full gender recognition certificate is that the applicant becomes a member of the acquired gender for all legal purposes (subject to any statutory exceptions). Following this, an entry must be made in the Gender Recognition Register, and the original entry in the birth register must be marked accordingly.[158]

## III. Adoption and Parental Orders Register

*63.* If a child is adopted, he or she will be registered in the Adopted Children's Register as the child of the adoptive parents. This replaces the earlier entry in the register of births, which will note that the child has been adopted. A parental order may be made in favour of the commissioning parents in surrogacy cases, if certain conditions are met.[159] All such orders are registered in a Parental Order Register. As with adoption, this entry, recording the commissioning parents as the legal parents, will replace the original entry in the register of births. In each case, the child concerned may, upon reaching the age of 18, apply for access to the original birth certificate.

---

154. *Ibid.*, s. 4(3).
155. *Ibid.*, s. 4(2), as amended by the *Marriage (Same Sex Couples) Act* 2013.
156. *Ibid.*, s. 4(3)(a), as amended by the *Marriage (Same Sex Couples) Act* 2013.
157. *Ibid.*, s. 5B, as inserted by the *Marriage (Same Sex Couples) Act* 2013.
158. *Gender Recognition Act* 2004, Sch. 1.
159. *Human Fertilization and Embryology Act* 2008, s. 54. For recent example of their application *see Re L (Commercial Surrogacy)* [2010] EWHC 3146 (Fam) and *A and A v. P, P and B* [2011] EWHC 1738 (Fam).

## IV. Marriages and Civil Partnerships

*64.* All marriages and civil partnerships celebrated in England and Wales are required to be registered, although non-registration does not affect the validity of the union. The responsibility for registration lies with the person conducting the ceremony (e.g., the clergyman, in the case of an Anglican wedding) or appointed for the purpose of securing registration (such as the secretary of the synagogue, in the case of Jewish weddings, or the registering officer of the Society of Friends,[160] in the case of Quakers).[161] There is no requirement that marriages or civil partnerships celebrated overseas should be re-registered in this jurisdiction, even if the parties travelled abroad only for the purpose of formalizing their relationship.

## V. Deaths

*65.* The law requires that a death be registered at the local register office within five days of it occurring. The person responsible for registering the death must take the medical certificate setting out the cause of death which will have been issued by the medical practitioner treating the deceased. If there is no doctor who can issue a medical certificate of cause of death, then the registrar is required to report the death to a coroner. If the coroner decides that further investigation into the cause of death is necessary, an inquest will be held, and the death certificate will not be issued until a formal decision as to the cause of death has been reached.

## §2. REGISTERS AND CERTIFICATES

*66.* The system of registration in England and Wales is both local and national. The actual process of registration of births and deaths takes place at the register office for the district where the event occurred. Each registrar is required to make quarterly returns to the superintendent registrar and to deliver a certified copy of all relevant entries made in the previous three months.[162] The superintendent registrar in turn is required to make quarterly returns to the Registrar General,[163] and it is the Registrar General who has overall responsibility for the system of registration.

Certificates of the relevant events may be obtained at the time of registration (or, at a later date, from the General Register Office). A certified copy of an entry in the register is accepted as evidence of the facts stated therein.[164]

---

160. *Marriage Act* 1949, s. 47.
161. *See* R. Probert, 'The Registration of Marriages' [2017] Fam. Law 1103.
162. *Births and Deaths Registration Act* 1953, s. 26.
163. *Ibid.*, s. 27.
164. *Ibid.*, s. 34.

# Chapter 3. Personality Rights

## §1. Introduction

*67.* The different types of legal persons were set out in Chapter 1. In general, a human being of full age and capacity who has the power to enter into any legal transaction may be sued in tort or prosecuted for criminal activities. A person may lack capacity to enter into legal transactions due to mental incapacity or the temporary influence of alcohol or drugs. The fact that a person was intoxicated when engaging in criminal activities is not a defence in itself, but will be relevant to the question of whether the accused had formed the necessary *mens rea*, if this is a component of the offence in question.

*68.* The powers of different types of legal corporation will depend on the terms under which they were established: the Royal Charter, statute or, in the case of a company, its articles of association. However, the Companies Act 2006 specifically provides that the validity of an act done by a company 'shall not be called into question on the ground of lack of capacity by reason of anything in the company's constitution'.[165] If a person deals with a company in good faith, then the actions of directors or those authorized by them will be binding on the company vis-à-vis that person, regardless of the terms of the company's constitution.[166] In general, a company does have the power to enter into contracts, which must be made in writing under the company's common seal.[167]

*69.* The circumstances in which minors may enter into contracts, sue and be sued in tort, own property, and be criminally responsible for their actions, require more detailed consideration.

## §2. Minors' Contracts

*70.* At one time, the ability of a minor to enter into a valid contract depended on the nature of the contract and the age of the child, but as a more unified law of contract was developed, minority became 'more of a consistent boundary'.[168] As the ability to enter into a contract became linked to the exercise of reason and judgment, the contractual capacity of minors diminished accordingly. Indeed, legislation passed in 1874 provided that certain classes of contracts – those 'for the repayment of money lent or to be lent, or for goods supplied or to be supplied (other than contracts for necessaries), and all accounts stated with infants' – were 'absolutely void'.[169] That Act was, however, repealed in its entirety by the Minors' Contracts

---

165. *Companies Act* 2006, s. 39(1).
166. *Ibid.*, s. 40(1); but *see* s. 41 on the liabilities of directors in cases of this kind.
167. *Ibid.*, s. 43.
168. H. Brewer, *By Birth or Consent: Children, Law & the Anglo-American Revolution in Authority* 247 (U. N. Carolina Press 2005).
169. *Infants' Relief Act* 1874, s. 1.

Act 1987, reviving the common law rule that contracts of this kind would be unenforceable against, although enforceable by, a minor.

Before the Family Law Reform Act 1969, which lowered the age of majority from 21 to 18, this rule meant that most undergraduates – and many people who had been in paid employment for a number of years – lacked the capacity to enter into a contract that would be binding upon them. Today individuals aged 18 and over have full contractual capacity.

*71.* Today, the basic rule is that an individual may enter into a binding contract at the age of 18 but a contract entered into by a minor is voidable at the option of that minor; i.e., it is binding on the other party to the contract, but the minor can choose whether or not to adhere to its terms.[170]

There are, however, certain exceptions to this rule. First, two types of contracts are enforceable against a minor: contracts for 'necessaries' and contracts for apprenticeship, employment and service. Second, certain types of contracts are valid unless repudiated by the minor. It should be noted that even an unenforceable contract may have some legal effects. These points will be considered in turn.

## I. Valid Contracts

*72.* A contract for necessaries will be valid even if one of the contracting parties is a minor. As one early text on the topic noted, 'an Infant shall not be bound by his Contract or Bargain for any Thing but for his Necessity (viz.) Diet, Apparel, Learning, and necessary Physic'.[171] The reason for exempting goods and services deemed to be necessary is plain: a rule that states that a minor cannot be held to the terms of a contract may appear to be protecting the minor, but a side effect of such a rule will be that adults will be unwilling to enter into contracts for the supply of necessary goods or services with minors; the exception is essential to ensure that minors can enter into contracts for the items they need.[172] As Lord Hardwicke put it in *Brooke v. Gally*, '[t]he law lays infants under a disability of contracting debts, except for bare necessaries, and even this exemption is merely to prevent them from perishing.'[173]

*73.* Less obviously, it is a rule with a distinct class bias. At the time the exception was carved out, it was only those at the higher end of the scale who were likely to enter into contracts involving deferred payment. The courts explicitly recognized that the concept of 'necessaries' was a relative one that varied according to the standard of living of the minor in question. This relative concept of necessaries was later enshrined in statute. The Sale of Goods Act 1979 defines them as 'goods suitable to

---

170. *See* generally E. Cooke, *Don't Spend It All At Once! Parental Responsibility and Parents' Responsibilities*, in *Respect of Children's Contracts and Property* Ch. 11 in R. Probert, S. Gilmore & J. Herring, *Responsible Parents and Parental Responsibility* (Hart 2009).

171. Anon, *The Infants Lawyer: or the Law (Ancient and Modern) Relating to Infants* 170 (3rd ed. 1726).

172. *Ryder v. Wombwell* [1868] L.R. 4 Ex. 32, at 38.

173. (1740) 2 Atk. 34.

the condition in life of the minor'.[174] However, even though it was a relative concept, it was not an indefinitely expandable one. One senses the note of judicial disapproval in comments such as 'Balls and Serenadoes at Night must not be accounted Necessaries' or 'Satin, with Silver and Gold Lace, etc., are not necessary Apparel for a Gentleman'.[175] What are considered necessaries can evolve with the times and could today include high value items such as smartphones, tablets and PCs.

74. Two further constraints on the exception should be noted. First, the Sale of Goods Act 1979 also makes clear that the goods supplied to a minor must be suited to 'his actual requirements at the time of sale and delivery'.[176] This draws a distinction between what a minor might need, and what that particular minor actually needs at the time of the contract. Second, even a contract for necessaries will not be enforceable against a minor if it contains harsh and onerous terms; it must, on balance, be for the benefit of the minor. The Sale of Goods Act 1979 provides that 'where necessaries are sold and delivered to a minor ... he must pay a reasonable price for them'.[177]

75. The second exception to the general rule that contracts entered into by minors are voidable applies when a minor is bound by contracts of employment, apprenticeship or service. Again, the rationale is that it is beneficial to the minor to enter into a contract that provides training in skills that will be needed in adulthood (although in some of the older cases the benefit to the poorer children of the parish, apprenticed by the parish authorities, may not be immediately obvious).

The contract will not be binding if it is oppressive in its terms. The courts have stressed that the contract in question should be construed as a whole. As it was pointed out in *De Francesco v. Barnum*, 'it is obvious that the contract of apprenticeship or the contract of labour must, like any other contract, contain some stipulations for the benefit of the one contracting party, and some for the benefit of the other'.[178] The question for the court is not whether every term of the contract is for the benefit of the minor, but whether the effect of the contract, viewed as a whole, will be for the benefit of the minor.[179]

76. The exception has been held in more recent times to extend by analogy to contracts that enable the minor to earn a living. Courts have on this basis upheld a contract between a boxer and the British Boxing Board of Control,[180] a contract between a minor and a publisher for the publication of the minor's memoirs[181] and a contract between a group of musicians (The Kinks) and a company that was to act

---

174. *Sale of Goods Act* 1979, s. 3(3).
175. *The Infants Lawyer*, 166, 167.
176. *Sale of Goods Act* 1979, s. 3(3).
177. *Ibid.*, s. 3(2).
178. (1890) 45 Ch. D. 430, at 439.
179. See also *Clements v. London and North Western Railway Co* [1894] 2 QB 482.
180. *Doyle v. White City Stadium* [1935] 1 KB 110.
181. *Chaplin v. Leslie Frewin (Publishers) Ltd* [1966] Ch. 71.

as their manager.[182] By contrast, a player representation agreement with a young footballer was held not to fall within this exception, as the minor already had a separate contract with a football club that enabled him to earn substantial sums. The court in this latter case distinguished the role of a company representing a music group from the role of a company representing a sporting personality on the basis that '[m]usic group managers organize matters that are essential to the very business of the musical artiste. Players' representatives do not undertake matters that are essential to the player's training or his livelihood.'[183]

77.    In such cases the two exceptions may blur into each other. In *Proform Sports Management Ltd v. Proactive Sports Management Ltd*, e.g., it was suggested that the meaning of necessaries could in one sense extend 'to contracts for the minor's benefit and in particular to contracts of apprenticeship, education and service'.[184] Thus the contract in *Roberts v. Gray* – in which the minor agreed to go on tour as a professional billiards player – was held to be one for teaching, instruction and employment, on the basis that 'playing billiards in company with a noted player … must be instruction of the most valuable kind for an infant who desired to make playing billiards the occupation of his life'.[185] Similarly, the contract between the band 'The Kinks' and their manager was construed as being for necessaries – in that case the means of the musicians earning a living.

78.    Although the rationale for the two exceptions may be that contracts that are beneficial to the minor should be enforceable against him or her, it is not the case that any contract that is beneficial to a minor will be enforceable.[186] This was reiterated by the court in *Proform Sports Management Ltd v. Proactive Sports Management Ltd*: 'merely because a contract is beneficial to a minor, if such is the case, it is not binding on him unless it falls within a particular category'.[187]

## II.    Contracts That Will Be Valid until Repudiated

79.    A further category of contracts are those that are valid unless repudiated by the minor (either before the age of majority or within a short period of attaining majority). This comprises contracts relating to land, shares, partnership agreements, and marriage settlements.[188] The inclusion of the last item hints at the fact that these exceptions were carved out at a time when social conditions were very different to those that prevail today.

---

182. *Denmark Productions Ltd v. Boscobel Productions Ltd* (1967) 111 S.J. 715.
183. *Proform Sports Management Ltd v. Proactive Sports Management Ltd* [2006] EWHC 2903 (Ch), para. 39.
184. [2006] EWHC 2903 (Ch), para. 34.
185. [1913] 1 KB 520, 527.
186. *Cowern v. Nield* [1912] 2 KB 419, at 422.
187. [2006] EWHC 2903 (Ch), para. 39.
188. G.H. Treital, *The Law of Contract*, 545–547 (11th ed., Sweet & Maxwell 2003).

### III. The Legal Effects of Minors' Contracts

*80.* Even if a contract cannot be enforced against a minor, it is not necessarily devoid of legal effect. Property in goods delivered to a minor under a contract of sale will pass to the minor, even if the contract is unenforceable against the minor.[189] This does not mean, however, that the minor will necessarily be entitled to retain the property in question. The Minors' Contracts Act 1987 provides that if a contract is either unenforceable against, or repudiated by, a minor, 'the court may, if it is just and equitable to do so, require the defendant to transfer to the plaintiff any property acquired by the defendant under the contract, or any property representing it'.[190] To date, there are no reported cases on the interpretation of this provision.[191]

*81.* The courts have also considered whether an action in tort should lie where the minor has damaged goods supplied under a contract that is not enforceable against the minor. Again, the protection afforded to minors has developed over time. In the eighteenth century it was 'generally agreed … that infants should be liable in cases where they intentionally caused damage or acted deceitfully, such that they, e.g., sought to sell goods not their own or pretended that they were of age'.[192] By the early nineteenth century, the liability of a minor was denied even in cases of this kind. The basic rule today is that a child is not liable for a tort which is founded on a contract on which he or she cannot be sued. However, a minor will be liable if the tort committed is effectively independent of the contract. For example, if it arises out of actions that were either not contemplated by the contract or were expressly forbidden by it.[193]

§3. Minors' Responsibility for Torts

*82.* A child of any age may be sued in tort. However, although minority per se is no defence, the fact that the defendant is a child will be relevant in determining whether any tort has been committed.

In order to succeed in an action for negligence, it must be shown that the defendant did an act which it was reasonably foreseeable would cause injury to the claimant, that the relationship between the claimant and the defendant was such as to give rise to a duty of care, and that the act was one which caused injury to the claimant. In *Mullin v. Richards*,[194] the Court of Appeal was required to consider the issue of foreseeability in a case involving two 15-year-old girls who had engaged in a mock fight with plastic rulers. One of the rulers had snapped during the course of the game

---

189. *Stocks v. Wilson* [1913] 2 KB 235, at 246.
190. *Minors' Contracts Act* 1987, s. 3(1)(b).
191. For discussion of the Act, and of the earlier law, *see* J. Holroyd, *The Minors' Contracts Act 1987*, 84 L.S.G. 2266 (1987).
192. H. Brewer, *By Birth or Consent: Children, Law & the Anglo-American Revolution in Authority* 267 (U. N. Carolina Press 2005).
193. *See*, e.g., *Burnard v. Haggis* [1863] 14 CB (NS) 45; *Ballett v. Mingay* [1943] KB 281.
194. [1998] 1 W.L.R. 1304.

and had pierced the eye of one of the participants, with the result that she lost all useful sight in that eye. The Court of Appeal held that the accident had not been foreseeable. Hutchison L.J. explained how the age of the defendant was relevant to this determination:

The test of foreseeability is an objective one; but the fact that the first defendant was at the time a 15-year-old schoolgirl is not irrelevant. The question for the judge is not whether the actions of the defendant were such as an ordinarily prudent and reasonable adult in the defendant's situation would have realized gave rise to a risk of injury, it is whether an ordinarily prudent and reasonable 15-year-old schoolgirl in the defendant's situation would have realized as much.[195]

The age of a child will also be taken into account in determining the extent to which a child is guilty of contributory negligence.[196]

83. Parents are not, in general, liable for the torts committed by their children.[197] However, a parent who has authorized the actions that gave rise to tortious liability will be vicariously liable. A parent, or other person having care of a child, may be found to be negligent in failing to prevent the child from committing a tortious act. Thus in *Newton v. Edgerley,* a father was held to be personally liable in negligence for the injury that his son had caused to another boy by accidentally shooting him in the leg with a shotgun.[198] Although he had told his son not to take the gun off the farm and not to use it when other children were present, the court was of the opinion that these 'were instructions which he, the father, could not possibly see were always obeyed'.[199] In addition, the father had not instructed the son how the gun should be held if others were present. The court did emphasize, however, that each case would turn on its own facts. It noted that in the earlier case of *Donaldson v. McNiven,*[200] the father had not been liable for the injury that his 13-year-old son had caused to another boy: in this case the father had similarly instructed his son not to use the air rifle outside the house, but the case was distinguished in part on the basis that an air rifle was a less dangerous weapon than a shotgun. Similarly, in *Gorely v. Codd,*[201] it was held that the father was not negligent as he had given his son 'proper and sufficient instruction' in using the air rifle and had pointed out the dangers inherent in its use.[202]

---

195. *Ibid.,* at 1308. *See also Orchard v. Lee* [2009] EWCA Civ 295.
196. *See,* e.g., *Toropdar v. D* [2009] EWHC 2997 (TCC).
197. *See* generally P. Giliker, *Responsible Parents and Parental Responsibility* Ch. 18 (R. Probert S. Gilmore & J. Herring, eds, Hart 2009).
198. [1959] 1 W.L.R. 1031.
199. *Ibid.,* at 1033.
200. [1952] 2 All E.R. 691.
201. [1967] 1 W.L.R. 19.
202. *Ibid.,* at 26.

## §4. MINORS AND PROPERTY

*84.* It was noted earlier that a minor may not hold a legal estate in land,[203] and that a contract by a minor relating to land may be repudiated during that person's minority.[204] A child may, however, own an equitable interest in land,[205] and if a child becomes entitled to a legal estate it will therefore be held on trust for that child until adulthood.[206] In *Kingston BC v. Prince*, e.g., it was held that the 13-year-old granddaughter of the tenant was entitled to succeed to the tenancy in equity, the girl's mother accepting the role of trustee.[207]

*85.* Yet the rights of a minor beneficiary differ in a number of respects from those of an adult beneficiary. Many provisions of the Trusts of Land and Appointment of Trustees Act 1996 confine rights to those beneficiaries who are of 'full age and capacity'.[208] Minors are in general excluded from any decision-making role. Indeed, there is no requirement that they should even be consulted,[209] and in cases of dispute it is the 'circumstances and wishes of any beneficiaries of full age' that are to be taken into account.[210] Even if there is a specific provision that the consent of a beneficiary is needed, the minor cannot give a valid consent and it is the consent of a parent or guardian with parental responsibility that will be needed.[211]

*86.* The rights of a child in occupation of property also differ from those of adults. It has been held that a child cannot be in actual occupation of property for the purpose of determining whether he or she has an overriding interest that may be binding on a third party.[212] Children in this situation are regarded as merely the 'shadows' of the adult occupiers, rather than exercising independent rights of occupation.[213]

## §5. MINORS' RESPONSIBILITY FOR CRIMES

*87.* There is an irrebuttable presumption that a child under the age of 10 years cannot be guilty of a criminal offence.[214] However, this does not mean that activities by a child under that age that would constitute crimes if committed by a child

---

203. *See supra* Part II, Ch. 1, para. 48.
204. *See supra*, para. 79.
205. Although the circumstances in a minor may acquire such an interest may be limited: *see, e.g., De Bruyne v. De Bruyne* [2010] EWCA Civ 519.
206. *Trusts of Land and Appointment of Trustees Act* 1996, Sch. 1, para. 1.
207. H.L.R. 31 (1999): 794.
208. *Trusts of Land and Appointment of Trustees Act* 1996, ss 6(2), 7(1), 9(1), 19(1)(b), 20(1)(b).
209. *Ibid.*, s. 11(1)(a).
210. *Ibid.*, s. 15(3).
211. *Ibid.*, s. 10(3).
212. *Hypo-Mortgage Services Ltd v. Robinson* [1997] 2 F.L.R. 71.
213. *Supra* n. 114.
214. *Children and Young Persons Act* 1933, s. 50, as amended by the *Children and Young Persons Act* 1963, s. 16(1).

over that age will be disregarded. Under the Crime and Disorder Act 1998, a magistrates' court may make a 'child safety order' if certain conditions are fulfilled, namely that the child has committed an act which, if he or she had been aged 10 years or over, would have constituted an offence, or that a child safety order is necessary for the purpose of preventing the commission by the child of such an act.[215] A child safety order may also be imposed if the child has acted in a manner that caused or was likely to cause harassment, alarm or distress to one or more persons not of the same household as himself or herself.[216]

The effect of making such an order will be to place the child under the supervision of the responsible officer – who may either be a local authority social worker or a member of a youth offending team – and to require the child to comply with such requirements as are stated in the order.[217] These may be such as the court considers desirable 'in the interests of ... securing that the child receives appropriate care, protection and support and is subject to proper control; or ... preventing any repetition of the kind of behaviour which led to the child safety order being made'.[218] The order may last for a maximum of twelve months.[219]

*88.* The fact that a child is engaged in activity that, but for his or her age, would be criminal, may also provide grounds for a care or supervision order being made. Under the Children Act 1989, such an order can only be made if the court is satisfied that the child concerned is suffering, or likely to suffer, significant harm, attributable either to lack of parental care or to the child being beyond parental control.[220] It had previously been possible to make a care order if a child safety order had been breached even if the threshold criteria set out in the Children Act 1989 were not satisfied, but this option was removed in 2004.[221]

*89.* If a child is in the care of a local authority – either under a care order or with the consent of those with parental responsibility for the child – a secure accommodation order may be made either if the child has a history of absconding and is likely to abscond from any other description of accommodation and thereby suffer significant harm, or if the child is likely to injure himself or herself or other persons if kept in any other description of accommodation.[222] It is significant that the potential for harm to the child is not the only ground on which such an order may be made. Nor is the welfare of the child in question the paramount consideration for the court in deciding whether to make such an order. However, it is a prerequisite for making the order that the child has legal representation in court, or at least has had the opportunity to apply for the provision of such representation.[223] In *Re SS*,[224]

---

215. *Crime and Disorder Act* 1998, s. 11(3).
216. *Ibid.*, s. 11(3)(d).
217. *Ibid.*, s. 11(1).
218. *Ibid.*, s. 11(5).
219. *Ibid.*, s. 11(4), as amended by the *Children Act* 2004, s. 60(3).
220. *Children Act* 1989, s. 31(2).
221. *Children Act* 2004, s. 60.
222. *Children Act* 1989, s. 25(1).
223. *Children Act* 1989, s. 25(6) as amended by the Legal Aid, Sentencing and Punishment of Offenders Act 2012, Sch. 5(1), para. 38.

Hayden J made it clear that restricting the liberty of a child by such an order is very rarely appropriate and remains a measure of last resort.

*90.* A child who has attained the age of 10 years will be criminally liable for his or her actions. The fact that the law of England and Wales sets such a low age of criminal responsibility has been criticized.[225] Until 1998, there was a rebuttable presumption that a child aged between 10 years and 14 years was incapable of committing a criminal offence, but this was abolished by the Crime and Disorder Act 1998.[226] The specific presumption that a boy under the age of 14 years is incapable of sexual intercourse – and therefore cannot be convicted of rape or other offences involving sexual intercourse – has also been abolished.[227]

*91.* However, it should be borne in mind that the fact that a child is criminally liable at this age does not mean that he or she will be treated in the same way as an adult who had committed a similar crime would be. Special rules apply at each stage of the process, from the circumstances under which a child may be detained before and after being charged, to the nature of the court in which the child will be tried, the procedural rules that apply in that court and the sentencing options available to the court.[228]

*92.* The extent to which a child's parents will be held liable for the crimes committed by the child also vary according to the age of the child.[229] A parenting order – requiring the parent to attend a counselling or guidance programme and to comply with such other conditions as may be specified – may be made by the court if the child has been convicted of an offence, or if a child safety order or antisocial behaviour order has been made in respect of the child.[230] If a child under the age of 16 years has been convicted of an offence, then the court must make a parenting order unless it gives reasons why such an order should not be made.[231] Parents may also enter into parenting contracts with the youth offending team to which their child has been referred, if it is thought likely that the child is likely to engage in criminal or antisocial behaviour.[232]

*93.* If a child under the age of 16 years is charged with an offence, the court will require the child's parent or guardian to attend the court hearing, unless this would

---

224. [2014] EWHC 4436 (Fam).
225. *See V and T v. UK* [2000] E.H.R.R. 121; J. Fortin, *Children's Rights and the Developing Law* 685–695 (3rd ed., Cambridge U. Press 2009).
226. *Crime and Disorder Act* 1998, s. 34.
227. *Sexual Offences Act* 1993, s. 1.
228. *See* J. Fortin, *Children's Rights and the Developing Law* Ch. 18 (3rd ed., Cambridge U. Press 2009).
229. *See* generally R. Leng, *Responsible Parents and Parental Responsibility* Ch. 17 (R. Probert, S. Gilmore & J. Herring eds, Hart 2009).
230. *Crime and Disorder Act* 1998, s. 8(1).
231. *Ibid.,* s. 9(1).
232. *Anti-social Behaviour Act* 2003, s. 25(2).

be unreasonable in the circumstances of the case.[233] If the child is 16 years or over, it may still require the child's parent or guardian to attend.[234]

94. If a child under the age of 16 years is convicted of a crime and a fine or cost is imposed or a compensation order is made, the court must order that the child's parent or guardian should pay the sum in question, unless the parent or guardian cannot be found or the circumstances of the case render it unreasonable to require him or her to pay.[235] If the child has attained the age of 16 years, the court may still make an order of this kind.[236]

95. If a child under the age of 16 years is convicted of an offence, the court must make an order requiring the child's parent or guardian to enter into a recognizance to take proper care of him or her and exercise proper control over him or her if it is satisfied that, in the circumstances of the case, this course 'would be desirable in the interests of preventing the commission by [the child] of further offences'.[237]

---

233. *Children and Young Persons Act* 1933, s. 34A(1)(b), as inserted by the *Criminal Justice Act* 1991.
234. *Ibid.*, s. 34A(1)(a).
235. *Powers of Criminal Courts (Sentencing) Act* 2000, s. 137(1).
236. *Ibid.*, s. 137(3).
237. *Ibid.*, s. 150(1).

# Chapter 4. Names

## §1. Composition of Names

96. A name is an important element of a person's self-identity; it also provides a means of identification.[238] It is composed of a forename (or forenames) and a surname. There are no statutory restrictions on the names that may be given to a child at birth or assumed at a later date. In practice, guidelines issued by the General Register Office provide that the name should consist of a sequence of letters and should not be offensive and must be able to fit in the space provided on the registration page. Names considered inappropriate by the registrar can be referred to the General Register Office for adjudication.

97. As a matter of convention, an adult male will be addressed as 'Mr', a married woman as 'Mrs', and an unmarried woman as 'Miss'. However, considerable flexibility exists in practice. Married and unmarried women may prefer to use the more neutral designation 'Ms'.

A peer of the realm – in descending order of rank, a duke, marquess, earl, viscount, or baron – is entitled to use the title associated with that peerage.

98. For most purposes, the name by which a person is known has no legal significance other than providing a means of identifying that person. This may be illustrated by a number of older authorities in which it was questioned whether the banns of marriage had been called in the correct names of the parties. The courts consistently held that the correct name was the name by which the person was generally known, since the purpose of calling the banns was to publicize the intended marriage.[239] A name assumed by a person – even for a relatively short period – could thus supplant the baptismal name. Even a name that was only used for the purpose of the marriage might be the 'true' name, if the person using it had genuinely believed that it was the correct name to use in the circumstances, and had not intended to conceal his or her identity.[240]

## §2. Surname

### I. Acquisition of Surname

99. There is no legal requirement that a child born to married parents should be registered with the surname of the father, nor that a child born to unmarried parents should not be so registered. The parents may choose to register the child with the

---

238. *See* generally J. Herring, *Responsible Parents and Parental Responsibility* Ch. 6 (R. Probert, S. Gilmore & J. Herring eds., Hart 2009).
239. *Frankland v. Nicholson* [1805] 105 E.R. 607; *R v. Inhabitants of Billinghurst* [1814] 105 E.R. 603; *Wilson v. Brockley* [1810] 161 E.R. 937.
240. *Sullivan v. Sullivan (falsely called Oldacre)* [1805] 105 E.R. 607 (use of mother's maiden name).

surname of either party, or with the surnames of both, or indeed of neither. Some parents choose to invent a new surname that has elements of both their names.

## II. Change of Surname

*100.* A married woman will generally adopt her husband's surname, but there is no legal requirement that she should do so; nor, if she does take his name, is there any requirement that she should resume her maiden name upon the termination of the marriage by death or divorce.

*101.* An adult may use whatever surname or forename he or she chooses, as long as there is no intent to deceive. No formal procedure is necessary for a person to effect a change of name. However, in a modern bureaucratic state, official bodies may be unwilling to accept a change of name without documentary evidence. A person may provide such evidence by executing a deed poll, and causing it to be enrolled in the Central Office of the Supreme Court.[241]

*102.* The surname of a child can be changed with similar ease if all those with parental responsibility are in agreement. If the child is under the age of 16 years, the deed poll must be executed by a person with parental responsibility;[242] if the child is 16 or 17, then his or her consent is also required.[243]

*103.* If certain legal orders are in force, no person may cause the child to be known by a new surname without either the written consent of every person who has parental responsibility for the child or the leave of the court. These include a child arrangements order relating to where a child should live,[244] a special guardianship order,[245] an order placing the child in the care of the local authority[246] or, in the context of adoption, a placement order.[247]

It has been debated whether similar restrictions pertain where no such order is in place. The relevant legislation would seem to suggest that parental responsibility can be exercised unilaterally, without consultation between those who possess it.[248] However, it has been held that there are a number of situations in which the consent of all those with parental responsibility is necessary, and the change of a child's surname is one of these.[249] Holman J., e.g., argued in *Re PC (Change of Surname)*[250] that the Children Act 1989 must have been intended to preserve the earlier position

---

241. *Enrolment of Deeds (Change of Name) Regulations* 1994, S.I. 1994/604.
242. *Enrolment of Deeds (Change of Name) Regulations* 1994, Reg. 8(3).
243. *Ibid.*, Reg. 8(4).
244. *Children Act* 1989, s. 13(1)(a).
245. *Ibid.*, s. 14C(3)(a).
246. *Ibid.*, s. 33(7)(a).
247. *Adoption and Children Act* 2002, s. 28(3)(a).
248. *Children Act* 1989, s. 2(7).
249. *See*, e.g., *Re J (Specific Issue Order: Child's Religious Upbringing and Circumcision)* [2000] 1 F.L.R. 571.
250. [1997] 2 F.L.R. 730.

whereby the consent of both parents was necessary. It is true that the regulations governing the execution of a deed poll clearly envisage that the consent of all persons with parental responsibility is required.[251] It is worth noting, however, that the range of persons who may have parental responsibility extends far beyond the child's legal parents. From this perspective, the 1989 Act did not merely preserve existing restrictions but also extended them.

If an application is made to the court for the name to be changed (or not changed, if one parent is threatening to do so), the child's welfare will be the court's paramount consideration.[252] The matter may come before the court in a variety of different ways: if one of the orders mentioned above is in force, then the application should be made under the appropriate provision; if no such order is in force the appropriate course is to make an application for a specific issue order or prohibited steps order under section 8 of the Children Act 1989. The courts have, however, confirmed that the same principles will guide their decision whatever the precise form of the application.[253] The test for changing a child's name is purely based on the best interests of the child.[254] The courts have weighed the importance of maintaining a visible link with an absent father against the short-term issues of convenience and avoidance of confusion.[255] The court has also authorized a change of surname to protect the children from risk of abduction[256] the consequences of detrimental information being published about them on an Internet blog.[257]

*104.*  It should also be borne in mind that the name used by a person on a day-to-day basis need not be the name that appears on the birth certificate. The case of *Re S (Change of Names: Cultural Factors)*[258] involved a dispute between a Muslim mother and a Sikh father. Their son had been registered with Sikh names, which the mother wanted to change after their divorce. The court held that she could use Muslim names for her son to ensure his integration into the Muslim community, but that the child's names should not be formally changed because this would eliminate his Sikh identity.

---

251. *Enrolment of Deeds (Change of Name) Regulations* 1994, S.I. 1994/604.
252. *Children Act* 1989, s. 1(1).
253. *Dawson v. Wearmouth* [1997] 2 F.L.R. 629; *Re W (A Child) (Illegitimate Child: Change of Surname)* [2001] Fam. 1.
254. *Re W (Change of Name)* [2013] EWCA Civ 1488.
255. *Re R (Surname: Using Both Parents')* [2001] 2 F.L.R. 1358. *Re F (Children; contact, name, parental responsibility)* [2014] EWFC 4.
256. *Re B (Change of Names: Parental Responsibility: Evidence)* [2017] EWHC 3250.
257. *Re F (Children; contact, name, parental responsibility)* [2014] EWFC 4.
258. [2001] 2 F.L.R. 1005.

§3. FORENAME

*105.* The statutory prohibitions on a change of name apply only to a change of a child's surname. It has been recognized that given names 'have a much less concrete character',[259] and that the names that are registered by the child's parents may be supplanted in practice by different names.

The issue in *Re H (Child's Name: First Name)* was whether a mother had the right to use her choice of names when dealing with educational, health, and other authorities. The parents were married but had separated while the mother was pregnant. Each had registered the child independently with their own choice of names. The mother's registration was subsequently cancelled as the father had registered his choice of names first. At first instance, the court held that the mother was obliged to use the names that the father had registered when dealing with external agencies, but the Court of Appeal allowed her appeal, pointing out that there was no need for her to produce a birth certificate when dealing with external agencies, and that she should simply inform them of 'the given name that is customary in the primary home'.[260]

---

259. *Re H (Child's Name: First Name)* [2002] EWCA Civ 190, para. 14.
260. [2002] EWCA Civ 190, para. 15.

# Chapter 5. Nationality

## §1. Introduction

*106.* Nationality is a complex and multilayered concept, raising fundamental issues of identity and belonging both for the state itself and for the individuals. At present, there are a number of different levels of British nationality: British citizens, British Overseas Territories citizens, British Overseas citizens, British Nationals (Overseas),[261] British subjects, and British protected persons. The precise definition of each category lies outside the scope of this chapter, which will focus on the most important – because it is the most privileged – of these categories, that of British citizenship. Possession of British citizenship carries a right of abode in the UK, and confers on the possessor citizenship of the EU as well.

There are a variety of ways in which citizenship may be acquired, which differ according to the age and status of the individual in question.

## §2. Acquisition by Birth

*107.* Before 1983, any child born in the UK was automatically entitled to British nationality. The position was changed by the British Nationality Act 1981, which now provides that a child born in the UK will only be a British citizen if at least one of the child's parents is themselves a British citizen or settled in the UK,[262] or a member of the armed forces.[263] Initially, the term 'father' was in this context defined as referring only to a father who was married to the mother. This was subsequently amended by the Nationality, Immigration and Asylum Act 2002, which came into force in July 2006. The concept of father now includes both social and biological fathers, being defined as the mother's husband, a man who is treated as the father in the context of assisted reproduction,[264] or, if neither of these provisions is applicable, 'any person who satisfies prescribed requirements as to proof of paternity'.[265] The necessary proof of paternity may be provided by the fact that the man in question is named on the child's birth certificate, or by a court order or DNA test.[266] In the wake of the amendments effected by the Human Fertilization and

---

261. *Hong Kong (British Nationality) Order* 1986, S.I. 1986/948.
262. *British Nationality Act* 1981, s. 1(1). 'Settled' is defined as being ordinarily resident in the UK without being subject under the immigration laws to any restriction on the period for which one may remain: *British Nationality Act* 1981, s. 50(2).
263. *British Nationality Act* 1981, s. 1(1A), inserted by the *Borders, Citizenship and Immigration Act* 2009, s. 42(2).
264. *See* Part II, Ch. 5, paras 287–294.
265. *British Nationality Act* 1981, s. 50(9A), as amended by the *Nationality, Immigration and Asylum Act* 2002.
266. *British Nationality (Proof of Paternity) Regulations* 2006 (S.I. 2006/1496).

Embryology Act 2008,[267] a child may also acquire British nationality through the mother's same-sex partner or spouse, if the latter fulfils the criteria for legal parenthood.[268]

*108.* A child born outside the UK (or other specified qualifying territories)[269] to parents at least one of whom is a British citizen will also acquire British citizenship.[270] However, citizenship by descent, as it is termed, can only be transmitted across one generation. Children who are born overseas to a person who is a British citizen by descent will not themselves acquire British citizenship.[271]

§3. ACQUISITION OF CITIZENSHIP DURING CHILDHOOD

*109.* Although birth in the UK no longer automatically confers British citizenship upon a child, a child who is born here but whose parents are neither British citizens nor settled in the UK is entitled to be registered as a British citizen upon attaining the age of 10 years, as long as those first ten years were spent in the UK with absences of no more than ninety days each year.[272] Similarly, if the child's parents subsequently become British citizens or settled in the UK while the child is still a minor, the child is entitled to be registered as a British citizen.[273]

*110.* In line with the view that adoption constitutes a 'legal transplant' whereby the adoptee becomes the child of the adopting parents, the making of an adoption order in favour of a British citizen will confer British citizenship upon the child.[274] The making of a parental order to transfer the status of legal parenthood after surrogacy will also confer British citizenship on the child where the order is made in favour of a British citizen.[275]

§4. ACQUISITION OF CITIZENSHIP AS AN ADULT

*111.* Marriage to (or a civil partnership with) a British citizen carries no automatic right to British citizenship, but the non-citizen spouse or civil partner may apply to become a British citizen by naturalization.[276] This is subject to a number

---

267. *See* Part II, Ch. 5, para. 291.
268. *British Nationality Act* 1981, s. 50(9A)(ba), as inserted by the *Human Fertilisation and Embryology Act* 2008, Sch. 6(1) para. 22.
269. *See* the *British Overseas Territories Act* 2002.
270. *British Nationality Act* 1981, s. 2(1).
271. *Ibid.*, s. 2(1)(a).
272. *British Nationality Act* 1981, s. 1(4).
273. *Ibid.*, s. 1(3).
274. *British Nationality Act* 1981, s. 1(5A). *See* discussion of the effect of adoption on non-national children in *Re N* [2016] UKSC 15.
275. *Human Fertilisation and Embryology (Parental Orders) Regulations* S.I. 2010/985.
276. *British Nationality Act* 1981, s. 6(2). For a discussion of the restrictions placed on marriage in the context of immigration *see* H. Toner, *Immigration Law and Family Life – A Happy Marriage?* in *Family Life and the Law: Under One Roof* 197–221 (R. Probert ed., Ashgate 2007).

of conditions. First, a minimum period of residence must be completed. An application can only be made by a spouse or civil partner who has been resident in the UK for at least three years (although absences totalling less than 270 days may be disregarded).[277] Second, applicants must not be subject to any immigration restrictions on their length of stay in the UK.[278] Third, an applicant must be of 'full age and capacity',[279] and must show that he or she is of good character[280] and has sufficient knowledge of the national language[281] and life in the UK.[282] Formal ceremonies are held to confer citizenship upon those who satisfy the requisite conditions, at which the new citizen must pledge allegiance to the Crown and loyalty to the UK.

*112.* Other adults may also apply to become a British citizen by naturalization.[283] In this case a longer period of residence is required, namely five years without a total combined absence of more than 450 days,[284] and applicants must show that they intend to make their future home in the UK,[285] but otherwise the same conditions apply.

---

277. *British Nationality Act* 1981, Sch. 1, para. 3(a) and (b).
278. *Ibid.*, Sch. 1, para. 3(c).
279. *Ibid.*, s. 6(1).
280. *Ibid.*, Sch. 1, para. 1(1)(b).
281. English, Welsh or Scottish Gaelic: *British Nationality Act* 1981, Sch. 1, para. 1(1)(c).
282. *British Nationality Act* 1981, Sch. 1, para. 1(1)(ca).
283. *British Nationality Act* 1981, s. 6(1).
284. *Ibid.*, Sch. 1, para. 1(a).
285. *Ibid.*, Sch. 1, para. 1(1)(d).

# Chapter 6. Domicile and Habitual Residence

## §1. Introduction

*113.* As discussed in the previous chapter, a person's nationality will determine issues such as whether he or she has a right to live in England and Wales. The concept of domicile, by contrast, is more important in determining which system of national law is most applicable to that particular person. To say that a person is domiciled in a particular country is to say that he or she has the strongest connection with that country, that it is their permanent home and that therefore its laws should apply to that person. Thus while the concept of nationality is premised on a person's connection to a particular state, domicile is based on a person's connection to a particular legal system. One might therefore refer to a person as having British nationality but being domiciled in England and Wales, whose legal system differs from that of Scotland or Northern Ireland.

## §2. Domicile

*114.* Every person must be domiciled somewhere, but no person can be domiciled in more than one place at a time. Under the law of England and Wales, there are three ways in which domicile is determined: by birth, dependence or choice.

*115.* Every newborn child acquires a domicile of origin from one of his or her parents. Which parent's domicile is relevant for these purposes will depend on whether the parents were married to each other or not: if they were, and the father is alive at the time of the birth, the child will take his domicile; if they were not married, or the father died before the birth, the child will take the mother's domicile.[286] These distinctions derive from the purpose of the rule, which is to provide the child with the same domicile as the person on whom he or she is legally dependent, although they have not kept pace with the changes in the rules applicable to both married and unmarried parents nor is it clear what will happen if the child is born to a same-sex couple whether married or unmarried.

A domicile of origin is difficult to change.[287] It has been held that the standard of proof necessary to show that a domicile of origin has been lost 'goes beyond a mere balance of probabilities'.[288] Nor will it ever be entirely lost, in the sense that it may revive if a person who has acquired and then abandoned a new domicile would otherwise have no domicile.

*116.* Nevertheless, there are a number of events during a child's minority that will have the effect of altering his or her domicile of origin. Children who are

---

286. *Udny v. Udny* (1869) L.R. 1 Sc. & Div. 441.
287. *See*, e.g., *Re A & B (Parental Order Domicile)* [2013] EWHC 426 (Fam), at para. 24, in which Theis J referred to 'the tenacity of the domicile of origin'.
288. *Henderson v. Henderson* [1967] P. 77, at 80. *See also Steadman v. Steadman* [1976] A.C. 356; *R v. R (Divorce: Jurisdiction: Domicile)* [2006] 1 F.L.R. 389.

adopted are treated as if they were born to the adopting parents within wedlock.[289] The same is true of children who are the subject of a parental order.[290] In either case the child will thus take the domicile of the father. A domicile of dependence may be acquired if the parent from whom the domicile was derived acquires a new domicile. In cases involving married parents, the child will take the domicile of the mother if the father dies or the parents are living apart and the child 'has his home with her and has no home with his father'.[291] In this latter case, if the mother dies, the child will retain her domicile unless he or she subsequently makes a home with the father.[292] There are no specific provisions relating to domicile where the child has two legal fathers or two legal mothers.

*117.*  A child may acquire an independent domicile of choice upon attaining the age of 16 years or by marrying under that age[293] (the latter, of course, will only be possible if he or she is domiciled in a country that permits marriage under that age, which England and Wales does not). A domicile of choice may be obtained by residing in a country with the intention of doing so for the indefinite future. The two elements that need to be established are intertwined. As no minimum period of residence is required it may be possible for a person to establish a domicile by choice the moment they arrive in a country where they intend to remain; by contrast, even lengthy periods of residence in a country may not suffice if the person in question never formed the intention to live there permanently.[294] The concept of 'intention' in this context connotes a degree of realism, one cannot intend to do something that one will not be able to do. This means that a person may not be able to acquire a domicile of choice in England and Wales if the rules governing immigration dictate that he or she will not be able to legally reside there;[295] equally, yearnings for one's country of origin do not necessarily prevent a person from acquiring a domicile of choice in another country if they know that they will not be returning back there.[296] Again, domicile must be distinguished from nationality. A change of nationality does not necessarily indicate a change of domicile, although it will be a factor taken into account by the courts in determining whether a person has acquired a domicile of choice.

*118.*  It is implicit in the rationale of the concept of domicile that one's domicile of choice may itself change. In deciding whether there has been a change from one

---

289. *Adoption and Children Act* 2002, s. 67(1).
290. *Human Fertilisation and Embryology Act 2008,* s. 54.
291. *Domicile and Matrimonial Proceedings Act* 1973, s. 4(2)(a). The increasing tendency of the courts to make orders for residence to be shared between both parents (*see* Part II, Ch. 8, para. 385) will obviously have an impact on the scope of this provision.
292. *Domicile and Matrimonial Proceedings Act 1973,* s. 4(3).
293. *Ibid.,* s. 3(1).
294. *See,* e.g., *Winans v. Attorney-General (No. 1)* [1904] A.C. 287; *IRC v. Bullock* [1976] 1 W.L.R. 1178; *Cyganik v. Agulian* [2006] EWCA Civ 129; *Holliday v. Musa* [2010] EWCA Civ 335; *M v. M (Divorce: Domicile)* [2010] EWHC 982 (Fam).
295. *Mark v. Mark* [2005] UKHL 42.
296. *See,* e.g., *Sekhri v. Ray* [2013] EWHC 2290 (Fam).

domicile of choice to another, the standard of proof required is the usual civil standard of the balance of probabilities, rather than the enhanced burden imposed in cases where a change to the domicile of origin is asserted.

*119.* Marriage no longer effects a change to either spouse's domicile. Prior to 1974, a married woman acquired her husband's domicile upon marriage (as a domicile of dependence, rather than a domicile of choice). The Domicile and Matrimonial Proceedings Act 1973 allowed those who married after 1 January 1974 to retain or acquire an independent domicile.[297] It was, however, not retrospective in its effect, and a woman who was already married at that date retained her husband's domicile – as a domicile of choice – unless and until she acquired a new domicile of choice.[298]

As a result, there may still be the occasional case in which it is necessary to determine the domicile of a married woman according to the common law rules.

*120.* It is also possible that a person will lose a domicile of choice without acquiring a new one. A domicile of choice will only be lost if the person in question ceases to reside in the country and has no intention of returning to live there permanently. Unless a new domicile of choice has been acquired, the initial domicile of origin will revive.[299]

§3. HABITUAL RESIDENCE

*121.* The concept of habitual residence is commonly used as a basis of jurisdiction under EU regulations such as Brussels II Revised and is also used as a connecting factor in domestic English statutes.[300] The legal meaning given to 'habitual residence' by the English courts has differed depending on the statutory context in which it arises.

Within EU legislation, habitual residence means the place where the person has established his permanent or habitual centre of interests.[301] A person will only have one habitual residence. A minimum duration of stay in a country is not required but serves only as an indicator in the assessment of the permanence of the residence.[302] In relation to children, the CJEU has interpreted 'habitual residence' to mean the place where the child has achieved some degree of integration with the social and family environment.[303]

---

297. *Domicile and Matrimonial Proceedings Act* 1973, s. 1(1).
298. *Ibid.*, 1973, s. 1(2).
299. *Henwood v. Barlow Clowes International Ltd* [2008] EWCA Civ 577.
300. For example, The Family Law Act 1986; Child Abduction and Custody Act 1985.
301. C-90/97 *Swaddling v. Adjudication Officer* [1999] ECR 1-1075 [29]. C523/07 *Re A (Area of Freedom, Security and Justice)* [2009] 2 FLR 1.
302. C-376/14 *C v. M* [53]; C-497/10 *Mercredi v. Chaffe* [2011] 1 FLR 1293, [51].
303. C523/07 *Re Proceeding Brought by A* [2009] ECR I 2805; C-497/10 *Mercredi v. Chaffe* [2011] 1 FLR 1293; C-376/14PPU *C v. M* [2015] Fam. 116.

The English courts have accepted that for the purposes of Brussels II Revised, an autonomous meaning of habitual residence exists which is different to the traditional meaning given to 'habitual residence' in domestic law.[304] It is now clear that the test for determining the habitual residence of children derives from the EU approach of examining integration with the social and family environment, regardless of whether the issues arise in a domestic or international legislative context.[305]

When interpreting domestic statutes the courts have repeatedly described habitual residence as a 'question of fact',[306] rather than a legal concept, which is to be determined by reference to the individual circumstances of the case.[307] When determining the habitual residence of adults, the English courts require that the new abode has been adopted 'voluntarily'[308] and for a 'settled purpose'[309] of remaining in the country in question for the time being, rather than for an indefinite future. Thus a person, who moves to a country to take up employment under a fixed-term contract, or to undertake a course of study, will be habitually resident there, regardless of his or her long-term intentions.[310] English case law suggests that a person cannot become habitually resident in a new country in a single day and that there is a requirement for an appreciable period of time to establish habitual residence.[311] It has been suggested that an adult may be habitually resident in more than one place (if he or she consistently maintains two homes)[312] or in no place.[313]

In many English cases, the habitual residence of a child has followed that of the parent who has parental responsibility for the child,[314] but there is no automatic rule to this effect.[315] In *Re LC (Children)*,[316] the Supreme Court expressly considered to what extent the child's habitual residence was dependent on that of their primary caregiver. The court emphasized that it is the factual integration of the child into the new community that is under consideration. Once a child leaves the family environment and goes to school it may not be appropriate to determine his habitual residence solely by reference to the intentions of the adult with whom he lives. The idea of a rule that neither parent could unilaterally change the habitual residence of the

---

304. For example, *Marinos v. Marinos* [2007] 2 FLR 1018; *Z v. Z (divorce; jurisdiction)* [2010] 1 FLR 694.
305. *In the Matter of A* [2013] UKSC 60; *In the Matter of KL* [2013] UKSC 75 and *In the matter of LC (Children)* [2014] UKSC 1; *Re S* [2015] EWCA 2.
306. *In the Matter of A* [2013] UKSC 60, [34]. *Re J (A Minor) (Abduction: Custody Rights)* [1990] 2 A.C. 562, at 578; *ES v. AJ* [2011] EWCA Civ 265, at para. 17.
307. *See*, e.g., *Re M (Abduction: Habitual Residence)* [1996] 1 F.L.R. 887, at 895.
308. *DT v. LBT* [2011] 1 FLR 1215.
309. *Shah v. Barnet London Borough Council* [1983] 2 A.C. 309, at 344. *See*, e.g., *Re S (Habitual Residence)* [2009] EWCA Civ 1021; *A v. P (Habitual Residence)* [2011] EWHC 1530 (Fam).
310. *See*, e.g., *DT v. LBT* [2010] EWHC 3177 (Fam); *Re H-K (Children)* [2011] EWCA Civ 1100; *EF v. MGS* [2011] EWHC 3139 (Fam).
311. *Re J (A Minor) (Abduction: Custody Rights)* [1990] 2 A.C. 562, at 578; *Nessa v. Chief Adjudication Officer* [1999] 2 F.L.R. 1116;. *ES v. AJ* [2011] EWCA Civ 265.
312. *Ikimi v. Ikimi* [2001] 2 F.L.R. 1288; *Armstrong v. Armstrong* [2003] EWHC 777 (Fam).
313. *See*, e.g., *W & B v. H (Child Abduction: Surrogacy) (No. 1)* [2002] 1 F.L.R. 1008: *Al Habtoor v. Fotheringham* [2001] EWCA Civ 186. *In the matter of LC (Children)* [2014] UKSC 1, [63].
314. *Re M (Minors) (Residence Order: Jurisdiction)* [1993] 1 F.L.R. 495, at 500.
315. *See*, e.g., *W & B v. H (Child Abduction: Surrogacy) (No. 1)* [2002] 1 F.L.R. 1008; *Re A* [2013] UKSC 60, [54].
316. [2014] UK SC 1.

child without permission of the other where both parents share parental responsibility has been expressly consigned to history by the Court of Appeal in favour of a factual enquiry tailored to the circumstances of an individual child.[317]

A child cannot acquire a new habitual residence while physically resident elsewhere.[318] Therefore a change in a parent's habitual residence will not change a child's habitual residence if the child does not accompany the parent to the new country.[319] The question of whether a child can acquire habitual residence in the country of birth where the mother had been held there during pregnancy against her will, was raised in *Re A*.[320] The Supreme Court remitted the question of whether jurisdiction could be exercised in relation to the child as a British national to the High Court. However, it was left open to the parties to refer the question to the CJEU if jurisdiction on the basis of nationality was not exercised as this was not *acte claire* within EU law. Lady Hale[321] and Lord Hughes[322] expressed contrasting views on the issue.

The EU 'centre of interests' test has recently been adopted for establishing jurisdiction of the Court of Protection under the Mental Capacity Act 2005. In this case, Moylan J held that both the degree of integration into society and the person's state of mind were relevant factors when the court is undertaking a broad factual assessment of the habitual residence of an individual who lacked capacity to decide where to live.[323]

## §4. DOMICILE OR HABITUAL RESIDENCE?

*122.* Given that the concepts of domicile and habitual residence differ in so many respects, in what circumstances will one concept be preferred to the other? Thorpe L.J. acknowledged in *Al Habtoor v. Fotheringham* that:

> [i]n order to achieve essential collaboration internationally it has been necessary to relax reliance upon concepts understood only in common law circles. Thus our historic emphasis on the somewhat artificial concept of domicile has had to cede to an acknowledgement that the simpler fact-based concept of habitual residence must be the currency of international exchange.[324]

---

317. *Re H (Jurisdiction)* [2014] EWCA Civ 1101, [26]–[37].
318. *Re M (Abduction: Habitual Residence)* [1996] 1 F.L.R. 887; *Al Habtoor v. Fotheringham* [2001] EWCA Civ 186.
319. *ES v. AJ* [2011] EWCA Civ 265.
320. *Re A* [2013] UKSC 60.
321. *Ibid.,* [54]–[56].
322. *Ibid.,* [82]–[86].
323. *An English Local Authority v. SW and Another* [2014] EWCOP 43, [72].
324. [2001] EWCA Civ 186, at para. 42.

By contrast, the concept of domicile continues to determine an individual's capacity to marry[325] or enter into a civil partnership, or to make a will.[326] It also governs the essential validity of a will.

*123.* Yet there is not necessarily any contradiction between the two concepts, since they are used in different contexts. The fact that the courts of a particular country have jurisdiction to hear a case does not mean that the laws of that country will be applicable to the issue in question. For example, a court in England and Wales might have jurisdiction to hear an application for nullity of marriage on the basis that one of the parties was habitually resident in England and Wales,[327] but the parties' capacity to enter into the marriage would be determined by the law of their domicile.

*124.* In some contexts, the two concepts may be deployed as alternatives.[328] An example is provided by the Wills Act 1963, which provides that:

> [a] will shall be treated as properly executed if its execution confirmed to the internal law in force in the territory where it was executed, or in the territory where, at the time of its execution or the testator's death, he was domiciled or had his habitual residence, or in a state of which, at either of those times, he was a national.[329]

This reflects the presumption in favour of due execution: as long as the will was properly executed by the law of one of these jurisdictions, this will suffice. As Murphy has pointed out, this section 'makes formal invalidity a highly unlikely (if not altogether impossible) event'.[330]

---

325. *Cheni v. Cheni* [1965] P. 85; *R v. Brentwood Superintendent Registrar of Marriages ex p Arias* [1968] 2 Q.B. 956.
326. *Groos v. Groos* [1915] 1 Ch. 572.
327. For example, under Council Regulation (EC) No. 2201/2003, Art. 3(1)(a).
328. Article 3(2) Brussels II Revised.
329. *Wills Act* 1963, s. 1.
330. J. Murphy, *International Dimensions in Family Law* 174 (Manchester U. Press 2005).

# Chapter 7. Mental Incapacity

## §1. BASIC PRINCIPLES

*125.* In previous chapters, reference has been made to the rights of those of full age and capacity, and consideration has been given to the particular position of minors. This chapter will consider the position of those adults who lack capacity, which is governed by the Mental Capacity Act 2005.[331] The scope of the Act was helpfully explained by Lewison J in *In re P (Statutory Will)*:

> First it brings together under one common framework the former powers of the court to make decisions both about a person's property and his personal welfare. It thus applies to all manner of decisions from the relatively minor to the most important. Second, it applies not only to decisions that the court might make, but also to decisions that others (carers, doctors, deputies) might make. Third, the test of incapacity is finely calibrated. The Act recognizes that the test of capacity is issue specific. A person ('P') may well have capacity in relation to some matters (e.g., what to wear or what to eat), while lacking capacity as regards others (e.g., what to do with his savings or whether to undergo an operation). A person's capacity may also vary from time to time … Fourth, the overarching principle is that any decision made on behalf of P must be made in P's best interests.[332]

## I. The Assumption of Capacity

*126.* The starting point of the law is that a person does have capacity; he or she must be assumed to have capacity unless the contrary is established.[333] A lack of capacity must be established on the balance of probabilities,[334] and cannot be based solely on a person's age or appearance, or a condition that 'might lead others to make unjustified assumptions about his capacity'.[335] In relation to the making of specific decisions, it is further provided that a person 'is not to be treated as unable to make a decision unless all practicable steps to help him to do so have been taken without success'.[336] The fact that the decision taken is unwise does not of itself justify treating the person as unable to make a decision,[337] although it will be a factor to be taken into account in determining whether that person does have capacity.[338]

---

331. For full details *see Heywood & Massey's Court of Protection Practice* (D. Rees ed., 14th ed., Sweet & Maxwell 2007).
332. [2009] EWHC 163 (Ch), paras 36–37.
333. *Mental Capacity Act* 2005, s. 1(2).
334. *Ibid.*, s. 2(4).
335. *Ibid.*, s. 2(3).
336. *Ibid.*, s. 1(3).
337. *Ibid.*, s. 1(4). *See,* e.g., *PC & Anor v. City of York Council* [2013] EWCA Civ 478.
338. As in cases such as *Banks v. Goodfellow* [1870] L.R. 5 QB 549 and *Sharp v. Adam* [2006] EWCA Civ 449.

## II. Determining When a Person Lacks Capacity

*127.* A person who is unable to make a decision for himself or herself in relation to a particular matter because of an impairment of, or a disturbance in the functioning of, the mind or brain at the material time, is held to lack capacity in relation to that particular matter.[339] The disturbance or impairment may be permanent or temporary.[340] It is further provided that a person is unable to make a decision for himself or herself if he or she cannot understand the information relevant to the decision, retain that information, use or weigh that information as part of the process of making the decision, or communicate his or her decision (whether by talking, using sign language, or any other means).[341]

It is clear from this that the issue of capacity is specific both to the particular decision and to the time at which the decision is taken. At any given moment in time, a person might have capacity to make one kind of decision but not another; at another point he or she might have the capacity to make either decision – or alternatively might lack the capacity to make any decision. This retains the approach of the common law, which held that the level of understanding necessary for certain legal transactions was higher than that required for others.[342] For example, making a valid will required a higher level of understanding than that required to enter into a valid marriage.[343]

*128.* If it is determined that an individual lacked capacity at the time of making a particular decision, the effect may be to invalidate the act in question. Thus, a will made while a person lacks capacity to do so will be invalid, while a marriage or civil partnership entered into by a person who lacks capacity will be voidable.[344] A contract will be voidable at the election of the person who lacks capacity, although if the other party was unaware of the lack of capacity it will be binding. Like minors, those who lack capacity are liable to pay a reasonable price for any goods or services provided under a contract that are deemed to be necessaries.[345]

## III. Making Decisions on Behalf of a Person Who Lacks Capacity

*129.* It may be decided that an individual lacks capacity to make decisions concerning his or her personal welfare or property and affairs. In this case, the Court of Protection may exercise its powers to make those decisions on that individual's behalf, or to appoint a deputy to make such decisions.[346] The 2005 Act stated that any act done or decision made, under the Act 'for or on behalf of a person who lacks

---

339. *Mental Capacity Act* 2005, s. 2(1). For discussion *see R v. C* [2009] UKHL 42.
340. *Ibid.*, s. 2(2).
341. *Ibid.*, s. 3(1).
342. *See*, e.g., *Re Beaney* [1978] 1 W.L.R. 770 at 774; *Singellos v. Singellos* [2010] EWHC 2353 (Ch).
343. *See*, e.g., *Re Park's Estate* [1953] 2 All E.R. 1411.
344. *Matrimonial Causes Act* 1973, s. 12(c), Part II, Ch. 1, para. 199; *Civil Partnership Act* 2004, s. 50(1)(a), Part II, Ch. 2, para. 234.
345. *Mental Incapacity Act* 2005, s. 7.
346. *Ibid.*, s. 16(2).

capacity must be done, or made, in his best interests',[347] substituting a 'structured decision-making process' for the 'mental gymnastics' involved under the previous law.[348] The person making the decision is required to consider whether the person lacking capacity is likely to have the capacity to make that decision at any point in the future,[349] to encourage his or her participation in the decision as far as possible,[350] and to consider such matters as 'the person's past and present wishes and feelings ... the beliefs and values that would be likely to influence his decision if he had capacity ... and the other factors that he would be likely to consider if he were able to do so'.[351] In other words, the statutory scheme emphasizes the need 'to see the patient as an individual, with his own values, likes and dislikes, and to consider his best interests in a holistic way'.[352]

*130.* The legislation also adopts the principle that before any act is done or decision is made, 'regard must be had to whether the purpose for which it is needed can be as effectively achieved in a way that is less restrictive of the person's rights and freedom of action'.[353] This applies both to the process of deciding who is to make the decision and what the content of that decision should be. It will, for example, be preferable for the Court of Protection to make a one-off decision on behalf of a person who lacks capacity than to appoint a deputy to make ongoing decisions on behalf of that person.[354] However, as Lewison J pointed out in *In re P (Statutory Will)*, there is no requirement that the least restrictive route be followed: '[t]he only imperative is that the decision must be made in P's best interests.'[355]

*131.* Since it is a basic presumption of the legislation that a person does have capacity, the mere fact that a deputy has been appointed does not mean that the decision of the deputy will override the decision of the person on whose behalf the decision is being made. A deputy does not have the power to make a decision on behalf of a person if there are reasonable grounds for believing that that person has capacity in relation to that particular matter.[356]

*132.* Those who realize that their capacity is diminishing may create a lasting power of attorney conferring on a specified donee the authority to make decisions once the donor no longer has capacity.[357] The decision-making capacity conferred on the donee may relate to all matters concerning the donor's personal welfare and property, or be confined to matters specified by the donor.[358]

---

347. *Ibid.*, s. 1(5).
348. *In re P (Statutory Will)* [2009] EWHC 163 (Ch), at para. 38.
349. *Mental Incapacity Act* 2005, s. 4(3).
350. *Ibid.*, s. 4(4).
351. *Ibid.*, s. 4(5).
352. *Aintree University Hospitals NHS Foundation Trust v. James* [2013] UKSC 67, para. 26.
353. *Mental Incapacity Act* 2005, s. 1(6).
354. *Ibid.*, s. 16(4).
355. [2009] EWHC 163 (Ch), para. 46.
356. *Mental Capacity Act* 2005, s. 20(1).
357. *Ibid.*, s. 9(1).
358. *Ibid.*, s. 9(1).

The donor of a lasting power of attorney must have sufficient capacity to execute the document.[359] Lasting powers of attorney must be made in a prescribed form,[360] and must be accompanied by a certificate by an appropriate person that the donor understood the purpose of the instrument creating the lasting power of attorney and the scope of the authority it conferred, that no fraud or undue pressure was used to induce the donor to confer such authority on another, and that there are no other reasons to prevent a lasting power of attorney from being created.[361] An application to register the instrument intended to create a lasting power of attorney must then be made to the Public Guardian,[362] who will register it unless there are statutory grounds not to do so.[363] A lasting power of attorney cannot be relied upon until it has been registered. A donor who retains capacity may revoke a lasting power of attorney.[364]

## IV. Decisions That May Not Be Made on Behalf of a Person Who Lacks Capacity

*133.* The Mental Capacity Act 2005 sets out a number of 'excluded decisions': nothing in the Act gives a person the power to give a consent on behalf of a person who lacks capacity to marriage or civil partnership,[365] to the ending of such a relationship on the basis of two years' separation plus consent,[366] or to sexual relations.[367] Restrictions are also placed on consent to adoption[368] or under the Human Fertilization and Embryology Acts 1990 or 2008,[369] and on the exercise of parental responsibility in matters not relating to a child's property.[370] Further provisions constrain the giving of treatment for mental disorder.[371]

---

359. *Ibid.*, s. 9(2)(c).
360. *Ibid.*, Sch. 1, para. 2(1).
361. *Ibid.*, Sch. 1, para. 2(1)(e).
362. *Ibid.*, Sch. 1, para. 4.
363. *Ibid.*, Sch. 1, para. 5.
364. *Ibid.*, s. 13(2).
365. *Mental Incapacity Act* 2005, s. 27(1)(a).
366. *Ibid.*, s. 27(1)(c) and (d).
367. *Ibid.*, s. 27(1)(b).
368. *Ibid.*, s. 27(1)(e) and (f). Note, however, that the court may decide in certain circumstances to dispense with a parent's consent: *see* Part II, Ch. 7, para. 352.
369. *Mental Capacity Act* 2005, s. 27(1)(h) and (i).
370. *Ibid.*, s. 27(1)(g).
371. *Ibid.*, s. 28.

# Part II. Family Law

## Chapter 1. Marriage

### §1. THE NATURE OF MARRIAGE

*134.* The law's concept of marriage – both in terms of who may marry and what the obligations of marriage are – has undergone profound changes over the years. Same-sex couples have been entitled to marry in England and Wales since March 2014, and the law is – in theory at least – largely gender neutral as regards the respective obligations of the spouses. The best summary of these different elements is that provided by Munby J in *Sheffield City Council v E and S*.[372] As he put it, marriage 'whether civil or religious, is a contract, formally entered into', that confers the status of married persons on the parties. The essence of this contract is an agreement 'to live together ... and to love one another ... to the exclusion of all others' and it creates 'a relationship of mutual and reciprocal obligations' that typically involves 'the sharing of a common home and a common domestic life and the right to enjoy each other's society, comfort and assistance'. As this chapter will show, however, many of these elements reflect social expectations rather than legal obligations.

### §2. THE CAPACITY TO MARRY

*135.* The topic of capacity to marry can be divided into two: those factors affecting the individual (e.g., age, existing marital status) and those factors affecting the couple (e.g., are they too closely related to each other). The law provides that a marriage is void if the parties do not have capacity to marry each other.[373]

### I. Age

*136.* Both parties to the marriage must be aged 16 years or over.[374] This is an absolute restriction. The marriage of a person who honestly believes that he or she has attained this age but in fact has not will still be void.

---

372. [2004] EWHC 2808 (Fam), at para. 132.
373. *See infra*, s. 5, Void, Voidable and Non-Existent Marriages.
374. *Matrimonial Causes Act* 1973, s. 11(a)(ii); *Marriage Act* 1949, s. 2.

It is not possible to escape this restriction by marrying overseas. In addition, the marriage of a person domiciled in England and Wales to someone under the age of 16 years will be void under English law even if the latter has capacity to marry by the law of their own domicile and even if the marriage takes place in a country that permits such marriages.[375] The key point is that a person domiciled in England and Wales does not have capacity to enter into a marriage with a person who is under the age of 16 years.

*137.* The consent of a parent or person with parental responsibility is required for the marriage of a 16- or 17-year old, but the absence of such consent does not invalidate the marriage. This requirement is considered further below.[376]

## II. Marital Status

*138.* An individual does not have capacity to marry if he or she is already married to, or in a civil partnership with, someone else at the time of the ceremony.[377] Again, this requirement is absolute. An honest belief that the previous marriage or civil partnership has been terminated, or that the previous spouse or partner has died is irrelevant for these purposes.

*139.* This means that a person whose first spouse or partner is still alive is not free to marry again until the decree of divorce or order of dissolution has been made absolute or the previous marriage or civil partnership has been annulled. There may, of course, be some cases in which it is uncertain whether the first spouse or civil partner is still alive. In such cases, the court may grant a decree of presumption of death and dissolution of marriage if it is satisfied that there are reasonable grounds for supposing the first spouse to have died.[378] The legislation provides that 'the fact that for a period of seven years or more the other party to the marriage has been continually absent from the applicant[379] and the applicant has no reason to believe that the other party has been living within that time shall be evidence that the other party is dead until the contrary is proved'.[380] The grant of a decree absolute terminates the marriage, and the applicant may remarry even if it transpires that the former spouse is still alive.

It should be noted that while a prior marriage always renders a later marriage void, the spouse who goes through a second ceremony of marriage is not necessarily guilty of the crime of bigamy, since he or she may lack the necessary *mens rea*.

---

375. *Pugh v. Pugh* [1951] P. 482.
376. *See infra*, s. 3, Formalities of Marriage.
377. *Matrimonial Causes Act* 1973, s. 11(b).
378. *Matrimonial Causes Act* 1973, s. 19; *see also Civil Partnership Act* 2004, s. 55.
379. In the light of the modernization of language by the Family Procedure Rules 2010, the terms 'applicant' and 'apply' are used throughout in preference to the older 'petitioner' and 'petition' save where quoting directly from the relevant legislation.
380. *Ibid.*, s. 19(3).

*140.* English law also provides that a person who is domiciled in England and Wales does not have capacity to enter into a polygamous marriage overseas, even if the marriage is celebrated in a country that permits polygamy.[381]

## III. Consanguinity and Affinity

*141.* The intending spouses must not be related to each other within the prohibited degrees of consanguinity (blood relationships) or affinity (relationships by marriage).[382]

At one time, the degrees within which marriage was prohibited were extremely wide; under the Canon law even those related to the seventh degree were unable to marry, and sex, as well as marriage, created relationships of affinity (so, e.g., Henry VIII could annul his marriage to Anne Boleyn on the basis that he had previously had sexual intercourse with her sister).

*142.* The prohibited degrees have been progressively narrowed. The law now states that a person may not marry his (or her) grandparent, parent, child, grandchild, sibling, aunt/uncle, or niece/nephew.[383]

*143.* The only restrictions now created by marriage are those that prohibit marriage between a step-parent and his or her stepchild and between a step-grandparent and step-grandchild.[384] In such cases, the prohibition is not absolute: a marriage may take place if both parties are over 21 years and have not lived together as parent and child at any time before the child was 18 years. The restriction is intended to protect minors from potentially exploitative relationships with a person who has been as a parent to them; if, by contrast, the parties met when both were adults there is no such policy reason for prohibiting a marriage between them. Of course, the restriction on a marriage taking place between step-parent and stepchild only prevents the formalization of the relationship, rather than the relationship itself; the latter is a matter for the criminal law.[385]

*144.* The restrictions on marriage between former in-laws were only gradually eliminated from the law, with the last of these restrictions being abolished as late as 2007. This last reform was in response to a legal challenge by a couple – a man and his former daughter-in-law – who wished to marry. The European Court of Human Rights held that English law – which prohibited such marriages unless both parties were over the age of 21 years and, more significantly, their former spouses were both dead – was in breach of Article 12 of the European Convention on Human Rights.[386] One of the justifications for this finding was that the restriction could be dispensed with by a private Act of Parliament. The European Court felt that this

---

381. *Matrimonial Causes Act* 1973, s. 11(d).
382. *Matrimonial Causes Act* 1973, s. 11(a)(i); *Marriage Act* 1949, s. 1 and Sch. 1.
383. *Marriage Act* 1949, Sch. 1, Part I.
384. *Ibid.*, Part II.
385. *Sexual Offences Act* 2003, s. 25.
386. *B and L v. UK* [2006] 1 F.L.R. 35.

undermined the rationality and logic of the restriction. The law was subsequently amended to remove the offending restriction,[387] and former in-laws may now marry each other.

*145.* While the trend in the twentieth century was to remove restrictions on marriage, the introduction of adoption as a legal concept in 1926 meant that new rules had to be formulated to deal with this particular situation. The rules relating to adopted children aim to reflect both biological and social realities. The restrictions on marriage to members of one's biological family apply just as if the adoption had never occurred. To this extent the law deviates from the idea of adoption as a 'legal transplant' whereby the child becomes, for all legal purposes, the child of the adoptive parents. There are additional restrictions on marriage between the child and the adoptive parents,[388] reflecting the policy that it is inappropriate for a marriage to take place between persons whose relationship has been that of parent and child. However, adopted children are able to marry any other members of their adoptive families.

§3. FORMALITIES OF MARRIAGE

*146.* There are three key stages to the solemnization of a marriage in England and Wales: preliminaries, celebration and registration. The law governing these three stages is complex, as it still retains the imprint of the law of earlier centuries, and the opening up of marriage to same-sex couples has added an extra layer of complexity.

*147.* Anglican ceremonies retain certain privileges reflecting the importance of the Established Church; Jews and Quakers, as a result of their exemption from the first legislation to regulate marriage in 1753, also enjoy special treatment; marriages according to other religious rites may take place but must satisfy a number of further hurdles. Couples may also choose to marry in a civil ceremony, and this option is now the most popular, largely due to the fact that a wider choice of venues is available for civil weddings. Different rules again apply to the marriages of prisoners, those in psychiatric hospitals, the housebound, and those who are terminally ill and not expected to recover. The precise legal formalities to be followed thus depend on the way in which the marriage is celebrated, as well as the parties marrying.

---

387. *Marriage Act 1949 (Remedial Order)* 2007, S.I. 2007/438.
388. *Marriage Act* 1949, Sch. 1, Part I.

## I.  Preliminaries

### A.  Parental Consent

*148.*  If a 16- or 17-year old wishes to marry then he or she will need to obtain the necessary consents.[389] While the lack of such consent does not invalidate the marriage once it has been celebrated, it is possible for those whose consent is required to prevent the marriage from going ahead.

Precisely whose consent is necessary will depend on the circumstances of the child. In most cases, it is parental consent that is required, although only a parent with parental responsibility is entitled to give such consent. If a guardian has been appointed, then he or she must also consent. The consent of other persons or institutions may be required if any of the following orders are in place: a special guardianship order (the special guardian); a care order or placement order (the local authority); a residence order (the person with whom the child resides under the order). In addition, if an adoption agency has been authorized to place a child for adoption, its consent will be required, and if the child has actually been placed with prospective adopters, their consent will be required. If any person whose consent is required refuses to give it, or is unable to do so (by reason of absence, inaccessibility, or disability), then the court may consent to the marriage.

### B.  Publicizing the Intention to Marry

*149.*  The preliminaries required by the law are intended to publicize the intended marriage so that any legal obstacles will be discovered before the marriage actually takes place.

Heterosexual couples who choose to marry according to the rites of the Church of England have a choice as to which preliminaries to observe.[390] Most choose to have banns called in the parish(es) where they reside. This ancient procedure, which dates from the first millennium, involves the minister announcing the intended marriage during a church service on three successive Sundays. Couples who wish to avoid this publicity may opt instead to be married by license. In this case they are required to make certain declarations as to their freedom to marry before the relevant church authorities. A third possibility is a special license. This can only be obtained from the Archbishop of Canterbury and is more expensive than the other preliminaries but, unlike banns or common license, allows the parties to be married at any time or place.

*150.*  A marriage in the Church of England may also be preceded by civil preliminaries,[391] as must civil weddings and those which are to be celebrated according to non-Anglican rites. Since the option of an Anglican wedding is not open to

---

389. *Marriage Act* 1949, s. 3.
390. *Ibid.*, s. 5.
391. *Ibid.*, s. 17.

same-sex couples, they too must follow the civil preliminaries.[392] Both parties are required to give notice of their intention to marry in person (although not necessarily together) to their local superintendent registrar.[393] The details of the parties will be displayed at the superintendent registrar's office for twenty-eight days, after which (assuming no objections have been made) the superintendent registrar will issue a certificate authorizing the marriage to go ahead.

*151.* There is special provision for the superintendent registrar to attend those who are housebound or detained and therefore unable to give notice in person.[394] A person who is ill and not expected to recover may obtain a special license from the Archbishop of Canterbury (if the marriage is to be celebrated according to Anglican rites) or a license from the Registrar General.[395] A longer waiting period of seventy days also applies to non-nationals.

## II. Celebration

### A. The Place of Celebration

*152.* If the marriage is to take place according to the rites of the Church of England, it must take place in the Anglican Church, unless a special license has been obtained.[396] This option remains limited to opposite-sex couples, although provision has been made for this to be changed if the Governing Body of the Church in Wales resolves to allow the marriages of same-sex couples according to the rites of the Church in Wales.[397]

*153.* The legislation does not specify where Jewish and Quaker couples should marry, leaving it to the relevant religious authorities to set their own requirements. Same-sex couples may be able to celebrate their marriages according to Jewish or Quaker rites, but this will depend on whether the relevant governing authority has given written consent to this.[398]

*154.* Those who belong to other religions or denominations may validly marry according to the rites of that religion if their local place of worship has been registered as such and is licensed for marriages. If their local place of worship is not registered for marriage – and many mosques and temples are not – the couple will need to go through a civil ceremony of marriage, either in addition to or instead of

---

392. *Marriage Act* 1949, s. 26, as amended by the *Marriage (Same Sex Couples) Act* 2013.
393. *Ibid.,* s. 27.
394. *Marriage Act* 1949, s. 27(7).
395. *Marriage (Registrar-General's License) Act* 1970.
396. *Marriage Act* 1949, s. 12 (marriage by banns), s. 15 (marriage by common license), s. 17 (marriage under superintendent registrar's certificate).
397. *Marriage (Same Sex Couples) Act* 2013, s. 8.
398. *Marriage Act* 1949, s. 26B, as inserted by the *Marriage (Same Sex Couples) Act* 2013.

a religious ceremony. Again, whether or not same-sex couples are able to celebrate their marriages in a registered building depends on whether the relevant governing authority has given written consent.[399]

*155.* Until 1994 a civil ceremony could only take place in a register office, but the Marriage Act 1994 provided that it could be celebrated at any premises approved by the local authority. Many hotels and stately homes have taken advantage of these provisions to offer a full package of wedding-cum-reception, and the plethora of attractive venues now available has led to an increase in civil weddings. Same-sex couples are able to marry in any of the venues available for civil weddings.[400]

*156.* Provision is made for those who are terminally ill to marry at home or in hospital, as appropriate; while those who are housebound or detained may marry where they are confined.[401]

## B. *The Celebrant*

*157.* An Anglican marriage must be celebrated by a clergyman of the Church of England, and if the parties 'knowingly and wilfully consent to or acquiesce in the solemnization of the marriage by any person who is not in Holy Orders', their marriage will be void.[402]

*158.* A civil marriage must take place before a superintendent registrar, and there is an equivalent provision rendering void any marriage 'knowingly and wilfully' celebrated in the absence of such a person.[403]

*159.* The legislation does not regulate the marriages of Quakers and Jews, and the celebration of such marriages is a matter for the relevant religious authorities.

*160.* For other religious marriages celebrated in registered buildings, there must be present either an 'authorized person' – authorized by the trustees or governing body of the building and duly noted to the Registrar General[404] – or a registrar.[405]

## C. *The Content of the Ceremony*

*161.* The content of the ceremony is largely left to the relevant religious authorities or, in the case of civil marriages, to the parties themselves. Thus Anglican weddings, e.g., will be celebrated according to one of the forms for the solemnization of

---

399. *Ibid.,* s. 26A.
400. *Marriage Act* 1949, s. 26, as amended by the *Marriage (Same Sex Couples) Act* 2013.
401. *Marriage Act* 1949, s. 27, as amended by the *Marriage Act* 1983.
402. *Marriage Act* 1949, s. 25.
403. *Marriage Act* 1949, s. 49(g).
404. *Marriage Act* 1949, s. 43.
405. *Ibid.,* s. 49(f).

matrimony that have been approved by the Church of England. There are, however, certain words that must be included in civil ceremonies and in those religious weddings celebrated in registered buildings (i.e., those that are not Anglican, Jewish, or Quaker). At some point in the service, the parties must declare – in words prescribed by statute[406] – that they are free to marry each other and that they take one another as husband and wife. In addition, certain material is excluded from civil ceremonies: no religious service may be used,[407] and readings from religious texts or the singing of hymns are not allowed, although material that contains incidental religious references is permitted.

### D. When Is a Couple Married?

*162.* It is often assumed that a couple is married only when the celebrant declares them to be so. Under the current law, however, there is a strong case for arguing that the parties are married as soon as consent has been exchanged, reflecting the key role of consent in marriage. The precise timing is unlikely to have an impact in most cases – unless there is a repetition of the Australian case of *Quick v. Quick*,[408] where the bride changed her mind after the vows but before the vicar's pronouncement that they were husband and wife (but was too late to prevent the marriage).

## III. Registration

*163.* Although all marriages, however celebrated, should be registered, the validity of the marriage is not affected by non-registration.[409] This is because the parties are already married by the end of the service – assuming that there were no impediments – and the validity of the marriage cannot be affected by later events or non-events.

Of course, the validity of the marriage may be affected by a failure to comply with the other formalities set out above, although some of the statutory requirements are directory rather than mandatory and a failure to comply will not invalidate the marriage. The rather complex rules are discussed further below.[410]

## IV. Presumption in Favour of Marriage

*164.* The complexities of the rules described above may make any intending spouses fearful lest they fail to comply and their resulting marriage is invalid. Such

---

406. *Marriage Act* 1949, s. 44(3) and (3A) (Ceremonies in Registered Buildings) and s. 45(1) (Civil Ceremonies).
407. *Ibid.*, s. 45(1).
408. [1953] VLR 224.
409. R. Probert, 'The Registration of Marriages' [2017] Fam. Law 1103.
410. *See infra*, s. 5, Void, Voidable and Non-Existent Marriages.

fears may be assuaged by the statutory provision that, in general, only a 'knowing and wilful' failure to comply will invalidate the marriage (discussed further below), and by the common law presumption in favour of marriage.

*165.* The latter provides that if a couple has gone through a purported ceremony of marriage, and then live together and enjoy the reputation of married persons, the court will presume that the marriage was validly celebrated. As Lord Campbell noted in *Piers v. Piers* 'until the contrary is proved, we are bound to draw the inference that everything existed which was necessary to constitute a valid marriage'.[411] Over the years the presumption has been relied upon to presume that sufficient notice has been given of the marriage,[412] that the religious building in which the marriage was celebrated was duly registered,[413] or that the marriage had been subsequently registered.[414]

*166.* While any presumption can be rebutted by evidence to the contrary, the courts have taken the view that very clear evidence is required to rebut this particular presumption. In *Mahadervan v. Mahadervan,* it was suggested that the evidence rebutting the presumption must be such as to satisfy the court 'beyond reasonable doubt' that there was no marriage,[415] as compared to the normal civil standard of proof. More recently, however, the Court of Appeal in *Hayatleh v. Modfy* referred to the need for 'clear, positive or compelling' evidence.[416]

*167.* The ceremony in question must, however, be one that is prima facie capable of giving rise to a valid marriage by the *lex loci celebrationis*; otherwise, as the court in *Kalinowska v. Kalinowska* pointed out, 'proof of some ceremony, however bizarre, coupled with cohabitation, would give rise to an almost irrebuttable presumption'.[417] This explains the difference in treatment of different types of ceremonies in recent cases: those taking place in locations that could have been registered for marriage can be presumed to be valid, whereas those taking place in locations where the law would not have permitted a marriage of that type to take place cannot.[418] There is however a division of opinion in recent cases as to what happens if the ceremony is shown to be invalid. In *Chief Adjudication Officer v. Bath,* Robert Walker L.J. referred to the ceremony as 'irregular' and doubted whether it would have been upheld as valid had they separated shortly afterwards. He explicitly justified his decision in favour of the validity of the marriage on the basis of the duration of the parties' relationship. The problem with this reasoning is that it assumes that a marriage can become valid over time. A different approach was adopted in

---

411. *Piers v. Piers* [1849] 9 E.R. 1118, 1136.
412. *Russell v. AG* [1949] P. 391.
413. *R v. Manwaring* (1856) 169 E.R. 948; *Sichel v. Lambert* (1864) 143 E.R. 992.
414. *Hayatleh v. Modfy* [2017] EWCA Civ 70.
415. [1964] P. 233, 246.
416. *Hayatleh v. Modfy* [2017] EWCA Civ 70, at para. 49.
417. [1964] 108 S.J. 260. *See also Collett v. Collett* [1968] P. 482 and more recently *Al-Saedy v. Musawi* [2010] EWHC 3293 (Fam).
418. Contrast for example the different outcomes in *Chief Adjudication Officer v. Bath* [2000] 1 F.L.R. 8 and *Dukali v. Lamrani* [2012] EWHC 1748.

*A-M v. A-M*,[419] in which a second lawful marriage was presumed to have taken place. More realistic was the approach in *Al-Saedy v. Musawi*,[420] in which it was stressed that there would have to be some evidential foundation for the possibility that a marriage had taken place. The judge quoted with approval the words of the Australian court in *Lister v. Lister*[421] to the effect that 'the application of the presumption must be consonant with the evidence in the case, not sit, as it does here, in an evidentiary vacuum'.[422]

*168.* It should also be noted that the significance attached to the cohabitation of the parties has changed over time. In earlier periods there was an assumption that a couple would be unlikely to live together unless they were married, and so it was the fact of cohabitation that was important, rather than its duration. That a lengthy period of time had passed since the celebration of the marriage might be regarded as an additional reason for wishing to find in favour of its validity, but it was not a prerequisite. Since *Chief Adjudication Officer v. Bath*, however, it has been assumed that the presumption will only arise where the parties have lived together for some time.[423] The logic of this depends on whether cohabitation is thought to provide an independent ground for upholding a marriage; if not then the duration of cohabitation should be immaterial.

§4. Effects of Marriage

*169.* The effect of a valid marriage under English law is largely a matter of inference. Nowhere in legislation do we find a convenient list of the obligations that spouses owe to one another (although Schedule 27 of the Civil Partnership Act 2004, which deals with the minor and consequential amendments necessitated by the introduction of a concept of civil partnership, provides an unrivalled overview of the occasions on which the word 'spouse' appears in legislation). Often the only way of inferring that an obligation is owed is the existence of a remedy in case of breach. For example, we may infer from the fact that a court will grant a divorce to one spouse upon evidence that the other has committed adultery that the spouses owe each other an obligation of sexual fidelity, but one would search in vain for any explicit statement to that effect in statute.

Modern judges appear to be equally wary of making sweeping statements about the effects of marriage. However, *Sheffield City Council v. E*[424] – dealing with the

---

419. [2001] 2 F.L.R. 6.
420. [2010] EWHC 3293 (Fam). *See also MA v. JA and the Attorney General* [2012] EWHC 2219 (Fam), in which it was correctly held that the presumption that the wedding had complied with all the stipulated formalities could not apply once it had been shown that this was not the case.
421. 2007 36 Fam. LR 438.
422. [2010] EWHC 3293 (Fam), at para. 70.
423. *AAA v. ASH* [2009] EWHC 636; *Dukali v. Lamrani* [2012] EWHC 1748; *Hayatleh v. Modfy* [2017] EWCA Civ 70.
424. [2004] EWHC 2808 (Fam).

issue of what a person should be able to understand in order to have capacity to enter into a valid marriage – provides a useful overview of what marriage usually involves:

> Marriage … confers on the parties the status of husband and wife, the essence of the contract being an agreement between a man and a woman to live together, and to love one another as husband and wife, to the exclusion of all others. It creates a relationship of mutual and reciprocal obligations, typically involving the sharing of a common home and a common domestic life and the right to enjoy each other's society, comfort, and assistance.[425]

Of course, while useful in its specific context, this has its deficiencies as a definition of the legal effects of marriage. If one were to subject each of the points stated by the judge to strict legal analysis, one might quibble that there is no legal 'duty' of love; that spouses may live 'together apart'; and that there is no guarantee that they will enjoy each other's company, still less that there is an enforceable right to it.

To determine the legal effects of marriage, then, it is necessary to piece together rules from a variety of sources on a range of topics. Two broad sets of rules need to be distinguished: first, those that originated in the common law (into which category fall the doctrine of unity and the common law concept of consortium, both broad concepts that have been whittled down by statute, as well as a number of specific rights); second, the specific statutory provisions imposing duties or providing remedies to spouses whose partners have fallen short of implied duties. These will be considered in turn. A number of areas in which marriage does not have any automatic consequences would thereafter be considered, and the section closes with a brief discussion of the consequences of an engagement to marry.

## I. Common Law Concepts

### A. The Doctrine of Unity

*170.* The doctrine of unity was the legal equivalent of the Christian tenet that husband and wife were 'one flesh';[426] according to the eighteenth century jurist Blackstone:

> By marriage, the husband and wife are one person in law: that is, the very being or legal existence of the woman is suspended during the marriage, or at least is incorporated and consolidated into that of the husband; under whose wing, protection, and cover she performs everything … Upon this principle of a union in person in husband and wife, depend almost all the legal rights, duties, and disabilities that either of them acquires by the marriage.[427]

---

425. At para. 132.
426. Matthew 19:5–6.
427. W. Blackstone, *Commentaries on the Laws of England*, vol. I.

The doctrine had a number of practical consequences: when it was applied in its full force, a married woman had limited rights to own property, to enter into contracts, or to bring an action in the courts. The position of the married woman was gradually ameliorated by statute,[428] and today a wife has almost identical rights and responsibilities to those of a husband. Should a court today be required to consider whether the doctrine of unity has any lingering practical effect, it is likely that it would adopt the same approach as the Court of Appeal in *Midland Bank v. Trust Co Ltd v. Green*.[429] The judges hearing the case robustly rejected the argument that a husband and wife could not commit the tort of conspiring with one another as they were one person in law.[430] Lord Denning M.R. declared that husbands and wives were 'two persons' both in law and in fact, and 'the doctrine of unity and its ramifications should be discarded altogether' except insofar as it explicitly formed part of the law.

## B. The Concept of Consortium

*171.* While the common law concept of consortium has not been as comprehensively cut down by statute as the doctrine of unity has been, this simply reflects the fact that it is, or was, such a nebulous concept that it would be difficult to say what rights and responsibilities it actually encompasses. Judicial references to consortium as 'a bundle of rights' do little to assist.[431] If the term 'consortium' is used solely as shorthand for the relationship of living together as husband and wife, and the legal rights and responsibilities that flow from that status, then it could be said to remain a relevant, if unhelpful, concept.

It is doubtful, however, whether the concept of consortium has any specific consequences beyond those conferred by, or implied from, the statutory provisions considered below.

One could say, e.g., that each spouse has a right to the company and society of the other, on the basis that it is possible for one spouse to obtain a divorce on the basis of the other's desertion. Yet this is not a right that the law actually allows an individual to enforce, either by self-help[432] or by court order.[433] Moreover, the courts have been willing to distinguish between the capacity to marry and the capacity to cohabit with one's spouse.[434]

*172.* In the past it was possible for a spouse to sue a third party who had 'enticed' the other spouse into abandoning the matrimonial home, the ground of the complaint being that the third party had deprived the plaintiff of the consortium of

---

428. *See*, e.g., *Married Women's Property Act* 1882; *Law Reform (Married Women and Tortfeasors) Act* 1935.
429. [1982] Ch. 529.
430. Although see now the explicit provision to this effect in the *Criminal Law Act* 1977, s. 2(2)(a).
431. *Best v. Samuel Fox & Co Ltd* [1952] A.C. 716, 736.
432. *See R v. Jackson* [1891] 1 Q.B. 671.
433. The action for restitution of conjugal rights was abolished in 1970: *see* below.
434. *See*, e.g., *PC v. City of York* [2013] EWCA Civ 478.

the other spouse. Similarly, a husband whose wife was injured as the result of another's negligence could sue the negligent party for loss of the wife's consortium. The anomalous nature of this action was highlighted in *Best v. Samuel Fox & Co Ltd*,[435] in which the House of Lords held that a wife was not entitled to bring an action for loss of consortium where her husband had been injured by the negligence of a third party. Lord Goddard explained this distinction on the basis that the authorities showed that 'the action which the law gives to the husband for lack of consortium is founded on the proprietary right which from ancient times it was considered the husband had in his wife'.[436] Both actions have now been abolished: that for enticement in 1970[437] and that for loss of consortium in 1982.[438]

## C. Keeping Confidences

*173.* Alongside the archaic concepts of unity and consortium is an area of the law that has seen considerable growth in recent years, namely the action for 'breach of confidence' or, to use the more modern term, 'misuse of private information'.[439] Such an action, of course, may be relied on in respect of a wide range of persons and indeed institutions. For present purposes its relevance lies in the fact that the relationship of husband and wife is one that gives rise to an obligation of confidence. As was declared in *Argyll v. Argyll*, '[t]he confidential nature of the relationship is of its very essence and so obviously and necessarily implicit in it that there is no need for it to be expressed.'[440] This means that an action will lie where confidential information has been communicated by one spouse to the other who then proceeds to make unauthorized use of it to the detriment of the former. This is not, however, unique to spouses, and will also apply to other intimate personal relationships.[441]

It has also been held that spouses have rights of confidentiality that are enforceable against each other. In *Tchenguiz v. Imerman; Imerman v. Imerman*,[442] the Court of Appeal held that a spouse had a right of confidentiality in relation to financial information during the marriage. Marriage does not, therefore, accord a spouse the right to know the income or assets of the other, which may lead to the weaker spouse settling for much less than they might otherwise be entitled to upon divorce.[443]

---

435. [1952] A.C. 716.
436. *Ibid.*, at 731.
437. *Law Reform (Miscellaneous Provisions) Act* 1970, s. 4.
438. *Administration of Justice Act* 1982.
439. *Campbell v. MGN Ltd* [2004] UKHL 22, para. 14.
440. [1967] Ch. 302, 322.
441. *CC v. AB* [2008] EWHC 3083 (QB).
442. [2010] EWCA Civ 908.
443. *See*, e.g., R. Probert, *For Richer, for Poorer – but How Does One Find Out Which?* 127 L. Q. Rev. 27 (2011).

### D.  Contracts for Day-to-Day Living

*174.*  It is presumed that a married couple who is living together in amity do not intend to create legal relations when they enter into a contract dealing with their domestic arrangements.[444] Agreements regulating the day-to-day life of the parties – as opposed to contracts stipulating how assets are to be divided on breakdown – are thus presumed not to be enforceable as contracts.

### E.  Presumption of Advancement

*175.*  It used to be presumed that a transfer from a husband to his wife, a fiancé to his fiancée or a father to his child was in fact a gift. In recent decades, however, it was clear that this presumption could be rebutted by relatively slight evidence, and in 2010, it was finally stated to be abolished by the *Equality Act*.[445] At the time of writing, however, the provision has still not been brought into force, and doubts have been expressed as to whether it is either necessary or effective.[446]

## II.  Statutory Provisions: Express Rights and Responsibilities

### A.  Mutual Support

*176.*  At common law, a husband had an obligation to support his wife financially, as far as he was able to. The statute now provides that each spouse has a duty to support the other, and if one fails to do so, the other can apply to a court for an order for financial provision;[447] the sex-specific common law rule, by contrast, was to have been abolished by the sweeping Equality Act 2010 but as yet this provision has not been brought into force.[448] Often such an application will be a preliminary to divorce proceedings – whereupon the court has considerably greater powers to reallocate assets between the parties.[449]

### B.  Occupation of the Matrimonial Home

*177.*  A spouse will always have the right to occupy the matrimonial home, whether as a result of a beneficial interest or statutory 'home rights'.[450] If, however, there is a dispute with a third party such as a bank or creditor, it may be necessary

---

444. *Balfour v. Balfour* [1919] 2 KB 571; *Gould v. Gould* [1970] 1 Q.B. 275.
445. *Equality Act* 2010, s. 199.
446. J. Glister, *Section 199 of the Equality Act 2010: How Not to Abolish the Presumption of Advancement* 73 M.L.R. 807 (2010).
447. *Domestic Proceedings and Magistrates' Courts Act* 1978; *Matrimonial Causes Act* 1973, s. 27.
448. *Equality Act* 2010, s. 198.
449. *See* further Part III, Ch. 2.
450. *See infra* Part III, Ch. 1, para. 435.

for the property to be sold, and spousal status will have little relevance (save to confer limited rights in the context of the other spouse's bankruptcy).[451]

## C. Evidence

*178.* At common law, a spouse was, as a rule, neither competent nor compellable as a witness for or against the other spouse in either civil or criminal proceedings. Over the last century and a half, rules have gradually been amended, with the result that spouses are now competent to give evidence in both civil and criminal proceedings.[452] They may also be compelled to give evidence in civil proceedings,[453] and for the defence in criminal proceedings.[454] Restrictions still remain on the extent to which a spouse may be compelled to give evidence for the prosecution in criminal proceedings. Under the Police and Criminal Evidence Act 1984, a spouse can only be compelled to give evidence for the prosecution if the offence charged is one of the following: first, an assault on, or injury or threat of injury to, the spouse himself or herself or a person under the age of 16 years; second, a sexual offence against a person under the age of 16 years; third, an attempt or conspiracy to do any offence within the first two categories, or if the accused aided, abetted, counselled, procured, or incited the commission of any such offence.[455]

## D. Actions in Tort

*179.* Spouses now have the same right to sue each other in tort as if they were not married, subject to two exceptions: The court has a discretion to stay proceedings brought during the subsistence of the marriage if it appears either that no substantial benefit would accrue to either party from the continuation of the proceedings; or that the issue would more conveniently be dealt with under section 17 of the Married Women's Property Act 1882 (which provides for the determination of questions between husband and wife as to the title to or possession of property).

## E. Criminal Law

*180.* Until recently it was a defence for a wife (but not a husband) to show that the offence with which she was charged had been committed in the presence of, and under the coercion of, her spouse.[456] This defence applied to all offences except

---

451. *See infra* Part III, Ch. 1, para. 439.
452. *Evidence Amendment Act* 1853; *Youth Justice and Criminal Evidence Act* 1999, s. 53.
453. *Evidence Amendment Act* 1853.
454. *Police and Criminal Evidence Act* 1984, s. 80(2).
455. *Ibid.*, s. 80(3).
456. *Criminal Justice Act* 1925, s. 47.

murder and treason. Following calls for reform by the Law Commission,[457] however, this defence was eventually abolished by the Anti-social Behaviour, Crime and Policing Act 2014.

### F. Taxation

*181.* At one time, the income of a wife was taxed as that of her husband,[458] but separate taxation was introduced in 1988 and has applied to all couples since 1990–1991.[459] Marriage also used to bring an entitlement to a married couples' allowance, but this was restricted in 1999 and today it is only spouses aged over 70 years who are entitled to the allowance.[460] Spouses and civil partners do now have the option of transferring part of their personal allowances to each other.[461]

Marriage also brings with it certain other tax benefits, in that spouses enjoy higher rates of exemption from capital gains tax on lifetime transfers to each other and no inheritance tax is paid on gifts or bequests to or transfers between spouses.

### G. Rights on Death

*182.* When one spouse dies, the survivor has an automatic right to receive assets from the estate of the deceased (if he or she died intestate), or to apply for financial provision from the estate (if the provision made for the survivor is inadequate).

If the other spouse's death is attributable to the wrongful act of another, then the survivor is entitled to bring an action for compensation.[462]

## III. Statutory Provisions: Implied Rights and Responsibilities

### A. Sexual Intercourse

*183.* At one time, the law held that a husband could not be guilty of raping his wife, on the basis that marriage itself signified the wife's consent to sexual intercourse. This rule has now been abolished,[463] and neither spouse has the right to insist on sexual intercourse against the other's wishes. Nor does marriage legitimate

---

457. Law Commission, *Criminal Law: Report on Defences of General Application* (1977), Law Com. No. 83 and *Legislating the Criminal Code: Offences against the Person and General Principles* (1993) Law Com. No. 218.
458. *Income Tax Act* 1799.
459. *Finance Act* 1988, s. 32.
460. *Income and Corporation Taxes Act* 1988, s. 257A.
461. *See* https://www.gov.uk/government/publications/transferable-tax-allowances-for-married-couples-and-civil-partners. Only GBP 1,150 of the allowance can be transferred, however, and only if the transferor is not liable to income tax, and the recipient is not liable to tax above the basic rate.
462. *Fatal Accidents Act* 1846; *see* now *Fatal Accidents Act* 1976, s. 1(3).
463. *R v. R* [1992] 1 A.C. 599; *see* now s. 1 of the *Sexual Offences Act* 1956, as amended by the *Criminal Justice and Public Order Act* 1994.

sexual relationships that would otherwise be unlawful, for example, where one spouse lacks capacity to consent.[464] That sexual intercourse is an important component of marriage can be inferred from the fact that a marriage may be annulled on the basis of one party's inability or wilful refusal to consummate the marriage; that only one act of intercourse is required for these purposes illustrates the limitations of this remedy.[465] Courts have, however, been willing to hold that a spouse's subsequent refusal of sexual relations is behaviour that would justify the grant of a divorce at the behest of the other.[466]

## B. Living Together

*184.* Again, while the law contains no explicit direction that spouses should live together, this is seen as being the 'essence' of the marriage contract.[467] More specifically, one can infer that this is part of the legal concept of consortium from the fact that a spouse may apply for divorce on the basis of desertion if the other refuses to live with him or her. The fact that a spouse can obtain a decree of judicial separation relieving him or her of the duty to cohabit with the other[468] is a further illustration. It was once possible for the court to order the reluctant spouse to return to live with the other by means of an order for restitution of conjugal rights, but this remedy lost much of its force when the sanction of imprisonment was abolished in 1884,[469] and the order itself was abolished by statute in 1970.[470] The right of the husband to dictate the location of the matrimonial home has also been abrogated by judicial decision.[471]

It has generally been assumed that a person who has capacity to marry also has capacity to decide whether to live with their spouse, but recent litigation raises the possibility that this will not always be the case.[472]

## C. No Other Marriage

*185.* One obvious effect of a marriage is that neither party is entitled to marry or enter into a civil partnership with another person, unless and until the marriage has either been brought to an end by death or divorce, or annulled.

---

464. *See*, e.g. *Re Ch (By his Litigation Friend the Official Solicitor) v. A Metropolitan Council* [2017] EWCOP 12.
465. *Matrimonial Causes Act* 1973, s. 12(a) and (b) and *see infra*, s. 5. Void, Voidable and Non-Existent Marriages.
466. *See*, e.g., *Cackett (otherwise Trice) v. Cackett* [1950] P. 253 (husband's insistence on *coitus interruptus* affected wife's health).
467. *PC & Anor v. City of York Council* [2013] EWCA Civ 478, at para. 63.
468. *Matrimonial Causes Act* 1973, s. 17.
469. *Matrimonial Causes Act* 1884.
470. *Matrimonial Proceedings and Property Act* 1970, s. 2.
471. *Dunn v. Dunn* [1949] P. 98; *Walter v. Walter* [1949] 65 T.L.R. 680.
472. *PC & Anor v. City of York Council* [2013] EWCA Civ 478.

## IV. Areas in Which Marriage Has No Effect

*186.* There are a number of areas in which one might expect marriage to have an impact but where English law either makes no provision or requires extra criteria to be fulfilled.

### A. Name

*187.* There is no obligation on a wife to take her husband's surname, or vice versa, and it is increasingly common for each to retain their own name, or to combine their names. Either spouse may choose to adopt the other's surname, although it is still more common for the wife to take her husband's surname than for a husband to adopt his wife's surname. If a spouse does adopt the other's surname, he or she may continue to use it after the death of the other spouse or even if the marriage ends in divorce. The only exception to this is that an individual cannot use a name for fraudulent purposes. Thus a wife may continue to use her husband's surname, but not to pretend that she is still married to him.

### B. Citizenship

*188.* Marriage to a British citizen does not automatically confer British citizenship on the other spouse, although it does facilitate the process. The rules are considered in the chapter on nationality.[473] The spouse of a British citizen may, however, be granted leave to remain in the UK as a result of the marriage.

### C. Ownership of Assets

*189.* Although many couples choose to own their home as joint tenants, marriage, as such, has no impact on the property rights of the parties. Thus a spouse does not acquire any property interest in the assets of the other on marriage.

If it is necessary to determine who owns what during the marriage – e.g., if there is a dispute with a third party such as a bank or building society – this will be determined by applying rules of property law, subject to one or two statutory modifications.[474] It should be noted that on divorce the court has a wide discretion to override property rights in reallocating assets between the parties.

## V. Engaged Couples

*190.* Before 1754, if a couple had exchanged vows in words of the present tense – e.g., 'I take you as my wife/husband' – the agreement was regarded as binding

---

473. *See supra* Part I, Ch. 5, para. 111.
474. *See* the chapter on matrimonial property law.

upon them, and the ecclesiastical courts would require them to solemnize their union with a marriage in church.[475] When the Clandestine Marriages Act of 1753 put the regulation of the formation of marriage on a statutory footing, it abolished the option of enforcing such contracts. However, it remained possible for either party to sue the other for breach of a promise to marry until 1970, when the action was finally abolished by statute.[476] Today, the law simply provides that an ex-fiancé(e) may recover any gift that was made on the express or implied condition that it would be returned if the marriage did not take place.[477] The gift of an engagement ring is presumed to be absolute, although it is possible for the giver to rebut this and show that it was in fact conditional.[478]

§5. VOIDABLE, VOID AND NON-EXISTENT MARRIAGES

*191.* In English law, a marriage must fall into one of the following categories: valid, voidable, void, or non-existent. The need for the final category – which is a creation of the courts and has no statutory basis – arose because the relevant legislation only spells out the consequences of a 'knowing and wilful' failure to comply with certain formalities, leaving unstated the consequences of an innocent failure to comply with those formalities – or indeed a wilful failure to comply with other formalities.

*192.* The distinction between a marriage that is voidable and one that is void originated in the Canon law, as did many of the relevant grounds, but is now exclusively governed by statute. There are a number of important differences between a marriage that is void and one that is merely voidable. A void marriage is one that is deemed never to have existed, while a voidable marriage exists up until the point at which a court grants a decree of nullity. As a consequence, it is not strictly necessary to obtain a decree if the marriage is void, whereas if no decree is obtained in relation to a voidable marriage it is, to all intents and purposes, valid. Since the grounds that render a marriage void are regarded as fundamental to the institution of marriage, it is possible for a third party to apply for the marriage to be annulled, even after the death of the relevant parties, whereas if the marriage is merely voidable it is only the parties themselves that can challenge its validity. In addition, if the marriage is merely voidable, a decree may be barred in certain circumstances even if a relevant ground has been made out, while there are no bars to a decree being granted if the marriage is void.

## I. Voidable Marriages

*193.* A marriage is voidable on the following grounds only.

---

475. *Baxtar v. Buckley* [1752] 161 E.R. 17.
476. *Law Reform (Miscellaneous Provisions) Act* 1970, s. 1.
477. *Ibid.*, s. 3(1).
478. *Ibid.*, s. 3(2).

## A. Inability to Consummate

*194.* A marriage may be annulled if it has not been consummated owing to the incapacity of either party to consummate it.[479] It is possible for either party to apply on this ground – i.e., on the basis of their own or the other's incapacity to consummate the marriage – but only if the parties are of the opposite sex.[480] Consummation has a very specific meaning for this purpose, one 'ordinary and complete'[481] act of penile-vaginal intercourse after the marriage is required, no more and no less. 'Complete' does not require that either party should achieve an orgasm,[482] but it does require a reasonable degree of penetration, to a significant depth and for a reasonable period of time.[483]

*195.* The incapacity of the affected spouse may be either physical or psychological. The courts have used the term 'invincible repugnance' to describe the psychological factors that render one party incapable of having sexual relations with the other. A distinction, however, is drawn between inability and unwillingness; the latter will not be accepted as a ground for annulling the marriage.[484]

There are of course conditions that may render a spouse temporarily incapable of consummation, but this would not justify an annulment. The question for the court is whether the spouse's incapacity is incurable. If a simple operation would render the spouse capable of intercourse, then an annulment will not be granted; however, if the operation would be dangerous, or the affected spouse refuses to undergo it, then the incapacity will be regarded as incurable.[485]

*196.* The possibility of recognizing transsexuals in their acquired gender under the Gender Recognition Act 2004 raises a further question: Is a transsexual capable of consummating a marriage? This issue is not explicitly addressed in the legislation, and so one must turn to the common law for illumination. In *Corbett v. Corbett,*[486] it was held that a male-to-female transsexual was incapable of consummating the marriage, on the basis that intercourse using an artificially constructed cavity did not constitute 'ordinary and complete' intercourse. It was, in the words of the judge, 'the reverse of ordinary, and in no sense natural'. This, however, was rather at odds with an earlier decision of the Court of Appeal, *SY v. SY.*[487] This case involved a wife who needed surgery to enlarge her vagina in order to enable her to have sex. The Court of Appeal refused to find that she was incapable of consummating the marriage. The key point for current purposes is the suggestion of Willmer L.J. that it was difficult to see 'why the enlargement of a vestigial vagina

---

479. *Matrimonial Causes Act* 1973, s. 12(1)(a).
480. *Ibid.,* s. 12(2).
481. *D-E v. A-G* (1845) 163 E.R. 1039.
482. *Cackett (otherwise Trice) v. Cackett* [1950] P. 253.
483. *W v. W* [1967] 1 W.L.R. 1554.
484. *Singh v. Singh* [1971] P. 226.
485. *S v. S (otherwise C)* [1956] P. 1.
486. [1971] P. 83.
487. [1963] P. 37.

should be regarded as producing something different in kind from a vagina artificially created from nothing'.[488] How a modern court would resolve the issue on the basis of these authorities must remain a matter of speculation; as a matter of policy, it is submitted that a more generous interpretation of consummation would be preferable. Indeed, given that the requirement of consummation has been decoupled from the purpose of procreation,[489] and since the technical and somewhat minimal activities that will constitute consummation may do little to foster the relationship of the parties or prevent them from seeking sexual satisfaction elsewhere, one might question why inability to consummate remains a ground for annulling a marriage.

## B. Wilful Refusal to Consummate

*197.* A spouse may also apply for the marriage to be annulled on the basis that the marriage has not been consummated owing to the wilful refusal of the respondent to consummate it.[490] Again, this is only possible where the parties are of the opposite sex.[491] The definition of consummation is the same for applications under this heading, but a spouse cannot apply on the basis of his or her own refusal to consummate.

A single refusal will not be sufficient to satisfy this ground. The question posed by the court is whether the respondent's refusal connotes a 'settled and definite decision come to without just excuse'.[492] This reflects the fact that a spouse may have a valid reason for refusing to consummate the marriage – e.g., the fact that he or she is currently in prison and the rules forbid intercourse during spousal visits,[493] or the fact that the other spouse has failed to arrange the religious ceremony of marriage that both regard as a prerequisite for cohabitation.[494]

## C. Lack of Consent

*198.* A spouse may apply for the marriage to be annulled on the ground that he or she did not validly consent to the marriage, 'whether in consequence of duress, mistake, unsoundness of mind or otherwise'.[495] The onus is on the applicant to establish the lack of consent and the application must be issued within three years of the marriage.[496]

---

488. [1963] P. 37, 59.
489. *Baxter v. Baxter* [1948] A.C. 274.
490. *Matrimonial Causes Act* 1973, s. 12(1)(b).
491. *Ibid.*, s. 12(2).
492. *Horten v. Horten* [1947] 2 All E.R. 871 at 874.
493. *Ford v. Ford* [1987] Fam. 232.
494. *Kaur v. Singh* [1972] 1 All E.R. 292.
495. *Matrimonial Causes Act* 1973, s. 12(1)(c).
496. *Ibid.*, s. 13(2). However, the courts have been willing to resort to the concept of 'non-marriage' where the application is brought out of time: *see B v. I (Forced Marriage)* [2010] 1 FLR 1721.

*199.* It has long been accepted that a consent given under duress is no consent, and the UK has ratified the Convention on Consent to Marriage, which sets out that:

> [n]o marriage shall be legally entered into without the full and free consent of both parties, such consent to be expressed by them in person after due publicity and in the presence of the authority competent to solemnize the marriage and of witnesses, as prescribed by law.

The courts have, however, differed in their interpretation as to what constitutes duress in this context. At one time, it was suggested that only threats to 'life, limb, or liberty' would suffice to establish duress for these purposes.[497] The current consensus, however, is that the applicant does not need to show threats of a specific type, the question for the court being 'whether the threats, pressure, or whatever it is, is such as to destroy the reality of consent and overbears the will of the individual'.[498] While the matter is not beyond doubt, as both *Hirani v. Hirani* and the earlier, conflicting case of *Singh v. Singh*[499] are decisions of the Court of Appeal, it is submitted that the test set out in *Hirani* is to be preferred both as a matter of precedent and as a matter of policy. As a matter of precedent, it was pointed out in *NS v. MI* that the requirement that the applicant show a threat to 'life, limb, or liberty' was itself a departure from earlier authorities.[500] As a matter of policy, there is today a greater appreciation of the problem of forced marriages, and of the more subtle and insidious forms of pressure that may be exerted to force an unwilling child into marriage. This is reflected in the consideration that has been devoted to the issue at a policy level, in the attempts by the courts to fashion appropriate means of preventing forced marriages from taking place,[501] and in the phrasing of the Forced Marriage (Civil Protection) Act 2007, which stated that 'force' would include coercion 'by threats or other psychological means'.[502] It therefore seems preferable to conclude that a marriage may be annulled on the basis of duress where the will of the applicant was overborne, whatever the nature of the pressure brought to bear on him or her, and whether or not that pressure would have had a similar effect on a hypothetical 'reasonable' individual.[503] Since 2008, it has also been possible for a court to grant a forced marriage protection order to protect those at risk of being

---

497. *Szechter v. Szechter* [1971] P. 286.
498. *Hirani v. Hirani* [1982] F.L.R. 232, followed in *P. v. R (Forced Marriage: Annulment: Procedure)* [2003] 1 F.L.R. 661, *NS v. MI* [2006] EWHC 1646 (Fam) and *Re P. (Forced Marriage)* [2011] EWHC 3467 (Fam).
499. [1971] P. 226.
500. [2006] EWHC 1646 (Fam).
501. *See*, e.g., *Re SK (Proposed Plaintiff) (An Adult by way of her Litigation Friend)* [2004] EWHC 3202 (Fam); *M v. B, A and S (By the Official Solicitor)* [2005] EWHC 1681; *Re K (A Local Authority) v. N and Others* [2005] EWHC 2956 (Fam).
502. *Family Law Act* 1996, s. 63A(6), as inserted by *Forced Marriage (Civil Protection) Act* 2007, s. 1.
503. *See NS v. MI* [2006] EWHC 1646 (Fam) for the view that the test is subjective rather than objective.

forced into marriage, and since June 2014, it has been a criminal offence, punishable by up to five years' imprisonment, to breach such an order.[504] It is also now a criminal offence, punishable by up to seven years' imprisonment, to cause another to enter into a marriage without free and full consent by means of 'violence, threats or any other form of coercion',[505] or, if the victim lacked capacity to consent, by any means.[506]

200. A mistake as to the identity of the other party (i.e., a belief that X was in fact Y), or as to the nature of the ceremony (e.g., a belief that it was an engagement rather than a marriage,[507] or a ceremony intended to convert the applicant to a different religion)[508] will also justify an application on the basis of lack of consent. However, a mistake as to the character or attributes of the other party, or as to the legal effect of a marriage, will not.

201. An individual may be unable to give a valid consent to marriage if he or she is not capable of understanding what marriage entails; the test developed by the courts is whether a person is 'mentally capable of appreciating that it involves the responsibilities normally attaching to marriage'.[509] A general description of marriage and its accompanying responsibilities was set out in *Sheffield City Council v. E*;[510] more specifically, the courts have also held that capacity to marry 'must include the capacity to consent to sexual relations',[511] on the basis that a sexual relationship is usually implicit in marriage and one spouse may commit offences under the Sexual Offences Act 2003 if the other is unable to consent.[512] If there are concerns that an individual does not have the requisite ability to consent, an injunction or forced marriage protection order[513] may be granted to prevent a marriage from taking place;[514] moreover, in cases of obvious impairment it is highly unlikely that any registrar would allow the marriage to proceed.[515]

202. Finally, an applicant may claim that no valid consent to the marriage was given on the basis that he or she was under the influence of drugs or alcohol at the time of the ceremony.

---

504. *Family Law Act* 1996 s. 63CA, as inserted by *Anti-social Behaviour, Crime and Policing Act* 2014, s. 120; *Anti-social Behaviour, Crime and Policing Act 2014 (Commencement No. 2, Transitional and Transitory Provisions) Order* 2014, SI 2014 No. 949.
505. *Anti-social Behaviour, Crime and Policing Act* 2014, s. 121.
506. *Ibid.*, s. 121(2).
507. *Kelly v. Kelly* [1932] 49 T.L.R. 99.
508. *Mehta v. Mehta* [1945] 2 All E.R. 690.
509. *Re Park's Estate* [1953] 2 All E.R. 1411. *See supra* Part I, Ch. 7, para. 127.
510. *See supra*, §4 Effects of Marriage.
511. *X City Council v. MB, NB and MAB (By His Litigation Friend the Official Solicitor)* [2006] EWHC 168 (Fam), para. 53; *YLA v. PM, MZ* [2013] EWHC 4020 (COP).
512. *See*, e.g., *XCC v. AA & Anor* [2012] EWHC 2183 (COP).
513. *See*, e.g., *YLA v. PM, MZ* [2013] EWHC 4020 (COP) on the categorization of the marriage of an incapacitous person as a forced marriage.
514. *M v. B, A, and S (By Her Litigation Friend the Official Solicitor)* [2005] EWHC 1681.
515. *City of Westminster v. IC (By his Litigation Friend the Official Solicitor) and KC and NNC* [2008] EWCA Civ 198.

## D. Mental Disorder

*203.* The fact that at the time of the ceremony one party was suffering from a mental disorder, which made him or her unfit for marriage, offers an alternative ground for annulling a marriage.[516] In such cases the marriage is voidable even though the party in question was capable of giving a valid consent. 'Mental disorder' for these purposes has the same meaning as in the Mental Health Act 1983, and is broadly defined as 'mental illness, arrested or incomplete development of mind, psychopathic disorder, and any other disorder or disability of mind'.[517] 'Unfitted for marriage', by contrast, has been given a narrow interpretation in the case law. The question to be posed by the courts is similar to that relevant to ascertaining capacity to consent: 'is this person capable of living in a married state and of carrying out the ordinary duties and obligations of marriage?'[518] As Ormrod J. emphasized, '[i]t can only be those unfortunate people who suffer from a really serious mental disorder who can positively be stated in humane terms to be incapable of marriage.'[519]

## E. Venereal Disease

*204.* A spouse may apply for the marriage to be annulled on the basis that at the time of the ceremony he or she was unaware[520] of the fact that the respondent was suffering from a venereal disease[521] in communicable form.[522] The application must be issued within three years of the marriage.[523]

## F. Pregnancy by Another

*205.* A husband may apply for the marriage to be annulled on the basis that at the time of the ceremony he was unaware[524] of the fact that the respondent was pregnant by a third party.[525] The application must be issued within three years of the marriage.[526] A wife cannot, however, apply for the marriage to be annulled on the basis that at the time of the ceremony another woman was pregnant by her husband.

---

516. *Matrimonial Causes Act* 1973, s. 12(1)(d).
517. *Mental Health Act* 1983, s. 1(2). This has not been altered by the *Mental Capacity Act* 2005.
518. *Bennett v. Bennett* [1969] 1 W.L.R. 430, p. 434.
519. *Ibid.*
520. *Matrimonial Causes Act* 1973, s. 13(3).
521. *See*, e.g., *C v. C* (1962) 106 S.J. 959 (syphilis).
522. *Matrimonial Causes Act* 1973, s. 12(1)(e).
523. *Ibid.*, s. 13(2).
524. *Ibid.*, s. 13(3).
525. *Ibid.*, s. 12(1)(f).
526. *Ibid.*, s. 13(2).

## G. Gender Reassignment

*206.* The final two grounds for annulment were added by the Gender Recognition Act 2004. The first is that an interim gender recognition certificate has been granted to one of the parties after the date of the marriage.[527] This deals with the situation where one spouse has undergone gender reassignment and has applied to the Gender Recognition Panel for recognition of the acquired gender. In the wake of the Marriage (Same-Sex Couples) Act 2013, it will only be necessary to take this course where the other spouse does not consent to the continuation of the marriage after the grant of a full gender recognition certificate.[528] Once the applicant has obtained the interim certificate, this is a ground on which either party may rely to annul the marriage. The time limit on issuing an application is more restrictive than that which applies to other grounds: it must be issued within six months of the interim certificate being granted.[529]

The second ground allows a marriage to be annulled at the request of an applicant who has discovered, after the ceremony has taken place,[530] that the respondent had undergone gender reassignment prior to the marriage.[531] The application must be issued within three years of the marriage.[532] Opinions are divided on the need for such a provision. On the one hand, it has been argued that gender is an aspect of identity, and that a mistake as to the other spouse's gender would be a relevant mistake rendering the marriage voidable.[533] This argument perhaps does not give sufficient weight to the fact that the mistake relates to what the respondent's gender once *was*, rather than what it has been legally determined to be. It could also be argued that the possibility of annulling a marriage on the basis that the other spouse has undergone gender reassignment singles out this fact – along with pregnancy by a third party and suffering from venereal disease – as something that strikes at the basis of marriage to such an extent that the marriage should be invalidated. One might question whether this is really in line with the rule, articulated in the Gender Recognition Act, that the applicant becomes a member of the acquired gender for all legal purposes.

## II. Bars to an Application Where a Marriage Is Voidable

*207.* Even if the applicant succeeds in establishing that one of the above grounds has been satisfied, it is not automatic that a decree annulling the marriage will be granted. This is because there are certain bars that apply if the marriage is voidable.

---

527. *Ibid.*, s. 12(1)(g).
528. *See* further above at para. 60.
529. *Ibid.*, s. 13(2A).
530. *Ibid.*, s. 12(3).
531. *Ibid.*, s. 12(1)(h).
532. *Ibid.*, s. 13(2).
533. N. Lowe & G. Douglas, *Bromley's Family Law* 90 (10th ed. Oxford U. Press 2006).

*208.* The first is a general bar that applies to all of the grounds set out in section 12 of the 1973 Act: the respondent may oppose a decree on the basis that the applicant, knowing that it was open to him or her to have the marriage avoided, so conducted himself or herself towards the respondent as to lead the respondent reasonably to believe that he or she would not seek to annul the marriage, and that it would be unjust to the respondent to grant the decree.[534] If the court is satisfied on these points, it will not grant a decree. It should be noted that it is not the role of the court to investigate the applicant's conduct. It is up to the respondent to establish the facts justifying the bar. To date there has been only one reported case in which this bar was considered *D v. D (Nullity: Statutory Bar).*[535] In this case, the wife was incapable of consummating the marriage due to a physical impediment and had refused to undergo a surgery that would have cured the problem. The husband was aware that he could apply for nullity but did not do so, and agreed to adopt two children with the wife. He subsequently changed his mind, left his wife for another woman and sought to have the marriage annulled. The wife argued that the decree should be barred under section 13(1). The court held that by agreeing to the adoption he had conducted himself in such a way as to lead the wife to believe that he would not seek an annulment. However, as the wife had also changed her mind and was willing for the decree to be granted, it would not be unjust to grant it.

*209.* The other two statutory bars apply only to specific grounds and have been alluded to in the context of those grounds. Under section 13(2), an applicant seeking to annul the marriage on the basis of a lack of consent, mental unfitness, venereal disease, pregnancy by another or acquired gender must issue proceedings within three years of the date of the marriage. This is an absolute rule: if the husband does not discover until many years have passed that he is not the father of the child his wife was carrying at the time of the marriage he will not be able to apply for the marriage to be annulled. There is one narrow exception, whereby a judge may grant leave for proceedings to be commenced after the three-year limit if he or she is satisfied that the applicant has suffered a mental disorder within that time *and* it would be just to allow proceedings to be instituted.[536] The potential harshness of this may be mitigated by the court exercising its discretion under its inherent jurisdiction to hold that there never was a marriage capable of recognition in the UK.[537]

The time limit on applying for a marriage to be annulled on the basis that one party has been granted an interim gender recognition certificate is still shorter, being six months from the grant of the certificate, and there is no provision whereby this may be extended.[538]

*210.* Similarly, section 13(3), which relates to the applicant's awareness of the facts alleged, applies only to the grounds of venereal disease, pregnancy by another

---

534. *Matrimonial Causes Act* 1973, s. 13(1).
535. [1979] Fam. 70.
536. *Matrimonial Causes Act* 1973, s. 13(4).
537. *B v. I* [2010] 1 F.L.R. 1721; *Re P. (Forced Marriage)* [2011] EWHC 3467 (Fam).
538. *Matrimonial Causes Act* 1973, s. 13(2A).

or acquired gender. In such cases, a decree will be barred if the applicant was aware of the facts at the time of the marriage.[539]

## III. Void Marriages

*211.* A marriage celebrated in England and Wales will be void if either party lacks capacity to enter into it – i.e., if the parties are within the prohibited degrees, or either party is under the age of 16 years or already lawfully married or in a valid civil partnership at the time of the marriage.

The marriage will also be void if the parties have 'knowingly and wilfully' disregarded certain formalities; basically, if they did not comply with the preliminaries required to publicize the marriage; if the marriage was celebrated in the wrong place; or if the celebrant was not authorized to solemnize the marriage.[540] Additional provisions apply to the marriages of same-sex couples: their marriages will be void if they 'knowingly and wilfully' married in a registered place of worship without the relevant governing authority having given written consent,[541] or if they went through a ceremony of marriage in the Church of England (even if they genuinely believed it to constitute a marriage).[542]

## IV. Non-existent Marriages

*212.* The provision that a marriage will only be void for a 'knowing and wilful' failure to comply with the specified requirements of the Marriage Act 1949 raises a further question: what if the parties have failed to comply with any of the required formalities because they did not appreciate the necessity of doing so? It would be inappropriate for such a marriage to be valid: it would undermine the point of having formalities if the couple were to be legally married even though they had not complied with any of the necessary formalities. But could such a marriage be classified as void if the parties – perhaps recent immigrants – did not realize that such formalities were necessary? If the parties do not know what formalities are required, they cannot be said to be 'knowingly and wilfully' disregarding them,[543] but does this mean that a marriage should be upheld even if the parties failed to comply with any of the required formalities? The courts have addressed the issue by developing

---

539. *Matrimonial Causes Act* 1973, s. 13(3).
540. *Marriage Act* 1949, s. 25 (Anglican ceremonies), s. 49 (other ceremonies).
541. *Marriage Act* 1949, s. 49A, as inserted by the *Marriage (Same Sex Couples) Act* 2013, Sch. 7, Part 2, para. 15.
542. *Marriage Act* 1949, s. 25(4), as inserted by the *Marriage (Same Sex Couples) Act* 2013, Sch. 7, Part 2, para. 4.
543. *MA v. JA and the Attorney General* [2012] EWHC 2219 (Fam), addressing a point left open in *Greaves v. Greaves* [1872] L.R. 2 P. & D. 423.

the concept of the non-marriage: if the parties marry in a form that bears no resemblance to that prescribed by the Marriage Act 1949, then their union will be relegated to the non-status of a non-marriage.[544] If the marriage is close enough to the form prescribed but the parties knowingly and wilfully failed to comply with the requisite formalities, then it will be void.[545] And if it is close enough to the form prescribed and the parties innocently failed to comply with the requisite formalities, then it will be valid.[546]

213. In a number of recent cases, the courts have also used the tactic of declaring there to be no marriage in order to circumvent legal restrictions that might otherwise debar the granting of a decree. It has been used, e.g., where one of the parties to a marriage celebrated over the telephone clearly lacked capacity to marry,[547] where a marriage celebrated in Cape Town failed to comply with the formalities prescribed by the law of South Africa,[548] and in a case of mistake/duress brought more than three years after the marriage was celebrated.[549]

214. One might well question whether it matters whether a marriage is void or non-existent. Surely a void marriage is one that has never existed, just as a non-marriage is? In strict logic, this is true. However, certain rights have been attached to void marriages in order to alleviate any potential hardship, whereas a non-marriage has no legal consequences and the parties are, in the eyes of the law, no more than cohabitants.

## V. Consequences of Void and Voidable Marriages

215. The court has the same powers to award financial provision when annulling a marriage as it does when granting a divorce. This is one reason – in addition to legal certainty – why a party to a void marriage may wish to obtain a decree of nullity. It should however be noted that the fact that the court has the same powers does not necessarily mean that they will be exercised in the same way. The conduct of the parties may justify a lesser award or indeed no award at all.[550] This is a matter for the court's discretion rather than an absolute rule.[551]

216. Similarly, if a void marriage has not been annulled before the death of either party, then the survivor will be able to apply for financial provision from the estate of the deceased as a spouse, but only if he or she entered into the marriage in

---

544. *Gandhi v. Patel* [2001] 1 F.L.R. 603 (Hindu ceremony in a restaurant); *Al-Saedy v. Musawi* [2010] EWHC 3293; *El Gamal v. Al Maktoum* [2011] EWHC B27.
545. *Gereis v. Yagoub* [1997] 1 F.L.R. 854.
546. *Dukali v. Lamrani* [2012] EWHC 1748 (Fam).
547. *City of Westminster v. IC (By his Litigation Friend the Official Solicitor) and KC and NNC* [2008] EWCA Civ 198.
548. *Hudson v. Leigh* [2009] EWHC 1306 (Fam).
549. *B v. I* [2010] 1 F.L.R. 1721; *Re P. (Forced Marriage)* [2011] EWHC 3467 (Fam).
550. *See,* e.g., *S-T (formerly J) v. J* [1998] Fam. 103.
551. *Rampal v. Rampal* [2001] EWCA Civ 989.

good faith and did not remarry during the lifetime of the deceased.[552] Where the marriage has been annulled, a party to it can make a claim as a former spouse.

---

552. *Inheritance (Provision for Family and Dependants) Act* 1975, s. 25(4).

# Chapter 2. Civil Partnership

§1. The Nature of a Civil Partnership

*217.* In 2004, Parliament passed the Civil Partnership Act, which allowed same-sex couples in England and Wales (and in Scotland and Northern Ireland) to formalize their relationship and thereby obtain virtually all of the same rights and responsibilities as married couples. The terminology of 'civil partnership' neatly positions the UK between the 'civil unions' available in some US states and the 'registered partnerships' introduced in many European countries.

*218.* With the opening up of marriage to same-sex couples, new questions are being asked as to whether civil partnerships should be made available to opposite-sex couples, maintained for same-sex couples alone, or abolished altogether. Provision has been made for the conversion of a civil partnership into a marriage, but not vice versa.[553] The fact that civil parternships are limited to couples of the same sex has recently been the subject of a challenge via judicial review.[554] The couple's claim that their Article 8 rights had been infringed was dismissed at first instance but the Court of Appeal was more sympathetic, holding that the bar on entering into a civil partnership fell within the scope of Article 8 and that although the distinction between same-sex and opposite-sex couples could be justified while the options for the future were considered, this could not provide a long-term justification.[555] The couple have since appealed to the Supreme Court.

§2. The Capacity to Enter into a Civil Partnership

*219.* With the exception that the parties must be of the same sex,[556] the rules governing capacity to enter into a civil partnership are the same as relating to capacity to marry.

*220.* First, both parties must be aged 16 years or over,[557] with parental consent being required for a 16- or 17-year old to enter into a partnership.[558]

*221.* Second, both must be single; if either is already married to, or in a civil partnership with, someone else at the time of the ceremony then the civil partnership will be void.[559] An offending partner is not guilty of the crime of bigamy, but will effectively have committed perjury if he or she claimed to be free to enter into

---

553. *Marriage (Same Sex Couples) Act* 2013, s. 9.
554. For discussion *see* C. Draghici, *Equal marriage, unequal civil partnership: a bizarre case of discrimination in Europe* 29 Child & Fam. L. Q. 313 (2017).
555. *Steinfeld & Keidan v. Secretary of State for Education* [2017] EWCA Civ 81.
556. *Civil Partnership Act* 2004, s. 3(1)(a).
557. *Ibid.*, s. 3(1)(c).
558. *Ibid.*, s. 4; Sch. 2 Part I.
559. *Civil Partnership Act* 2004, s. 3(1)(b).

the partnership knowing that this was not the case.[560] It was argued that 'the criminal consequences of the relevant offence akin to perjury … together with the proposals to ensure the validity of civil partnerships would provide enough deterrent to the offender and provide enough protection to the public'.[561] A further minor distinction between the provisions relating to marriage and those governing civil partnerships is that the 2004 Act contains no equivalent of the provision that a person who is domiciled in England and Wales does not have capacity to enter into a polygamous marriage overseas: since no jurisdiction allows multiway civil partnerships there was no need for such a provision.

222. Third, the parties must not be related to each other within the prohibited degrees.[562] The transposing of these restrictions illustrates that their purpose is as much influenced by social considerations as by genetic concerns. In addition, a civil partnership creates relationships by affinity in exactly the same way as a marriage does, but this is of little significance now that the last remaining restriction on formalizing a relationship with a former in law has been removed. There are, however, restrictions on forming a civil partnership (or indeed marriage) with the children or grandchildren of one's civil partner unless both parties are over 21 years and have not lived together as parent and child at any time before the child was 18 years.

223. Finally, when determining whether the parties are indeed of the same-sex, the Gender Recognition Act 2004 will apply to civil partners in the same way as it does to spouses; thus a transsexual who undergoes gender reassignment during the course of a civil partnership will need to take steps to annul it before the reassigned gender can be recognized. There will then of course be the possibility of a marriage with the former civil partner.

224. A civil partnership will be void if the parties do not have capacity to enter into a civil partnership with each other.[563]

§3. Formalities for Entering into a Civil Partnership

225. The formalities for entering into a civil partnership are rather more streamlined than those for entering into a marriage, simply comprising certain specified preliminaries[564] (modelled on those required in the case of civil marriage) and registration. Although registration must take place in a licensed location, little else in the Act suggests any form of ceremony: no words are prescribed for use by the parties and it is simply stated that 'two people are to be regarded as having registered as civil partners of each other once each of them has signed the civil partnership

---

560. *Ibid.*, s. 80.
561. Women and Equality Unit, *Response to Civil Partnership: A framework for the Legal Recognition of Same-Sex Couples* 31–32 (November 2003).
562. *Civil Partnership Act 2004*, s. 3(1)(d); Sch. 1 Part 1.
563. *Civil Partnership Act 2004*, s. 49(a).
564. *Civil Partnership Act 2004*, s. 8. There are additional preliminaries for non-relevant nationals: *see* s. 8A, inserted by the *Immigration Act 2014*.

document' in the presence of a civil partnership registrar and witnesses.[565] One could scarcely imagine a more pared down celebration: signing the register is consent, ceremony and proof all rolled into one. In practice, however, it is likely that civil partnerships will be accompanied by readings and music in the same way as civil marriages, and the same broad spectrum of venues is available for the celebration of such unions.

226.  The legislation originally provided that the registration of a civil partnership could not take place on religious premises. In 2010, however, this prohibition was removed, although it was made clear that there would be no obligation on religious organizations to host civil partnerships.[566]

227.  The 2004 Act replicated the provision made for spouses in including options for the civil partnerships of prisoners,[567] those in psychiatric hospitals,[568] the housebound[569] and those who are terminally ill and not expected to recover.[570]

228.  It remains to be seen whether the courts will develop a 'presumption in favour of civil partnership' equivalent to that which operates in the context of marriage. It would be logical if the effect of registering a civil partnership and thereafter cohabiting was to raise a presumption that the civil partnership was valid. However, since the other strand of the presumption is based on a misunderstanding of the rules originally applicable to married couples, it is submitted that this mistake should not be transposed to a new context.

§4.  EFFECTS OF A CIVIL PARTNERSHIP

229.  The 2004 Act largely replicates the legislative provisions applicable to married couples, dealing with issues such as maintenance during a civil partnership,[571] 'home rights',[572] wills and inheritance rights,[573] evidence[574] and the possibility of an action in tort between the parties.[575] There is even a provision that an action will not lie for 'breach of a civil partnership agreement'[576] – i.e., an agreement to enter into a civil partnership – to preclude the rather unlikely scenario of 'breach of promise' actions between same-sex couples. Even some provisions that were initially

---

565. *Ibid.*, s. 2(1).
566. *Civil Partnership Act* 2004, s. 6A(3A) as amended by *Equality Act* 2010, s. 202(4). *See* R. Probert, *Fifty Years in Family Law: Essays for Stephen Cretney* (R. Probert & C. Barton eds., Intersentia 2012).
567. *Civil Partnership Act* 2004, s. 19.
568. *Ibid.*, s. 19.
569. *Ibid.*, s. 18.
570. *Ibid.*, ss 21–27.
571. *Civil Partnership Act* 2004, Part 9 of Sch. 5 and Sch. 6.
572. *Ibid.*, Sch. 4.
573. *Ibid.*, Sch. 2.
574. *Ibid.*, s. 84.
575. *Ibid.*, s. 69.
576. *Ibid.*, s. 73.

sex-specific have been extended to civil partners: it is provided that if one civil partner provides the other with a housekeeping allowance, any savings from that allowance belongs to them both in equal shares.[577] The effects of void and voidable civil partnerships are also equated to those of void and voidable marriages.

*230.* This process of transposition does, however, raise a question as to whether other doctrines – such as those originating in the common law – have any application to civil partners. It seems unlikely that the concept of consortium would ever be applied to civil partners, given its nebulous nature and the legislature's clear intention to draw some distinctions between marriage and civil partnership. It is even more unlikely that the doctrine of unity would be held to apply, given its limited relevance to modern married couples and the lack of any religious justification for regarding the two partners as one. There may be certain contexts in which civil partners are regarded as having unity of interests (such as keeping confidences and assuming a lack of any intention to create legal relations) but this is distinct from unity of persons.

*231.* Matters are more complex when one comes to consider the implied rights and responsibilities of civil partners. The fact that a civil partnership can be dissolved upon proof of one party's desertion, and the availability of a separation order enabling the parties to live apart, does suggest that there is an implicit obligation on civil partners to live together. On the issue of sex, matters are less straightforward. The inclusion of prohibited degrees is consistent with a context in which it is assumed that the parties will have a sexual relationship. Yet non-consummation is not a ground for annulling a civil partnership, and there is no explicit provision that the infidelity of one partner justifies dissolution of the union. This desexualization of civil partnerships has enabled some groups to accept them as mere partnerships. The Church of England, e.g., has stated that it is willing to accept its ministers entering into civil partnerships as long as they abstain from sex.[578] According to one spokesman: 'The Church's approach to civil partnerships will reflect the fact that they will not be marriages, nor based on the presumption of sexual relations between the two people making the legal agreement.'[579]

## §5. Void, Voidable and Non-existent Civil Partnerships

*232.* The Act sets out the grounds on which a civil partnership may be void or voidable, and the terms bear the same meaning that they do in the context of marriage. As noted above, a civil partnership will be void if the parties do not have capacity to enter into such a union; it will also be void if they both know that they

---

577. *Ibid.*, s. 70A, as inserted by *Equality Act* 2010, s. 201. This however has not yet been brought into force.
578. 'Civil Partnerships – A Pastoral Statement from the House of Bishops of the Church of England' issued on 25 Jul. 2005.
579. *Bishops Decide Clergy Can Register Gay Partnerships*, Church Eng. Newsp. (3 Jun. 2005).

have failed to comply with certain formalities.[580] Once again, this raises the question as to whether a further category of 'non-existent' civil partnerships will need to be created. The concept could in theory be applied to self-devised ceremonies (such as 'hand fasting', which has been appropriated as a pseudo-pagan marriage ceremony), but given that there could be no question of such ceremonies claiming legal status – or even, given the phrasing of the legislation, being classified as void – it is unlikely that the courts will ever need to consider the issue.

*233.* A civil partnership is not voidable on the basis of either inability or wilful refusal to consummate. The Women and Equality Unit explained these omissions on the basis that consummation had 'a specific meaning within the context of heterosexual relationships and it would not be possible or desirable to read this across to same-sex civil partnerships'.[581] One can readily perceive the difficulties in transposing the narrow legal definition of consummation, with its requirement of penile-vaginal sex, to same-sex relationships. More oddly, the fact that one party is suffering from a communicable venereal disease was also omitted from the list of grounds that might render a civil partnership voidable. The expressed view that it was not 'appropriate in present day circumstances to include [transmission of a venereal disease] as a ground to nullify a civil partnership'[582] is unhelpful, since the reason given – that men and women might carry certain venereal diseases for years without their knowledge – is equally applicable to spouses. It was suggested, however, that the absence of any sexual activity and the deliberate transmission of a sexually transmitted disease could be 'evidence of unreasonable behaviour leading to the irretrievable breakdown of a civil partnership',[583] but that this would be decided on an individual, case-by-case basis.

*234.* By contrast, a civil partnership may be annulled if one of the parties was pregnant (necessarily by a third party) at the time of registration and the other was unaware of this,[584] despite the fact that such a provision is obviously of limited application to same-sex couples.

*235.* A civil partnership may also be annulled on the basis of lack of consent,[585] mental disorder,[586] the discovery that the other partner has undergone gender reassignment,[587] or the fact that a gender recognition certificate has been issued to either party.[588] There are certain statutory bars to relief where a civil partnership is voidable, which are equivalent to those applicable in the context of marriage.[589]

---

580. *Civil Partnership Act* 2004, s. 49(b).
581. Women and Equality Unit, *Response to Civil Partnership: A Framework for the Legal Recognition of Same-Sex Couples* 36 (November 2003).
582. *Ibid.*
583. *Ibid.*
584. *Civil Partnership Act* 2004, s. 50(1)(c).
585. *Civil Partnership Act* 2004, s. 50(1)(a).
586. *Ibid.*, s. 50(1)(b).
587. *Ibid.*, s. 50(1)(e).
588. *Ibid.*, s. 50(1)(d).
589. *Ibid.*, s. 51.

# Chapter 3. Terminating a Marriage or Civil Partnership

## §1. Introduction

*236.* England and Wales were among the few protestant countries not to make provision for divorce after the Reformation. The ecclesiastical courts, which had jurisdiction over such matters until 1857, could grant a divorce *a mensa et thoro* upon proof of the other spouse's adultery, cruelty or desertion but this did not enable the parties to remarry. Members of the elite were able to bring their marriages to an end by a private Act of Parliament,[590] but judicial divorce did not become available until 1857.

This chapter considers both the law of divorce and the means of terminating a civil partnership, termed dissolution. Brief mention is also made of the alternative option of judicial separation, the successor to the divorce *a mensa et thoro*, which does not have the effect of terminating the marriage but does allow the parties to live separately.

## §2. Facts Justifying a Divorce

*237.* When divorce was first introduced in 1857, adultery was the only factor that justified a divorce,[591] and it was not until 1937 that the grounds of cruelty, desertion and incurable insanity were added.[592] More radical reform came in 1969, when the Divorce Reform Act provided that the sole ground for divorce was that the relationship between the parties had irretrievably broken down. Irretrievable breakdown, however, could only be proved by one of five facts, three of which bore more than a passing resemblance to the old 'matrimonial offences' under the 1937 Act. It remains the case, therefore, that even if the court is satisfied that the marriage has irretrievably broken down, it is unable to grant a divorce unless one of the five facts has been established.[593] In theory, it would be possible for a court to decide that the marriage had not broken down even though one of the five facts had been proved, but this is highly unlikely. The law was consolidated in the Matrimonial Causes Act 1973.

The five 'facts' are as follows.

### I. Adultery

*238.* Irretrievable breakdown of the marriage may be inferred from the fact that the respondent has committed adultery and the applicant finds it intolerable to live

---

590. *See*, e.g., R. Probert, *Landmarks in Family Law* Ch. 2 (S. Gilmore, J. Herring & R. Probert eds, Hart 2011).
591. *Divorce and Matrimonial Causes Act* 1857.
592. *Matrimonial Causes Act* 1937.
593. *See*, e.g., *Buffery v. Buffery* [1988] 2 F.L.R. 365; *Owens v. Owens* [2017] EWCA Civ 182.

with the respondent.[594] There are two elements to this: first, the adultery – i.e., voluntary sexual intercourse between the respondent and a third party of the opposite sex[595] – and, second, the intolerability of cohabitation. The courts have held that the second does not need to be linked to the first;[596] the respondent's adultery may therefore be the fact from which breakdown is inferred for legal purposes even if it was not the actual reason for the breakdown of the relationship. Empirical research has established that applications rarely elaborate on why the applicant finds it intolerable to live with the respondent: a mere assertion to this effect is sufficient.[597]

*239.* The respondent must formally admit to the adultery in order for an application to proceed. However, there is no need for applicants to name a co-respondent and the Family Procedure Rules now specifically discourage them from doing so.

*240.* No application may be brought on this ground if the spouses have continued to live together for six months or more (whether continuously or in an aggregate of shorter periods) after the adultery was discovered.[598] Clearly, it is desirable that the law should encourage reconciliation wherever possible; it would, however, be undesirable to allow one spouse to hold the threat of divorce over the other for the rest of their lives together. The bar is intended to strike a balance between these two elements, with any period of cohabitation shorter than six months being disregarded by the courts in determining whether the applicant does indeed find it intolerable to live with the respondent.[599]

## II. 'Unreasonable Behaviour'

*241.* The conventional abbreviation of section 1(2)(b) that appears in the heading is somewhat misleading: what it actually provides is that breakdown may be inferred if the other spouse 'has behaved in such a way that the applicant can no longer reasonably be expected to live with the respondent'. It is thus the expectation that the applicant will continue to live with the respondent, rather than the respondent's behaviour per se, that must be shown to be unreasonable. The test applied by the courts is therefore both objective and subjective: objective, in that the test is that of 'reasonableness'; subjective, in that the characteristics of the individual applicant will be taken into account. The central question was accordingly formulated as: would any right thinking person come to the conclusion that this husband has behaved in such a way that this wife cannot reasonably be expected to live with him, taking into account the whole of the circumstances and the characters and

---

594. *Matrimonial Causes Act* 1973, s. 1(2)(a).
595. This remains the case despite the introduction of same-sex marriage: *see Matrimonial Causes Act* 1973, s. 1(6), as inserted by the *Marriage (Same-Sex Couples) Act* 2013.
596. *Cleary v. Cleary and Hutton* [1974] 1 W.L.R. 73.
597. L. Trinder, D. Braybrook, C. Bryson, L. Coleman, C. Houlston and M. Sefton, *Finding Fault? Divorce Law and Practice in England and Wales* (Nuffield Foundation 2017).
598. *Matrimonial Causes Act* 1973, s. 2(1).
599. *Ibid.*, s. 2(2).

personalities of the parties?[600] A sensitive spouse may therefore obtain a divorce on the basis of facts that would not affect one more robust.[601]

*242.* The fact that the focus is on the effect of the respondent's behaviour on the applicant has a further implication: there is no need to show that the respondent was at fault or that the behaviour complained of was intentional. This means that a spouse who is mentally ill may be divorced under this heading even if the behaviour that so affects the applicant is the result of the respondent's illness.[602]

*243.* Research has demonstrated that the threshold for obtaining a divorce on the basis of the respondent's behaviour is a fairly low one and that in undefended cases 'even citing the mildest action or inaction that could be attributable to the respondent, would very likely be accepted'.[603] In the rare cases where the divorce is defended, however, it is clear that the courts do still attach importance to the objective part of the test.[604]

*244.* Again, the law tries to allow time for reconciliation, providing that continued cohabitation for a period or periods less than six months will not be taken into account when determining whether it is unreasonable to expect the applicant to continue living with the respondent.[605] Longer periods will be taken into account, but, unlike in the case of adultery, do not constitute an absolute bar.[606] It is also interesting to note that the court will only take into account periods of cohabitation since the last incident alleged in the application; the fact that the behaviour complained of has persisted over a long period of time is irrelevant.

### III. Desertion

*245.* The third fact from which the breakdown of a marriage may be inferred is that the 'respondent has deserted the applicant for a continuous period of two years immediately preceding the presentation of the petition'.[607] Despite the explicit reference to a continuous period, the legislation later qualifies this by providing that no account will be taken of any period or periods of cohabitation totalling less than six months.[608] The effect of a reunion is therefore merely to 'stop the clock' running against the respondent: any such periods of cohabitation do not count towards the

---

600. *Livingstone-Stallard v. Livingstone-Stallard* [1974] Fam. 47, 54, adopted by the Court of Appeal in *O'Neill v. O'Neill* [1975] 1 W.L.R. 1118.
601. *See,* e.g., *Birch v. Birch* [1992] 1 F.L.R. 564.
602. *Thurlow v. Thurlow* [1976] Fam. 32.
603. Trinder et al, *Finding Fault,* p. 79.
604. *See,* e.g., *Owens v. Owens* [2017] EWCA Civ 182.
605. *Matrimonial Causes Act* 1973, s. 2(3).
606. *See,* e.g., *Bradley v. Bradley* [1973] 1 W.L.R. 1291.
607. *Matrimonial Causes Act* 1973, s. 1(2)(c).
608. *Ibid.,* s. 2(5).

two years. If, however, the respondent returns after the two years have elapsed but before the other spouse has applied for divorce it will not be possible for the latter to apply on this ground.

*246.* Desertion involves both a physical and a mental element: there must be both physical separation and an intention to desert on the part of the respondent. It is possible for both to be satisfied even though the spouses remain living under the same roof, as long as they have established two separate households.[609]

*247.* Unlike the first two facts, which were modified in 1969 to fit with the new ethos of divorce law, the scope of desertion remained largely unaltered. Thus it is a defence for the respondent to show that he or she had a reasonable excuse for leaving the other.[610]

## IV. Living Apart for Two Years Plus Respondent's Consent

*248.* The first three facts have their roots in the earlier fault-based law, the fourth – that the spouses 'have lived apart for a continuous period of two years immediately preceding the presentation of the petition ... and the respondent consents to the decree being granted'[611] – was introduced only in 1969. It was an innovation in sharp contrast to the law's earlier approach: up until 1963, any agreement between the parties regarding their divorce would have been labelled collusion and would have justified the divorce being denied. It was hoped that the availability of this ground would reduce the bitterness of divorce by allowing divorce without the need to attribute blame. In practice, its popularity has never matched that of the first two facts, perhaps because spouses wish to attribute blame, or because those who are genuinely in agreement would rather concoct a story to obtain a quicker divorce than this fact allows.[612]

*249.* The practical problems of establishing this fact should also be borne in mind. Either one party must move out, or the pair must lead separate lives under the same roof.[613] As with desertion, the requisite 'continuous' period of separation may in fact be made up of shorter periods, as long as the interludes of cohabitation do not total more than six months.[614]

*250.* The respondent is only required to consent to the divorce, not to the separation. Indeed, although the courts have held that 'living apart' includes a mental element as well as a physical element, it is only necessary for one of the spouses to

---

609. *Le Brocq v. Le Brocq* [1964] 1 W.L.R. 1085.
610. *See*, e.g., *Quoreshi v. Quoreshi* [1985] F.L.R. 780.
611. *Matrimonial Causes Act* 1973, s. 1(2)(d).
612. *See* generally Trinder et al, *Finding Fault.*
613. *Mouncer v. Mouncer* [1972] 1 W.L.R. 321.
614. *Matrimonial Causes Act* 1973, s. 2(5).

be of the opinion that the marriage is at an end and that view need not be communicated to the other during the two-year period.[615]

## V. Living Apart for Five Years

*251.* The fifth and final ground – that the spouses 'have lived apart for a continuous period of five years immediately preceding the presentation of the petition'[616] – was also an innovation when the law was reformed in 1969, and a controversial one. For the first time it was possible to divorce an innocent spouse against his or her wishes, reflecting the higher priority being given to the legal termination of marriages that had ended in all but name. It was, however, deemed appropriate to confer further protection on the respondent in such cases: a divorce may therefore be opposed on the basis that the dissolution of the marriage would cause grave financial or other hardship to the respondent and it would in all the circumstances be wrong to dissolve the marriage.[617] In practice, this bar has been of limited effect: the hardship in question must be the result of the divorce, rather than of the breakdown of the marriage and consequent separation of the parties, and the allocation of assets on divorce may compensate for the loss of any pension rights that were contingent on spousal status. It is very rare for the court to exercise its discretion to deny a divorce on the basis of grave financial hardship,[618] and there are no reported cases in which a divorce has been denied on the basis of 'other' hardship.

## §3. Procedure for Obtaining a Divorce

## I. Jurisdiction

*252.* The first issue to be considered is whether a court in England and Wales actually has jurisdiction to entertain proceedings for divorce. For proceedings commenced since 1 March 2001 this issue will be determined by the terms of the relevant EC Council Regulation.[619] If no court of a Contracting State has jurisdiction under the terms of that regulation, then there is an alternative ground on which the courts of this country may exercise jurisdiction, namely that at least one of the parties was domiciled in England and Wales on the date the proceedings were commenced.[620]

---

615. *Santos v. Santos* [1972] Fam. 247.
616. *Matrimonial Causes Act* 1973, s. 1(2)(e).
617. *Ibid.*, s. 5(1) and (2).
618. *Julian v. Julian* [1972] 116 S.J. 763.
619. *European Communities (Jurisdiction and Judgments in Matrimonial and Parental Responsibility Matters) Regulations* 2005, S.I. 2005/265.
620. *Domicile and Matrimonial Proceedings Act* 1973, s. 5(2)(b).

*253.* Following the introduction of the single Family Court in 2014, a number of divorce centres were created to deal with uncontested applications for divorce. Divorce centres will also issue applications, serve documents and fix directions appointments for contested cases.

## II. Bar on Applications in the First Year of Marriage

*254.* No application for divorce can be brought before one year has elapsed from the date of the marriage. This is an absolute bar, and is intended as 'a useful safeguard against irresponsible or trial marriages and a valuable external buttress to the stability of marriages during the difficult early years'.[621] Whether it fulfils this function is open to doubt. There is nothing to prevent a couple from separating immediately after the ceremony, or indeed from seeking a judicial separation.[622]

## III. Undefended Divorces

*255.* If the application for divorce is undefended, the procedure is very simple. The applicant simply fills in the relevant forms and sends them to court. Neither party is required to attend in person: the decision as to whether or not a divorce is to be granted on the basis of written evidence alone and routine applications are dealt with by legal advisors rather than by judges.

## IV. Defended Divorces

*256.* In a very few cases, the respondent will give notice of his or her intention to defend the proceedings and file an answer. Since legal aid is not available for this purpose, defending the proceedings is likely to be an expensive and ultimately fruitless exercise. Even if the defence is successful, it is likely that this will only have the effect of preventing the divorce, rather than saving the marriage. However, judges have asserted that those who do choose to mount a defence should not be treated as if they are acting unreasonably. The law allows the respondent 'the right to oppose it and to have the allegations made against him properly proved to the satisfaction of the court to the civil standard of the balance of probabilities'.[623]

## V. Decree Nisi and Decree Absolute

*257.* Whether defended or undefended, the granting of a divorce is a two-stage process. First, a decree *nisi* will be pronounced. Six weeks and one day later, the

---

621. *See* Law Commission, *The Field of Choice* (1966) Law Com. No. 6 Cmnd. 3123, para. 19.
622. *Matrimonial Causes Act* 1973, s. 17.
623. *Butterworth v. Butterworth* [1997] 2 F.L.R. 336, 339.

applicant may apply for the decree to be made absolute. During this period it is open to any person to challenge the proceedings and 'show cause why the decree should not be made absolute'.[624]

258.   In addition, if the application is based on either of the separation grounds, a respondent may oppose the granting of the decree absolute on the ground that reasonable financial provision has not been made.[625] In such a case, the court may not make the decree absolute unless it is satisfied that reasonable financial provision has either been made or agreed or that there are circumstances requiring the decree to be made absolute without delay.[626] It has further been held by the courts that there is, in addition to these statutory powers, 'a discretionary power under the inherent jurisdiction to delay or stay an application to make a decree absolute'; however, it was also emphasized that 'this jurisdiction can only be exercised if the respondent is able to establish special or exceptional circumstances'.[627]

259.   Further delay may be occasioned if the parties married 'according to the usages of the Jews' and no *get*, or Jewish divorce, has been granted. The court may order that the decree is not to be made absolute until a declaration has been made by both parties that they have taken such steps as are required to dissolve the marriage in Jewish law.[628] This was intended to address the problem of so-called limping marriages: as a divorce granted in the English courts does not affect the parties' status under Jewish law, and as Jewish law requires the husband to grant the *get*, it was possible for the parties to be divorced in the eyes of the legal authorities but not in the eyes of their religious authorities. The solution adopted prevents this particular problem arising, but it can also prevent the divorce, as the husband cannot be compelled to grant the *get*.

260.   If the applicant chooses not to apply for the decree to be made absolute, the respondent may do so, but only after a further three months have elapsed from the day on which the applicant could first have applied.[629] If the decree is made absolute before the relevant period has expired, it is void, and the marriage remains in force.[630] If neither party applies, then, again, the marriage remains in force and the court may decide to rescind the decree *nisi*.[631] It is only once the decree of divorce has been made absolute that the parties are free to remarry.[632]

---

624. *Matrimonial Causes Act* 1973, s. 8(1). *See*, e.g., *Rapisarda v. Colladon (Irregular Divorces)* [2014] EWFC 35.
625. *Matrimonial Causes Act* 1973, ss 10(3) and (4)(a).
626. *Ibid.*, s. 10(4)(a).
627. *Miller-Smith v. Miller-Smith* [2009] EWHC 3623 (Fam) at para. 23. No such special or exceptional cases were established in that case.
628. *Matrimonial Causes Act* 1973, s. 10A(2).
629. *Matrimonial Causes Act* 1973, s. 9(2). *See*, e.g., *Evans v. Evans* [2012] EWCA Civ 1293.
630. *See*, e.g., *Dennis v. Dennis* [2000] 2 F.L.R. 231.
631. *See*, e.g., *Kim v. Morris* [2012] EWHC 1103 (Fam), in which the parties temporarily reconciled after the decree *nisi*.
632. Assuming that it was properly granted: *see Rapisarda v. Colladon (Irregular Divorces)* [2014] EWFC 35, at [35], in which it was established that the English courts had been 'induced by fraud

§4. JUDICIAL SEPARATION

*261.* The law provides an alternative to divorce, namely, a judicial separation.[633] This order, inherited from the practice of the ecclesiastical courts, does not terminate the marriage but merely enables the parties to live separately. It was obviously of more relevance when the duty of the parties to cohabit with each other could be enforced, but the courts' power to imprison a spouse who refused to do so was abolished in 1884, and their power even to order cohabitation was lost in 1970.[634] Today, the order is largely of relevance to those who have religious or other objections to divorce but who wish to live separately from their spouse and to take advantage of the court's extensive powers to reallocate assets. Only a hundred or so such orders are granted each year now.

*262.* A judicial separation may be granted where any of the five facts set out above are established. There is no need to prove that the marriage has irretrievably broken down.

§5. DISSOLUTION OF A CIVIL PARTNERSHIP

*263.* Despite the difference in terminology, the law governing the termination of a civil partnership is almost identical to the law of divorce.[635] The main difference is that adultery does not appear in the list of facts from which breakdown may be inferred. The reason for this is, as noted above, adultery has always been defined as sexual intercourse with a person of the opposite sex (although it is not beyond the bounds of possibility that civil partners might engage in liaisons with members of the opposite sex, just as some spouses may be unfaithful with those of the same-sex). Infidelity with a person of the same-sex may, however, show that the unfaithful party has behaved in such a way that the other can no longer reasonably be expected to live with him or her.[636] The parallels with marriage extend to the provision of a 'separation order' equivalent to a judicial separation – again, with the adultery 'fact' being omitted.[637] In 2016, there were 1,313 dissolutions of civil partnerships in England and Wales.[638]

---

to accept that it had jurisdiction to entertain the petition' and 91 decrees absolute were consequently set aside. *See also Grasso v. Naik* [2017] EWHC 2789 (Fam).

633. *Matrimonial Causes Act* 1973, s. 17.
634. *See supra*, para. 182.
635. *Civil Partnership Act* 2004, s. 44.
636. *Ibid.*, s. 44(5)(a).
637. *Ibid.*, s. 56.
638. Office for National Statistics, *Civil partnerships in the UK, 2016* (September 2017).

§6. LEGAL EFFECTS OF DIVORCE, DISSOLUTION, AND SEPARATION ORDERS

*264.* There is an enormous literature on the effects of divorce – on the parties themselves, on any children they might have, and on society as a whole. This section will focus solely on those legal effects of divorce that are not covered elsewhere (*see* Part III, Chapter 2, on the division of assets on divorce and Part II, Chapter 8, on the way that the courts resolve disputes relating to children).

*265.* The grant of a divorce affects any will previously made by either party. Any property left to the former spouse will pass as if he or she had died on the date that the divorce was granted, unless a contrary intention is expressed in the will.[639] It is of course possible to make a will after the divorce conferring rights on one's former spouse. A former spouse also has the right to apply for financial provision from the estate of the deceased.[640] The same rules now apply to former civil partners following the dissolution of the partnership.[641]

*266.* If a judicial separation or separation order remains in force until the death of one of the parties, and the parties were living separate at the time, there is an exception to the usual rule that the court should take into account what provision the survivor would have received had the union ended by divorce or dissolution on the date of the death.[642]

---

639. *Wills Act* 1837, s. 18C.
640. Under the *Inheritance (Provision for Family and Dependants) Act* 1975, s. 1(1)(b): *see* Part IV, Ch. 3.
641. *Wills Act* 1837, s. 18C; *Inheritance (Provision for Family and Dependants) Act* 1975, s. 1(1)(b), as amended by the *Civil Partnership Act* 2004.
642. *Inheritance (Provision for Family and Dependants) Act* 1975, s. 3(2).

# Chapter 4. Cohabitation Without Marriage

## §1. Introduction

*267.* As the previous chapters have shown, marriage and civil partnership confer a status and a bundle of rights upon those who opt in. By contrast, cohabitants have no formal legal status, and the way in which they are treated by the legal system is fragmented and inconsistent.[643] In some contexts – generally where this is to their disadvantage – cohabitants are treated as if they were married. In other areas, they have rights that are less generous than those accorded to spouses or civil partners. And in some contexts they have no rights at all, other than those accorded under the general law. Such inconsistency of treatment encourages misunderstandings: couples who are treated as if married in one context may well believe that they will have the same rights in another and, therefore, fail to put in place the arrangements that could have secured them some protection. A surprisingly high percentage of cohabitants believe that they have the same rights as married couples by virtue of a 'common-law marriage', a concept that has never existed in domestic English law and is based on a conflation of the American concept and the possibility of celebrating a marriage overseas with little formality.[644] Again, the effect of this mistaken belief is to deflect couples from entering into contracts, trusts and wills that would secure their legal position.

*268.* Until 2004 same-sex cohabitants were in an even worse position than opposite-sex cohabitants, since such legislation as had been passed focused explicitly on couples who were living together 'as if they were husband and wife'. The House of Lords then held that this phrase was capable of encompassing same-sex couples,[645] and the Civil Partnership Act subsequently conferred the same rights on same-sex cohabitants living together 'as if they were civil partners' as upon opposite-sex couples living together 'as if they were husband and wife'.

*269.* This chapter will consider, first, the steps that cohabiting couples can take to secure some legal protection; second, the existing patchwork of rights and, finally, the proposals for reform that have been put forward.

## §2. Options for Private Ordering

*270.* What rights can cohabitants confer on each other, and what steps should they take to do so? A couple who purchase a home in joint names will be directed to complete a declaration as to their beneficial interests in the property.[646] This will

---

643. *See* generally R. Probert, *Cohabitation: Current Legal Solutions*, Current Leg. Problems 316 (2009).
644. R. Probert, *Common-Law Marriage: Myths and Misunderstandings*, 20 Child & Fam. L. Q. 1 (2008).
645. *Ghaidan v. Goden-Mendoza* [2004] UKHL 30.
646. *See infra* Part III, Ch. 1, para. 432.

be conclusive in the absence of mistake or fraud and will determine the interest each has in the property. It is also possible for the legal owner or owners of a property to declare a trust in favour of another, thereby conferring a beneficial interest in the property. Such a declaration must, however, be evidenced in writing if it relates to land,[647] and few couples actually make such arrangements. Declarations of trust in relation to personal property do not need to be supported by written evidence, and may arise out of relatively informal conversations, such as the use of the word 'ours' when describing the property in question.[648]

*271.* Since a surviving cohabitant has no automatic right to any share of the estate of a deceased partner, couples would also be well advised to make provision for each other by way of a will.

*272.* All of the above arrangements are available under the general law, and the fact that the parties are cohabiting makes no difference to their ability to enter into them. The possibility of a cohabiting couple entering into a contract raises rather different issues. First, cohabitants may find it difficult to satisfy the general requirements for a valid contract: their intentions to create legal relations must be made clear, and there must be mutual consideration. Executing a deed will address both factors: it clearly demonstrates the parties' intentions to be bound and obviates the need for consideration. The second potential problem is more closely related to the nature of the parties' relationship. For a long time it was thought that a contract between cohabitants risked being struck down as contrary to public policy on the basis that to uphold such a contract would undermine marriage. It has now been confirmed that there is a distinction between a contract for cohabitation (i.e., a contract entered into to procure one party to cohabit with the other) and a contract between cohabitants regulating their financial affairs.[649] The former would be void, the latter – assuming other legal requirements had been observed – valid. As yet, however, there is no modern decision definitively upholding a cohabitation contract, and the Law Commission has recommended that the matter be clarified by legislation.

§3. EXISTING RIGHTS

## I. Equal Treatment

*273.* Since the general tendency of law reform has been to abolish the particular legal disabilities that once applied to spouses – e.g., to prevent them from suing one another in tort, or from giving evidence against one another – it could be argued that there are many areas of the law in which cohabitants have the same rights as

---

647. *Law of Property Act* 1925, s. 53(1)(b).
648. *Paul v. Constance* [1977] 1 W.L.R. 527; *Rowe v. Prance* [1999] 2 F.L.R. 787.
649. *Sutton v. Mishcon de Reya* [2003] EWHC 3166 (Ch).

spouses, simply because neither group enjoys any status-specific rights or disabilities. This section will focus on those areas in which cohabitants are treated in the same way as spouses or civil partners as a result of their status.

274. If a couple lives in rented accommodation, it is possible for the courts to order that the tenancy be transferred either from joint names to the sole name of one of the parties, or from the sole name of one to the sole name of the other.[650] The transferee may be required to compensate the transferor.[651] This is of more significance to cohabiting than married couples, since cohabitants are more likely to live in rented accommodation than their married counterparts.

275. The equation of cohabitation with marriage may not always be to the advantage of the cohabiting couple. So it is in the context of certain welfare benefits: if a particular benefit ceases upon the recipient's marriage (or remarriage), it will also cease if he or she cohabits; if the incomes of spouses and civil partners are aggregated for the purpose of assessing either party's entitlement to benefits, so too will the incomes of cohabiting partners. Even in the context of benefits, however, the law's treatment of cohabiting couples is not uniform: cohabitation may be a ground for disentitlement, but it is not a ground for entitlement to (e.g.,) a state retirement pension based on a former partner's contributions or bereavement benefits.

276. Cohabitants have the same rights to apply for a non-molestation order under the Family Law Act 1996 as do spouses and civil partners – but so do a whole range of other family members who fall within the long statutory list of 'associated persons',[652] including those as remote as a cousin by marriage. By contrast, when it comes to applying for an order to exclude the abusive party from the shared family home, spouses and civil partners are privileged above other applicants, as the next section will explain.

## II. Lesser Rights

277. Under the Family Law Act 1996, two classes of persons are entitled to apply for an occupation order regulating who lives in the family home: 'entitled' applicants – namely those who have an interest in the property or spouses and civil partners with 'home rights'[653] – and 'non-entitled' applicants – those former spouses/civil partners and current or former cohabitants who do not have an interest in the property. Thus a cohabitant will always be able to apply for an occupation order in relation to the shared family home, but only a cohabitant who has a legal or beneficial interest in the property will have the same rights as a spouse. Whether a cohabitant is entitled or non-entitled has two consequences: first, the test to be

---

650. *Family Law Act* 1996, Sch. 7.
651. *Ibid.*, Sch. 7, para. 10.
652. *Family Law Act* 1996, s. 62.
653. *See infra* Part III, Ch. 1, para. 435.

applied in deciding whether the order should be made differs between the two groups; and, second, the duration of an order in favour of a non-entitled cohabitant or former cohabitant is more limited. If the application is made by an entitled person, the court must make an occupation order requiring the other party to leave the home if the so-called balance of harm test is satisfied.[654] This test requires the court to consider whether the applicant or any relevant child is likely to suffer 'significant harm' attributable to the other party's conduct if the order is not made, greater than the harm likely to be suffered by the other party, or a child, if the order is made. If the application is made by a non-entitled person, the 'balance of harm' is merely a factor to be taken into account.[655] If the court has decided that an occupation order should be made, the duration of that order is at the court's discretion in the case of an entitled applicant, but limited to a maximum of six months in the case of a non-entitled cohabitant (with the possibility of one further extension for a further six months).[656]

278.   If a cohabiting relationship is ended by the death of one of the parties, the survivor may have the right to apply for financial provision from the estate of the deceased under the Inheritance (Provision for Family and Dependants) Act 1975.[657] There are, however, a number of important differences between the rights of a surviving spouse and those of a surviving cohabitant. First, a cohabitant must be able to show that he or she had been living with the deceased for at least two years immediately before the latter's death,[658] or, if the relationship was shorter in duration, that he or she had been dependant on the deceased.[659] Second, there is no provision for a former cohabitant – as opposed to a former spouse or civil partner – to apply for provision. Third, the court can only award such provision as is reasonable for the applicant's maintenance,[660] whereas there is no such limit on awards to spouses or civil partners. The courts have, however, been generous in their interpretation of this provision: thus maintenance may, e.g., include the provision of a home.[661]

279.   Certain rights are also conferred indirectly on cohabitants who have had children together. Payments from a former partner for the maintenance of their child will increase the amount of money coming into the household. The size of such payments may be agreed privately or assessed by the Child Maintenance Service under the Child Support Act 1991. Under Schedule 1 of the Children Act 1989, the court has the power to order periodical payments (in certain defined circumstances), the payment of a lump sum or the transfer or settlement of property. This may benefit a former cohabitant in two ways: first, an assessment of the child's needs may

---

654. *Family Law Act* 1996, s. 33(7).
655. *Ibid.*, s. 36(7) and (8).
656. *Ibid.*, s. 36(10).
657. *See further* Part IV, Ch. 3.
658. *Inheritance (Provision for Family and Dependants) Act* 1975, s. 1(1A), as amended by the *Law Reform (Succession) Act* 1995; and s. 1(1B), as inserted by the *Civil Partnership Act* 2004.
659. *Inheritance (Provision for Family and Dependants) Act* 1975, s. 1(1)(e).
660. *Ibid.*, s. 1(2)(b).
661. *Churchill v. Roach* [2002] EWHC 3230 (Ch); *Webster v. Webster* [2009] EWHC 31 (Ch).

include an allowance for the parent caring for the child;[662] second, the provision of a home for the child will obviously benefit the child's carer. Although the relevant legislation does not differentiate between parents who have been married to each other and those who have not, the fact that the court has more extensive powers upon divorce means that in practice it is only those who have never been married to each other that will need to rely on the provisions of Schedule 1. One noticeable difference between the two is that courts are far less willing to order the transfer of property between former cohabitants. The more common course is to order that property be settled on the child during his or her minority, to revert back to the settlor when the child reaches adulthood.[663] It is not unknown for a transfer of the property to be ordered, but a compensatory payment may be required from the transferee.[664]

## III. No Rights

*280.* Even those limited rights are not available to childless cohabitants. When a cohabiting relationship breaks down, the courts have no powers – other than the limited exceptions set out above – to override the property rights of the parties. In sharp contrast to the position on divorce or dissolution, each party will be entitled to the property that he or she owns, and the question of ownership will be determined by applying general rules of property law. These rules are set out in Part III, Chapter 1, in the context of the matrimonial home, and the only additional point to note relates to the effect of making improvements to the home. The statutory provisions on this point apply only to spouses, civil partners and those who have agreed to enter into such unions; the effect of improvements made by a cohabitant thus falls to be determined by the general law. In the past, contributions of this kind have been taken into account in quantifying the shares of the parties, or in showing detrimental reliance upon a promise that the contributing party will have a share,[665] but have not, by themselves, been sufficient to raise the inference that there was a common intention that the contributor should have an interest in the property.[666] The House of Lords did suggest that making improvements that added significant value to the property should be sufficient to generate an interest,[667] but to date no courts have followed this lead.[668]

*281.* If only one of the parties has an interest in the family home, then – subject to the provisions of the Family Law Act 1996 considered above – the other may be

---

662. *F v. G (Child: Financial Provision)* [2004] EWHC 1848 (Fam); *N v. D* [2008] 1 F.L.R. 1629.
663. *A v. A (A Minor: Financial Provision)* [1994] 1 F.L.R. 657.
664. *Francis v. Manning* [1997] EWCA 1231.
665. *Eves v. Eves* [1975] 1 W.L.R. 1338; *Cox v. Jones* [2004] EWHC 1486 (Ch). *See also Chapman v. Jaume* [2012] EWCA Civ 427, in which moneys paid by one cohabitant to the other for the purpose of making improvements to the latter's property were held to constitute a loan.
666. *Thomas v. Fuller-Brown* [1988] 1 F.L.R. 237.
667. *Stack v. Dowden* [2007] UKHL 17: Lord Hope (para. 12); Lord Walker (para. 36); Baroness Hale (para. 70).
668. *See*, e.g., the inconclusive comments in *Aspden v. Elvy* [2012] EWHC 1387 (Ch).

required to leave. If both have an interest, and disagree as to who should remain in the property, then the matter may be resolved either under the Family Law Act or the Trusts of Land and Appointment of Trustees Act 1996. Under the latter – which is applicable to all co-owners, regardless of their relationship – the courts are required to have regard to a number of factors in considering whether sale should be ordered: the intentions of the person or persons who created the trust; the purposes for which the property subject to the trust is held; the welfare of any minor who occupies or might reasonably be expected to occupy any land subject to the trust as his or her home; the interests of any secured creditor of any beneficiary; and the circumstances and wishes of any beneficiaries of full age and entitled to an interest in possession in the property or (in case of dispute) of the majority (according to the value of their combined interests).[669] The fact that a co-owner remains in the home with the minor children of the relationship does not guarantee that sale will be postponed until the children reach adulthood. In *W v. W (Joinder of Trusts of Land Act and Children Act Applications)*,[670] the Court of Appeal held that it had not been the intention of the parties to provide a home for the children at the time it was purchased (as they were born subsequently) nor had it been a purpose of the trust under which the property was held (as the parties had not explicitly agreed that this would be the case). The mother's need to realize capital in order to purchase a new home was accorded greater weight than the interests of the children.

§4. PROPOSALS FOR REFORM

*282.* Although there have been a number of reforms that have applied to cohabitants, to date there has been no reform devoted exclusively to their legal position. The Law Commission first considered the legal position of cohabitants in the late 1970s,[671] but decided against a wholesale review of the area. In the 1990s, it commenced a project on the property rights of all those who shared a home, but its final report made no recommendations for reform.[672]

*283.* It was not until 2006 that a consultation paper on the financial consequences of relationship breakdown was published,[673] with a report following in 2007.[674] Under the Law Commission's proposed scheme, eligible cohabitants (defined by reference to a minimum period of cohabitation or the fact that the parties had had a child together) would be able to apply to a court for financial relief upon separation. The mere fact that the couple had cohabited for a certain period, or the needs of the applicant would not, however, be a sufficient basis for the court to

---

669. *Trusts of Land and Appointment of Trustees Act* 1996, s. 15.
670. [2004] 2 F.L.R. 321; [2003] EWCA Civ 924.
671. Law Commission, *Fourteenth Annual Report 1978–1979* Law Com. No. 97 para. 2.32 (HMSO 1980).
672. Law Commission, *Sharing Homes: A Discussion Paper* Law Com. No. 278 (HMSO 2002).
673. Law Commission, *Cohabitation: The Financial Consequences of Relationship Breakdown: A Consultation Paper* Consultation Paper No. 179 (HMSO 2006).
674. Law Commission, *Cohabitation: The Financial Consequences of Relationship Breakdown*, Law Com. No. 307 (HMSO 2007).

grant relief: a claim would only succeed if the applicant had suffered an economic disadvantage or if the other party had retained a benefit as a result of contributions made by the applicant. The court would then have the power to make an order reversing the retained benefit and distributing the loss attributable to any remaining economic disadvantage between the parties, having regard to a number of discretionary factors. The rights cohabitants currently have on the death of a partner would also be enhanced.[675]

*284.* However, no action was taken to implement these proposals: the then Government simply announced that it intended to consider research findings on the Family Law (Scotland) Act 2006, which came into effect in 2007, before deciding whether to legislate for England and Wales. The previous Government subsequently indicated that it had no plans to introduce reform. Private members' bills have been introduced seeking to give effect to the Law Commission's proposals, or some version of them, but have made little progress.[676]

---

675. *See* Part IV, Ch. 3, and *see* further Law Commission, *Intestacy and Family Provision Claims on Death*, Law Com. No. 331 pt. 8 (HMSO 2011).
676. *See* most recently the Cohabitation Rights Bill 2017.

# Chapter 5. Establishing Parenthood and the Status of the Child

## §1. INTRODUCTION

*285.* This chapter has three purposes: first, to set out the legal rules that determine who are the legal parents of a child at the time of birth; second, to discuss how legal parenthood may be established in cases of dispute; and third, to examine the relationship between legal parenthood and the status of the child. It follows conventional usage in distinguishing between genetic parentage and legal parenthood: the former does not necessarily dictate the latter, the existing rules on the allocation of legal parenthood being based on both genetic fact and social fictions. It is possible for legal parenthood to be transferred at a later stage by adoption, but this is dealt with in Chapter 7. Where a child is created as part of a surrogacy arrangement, legal parenthood may be transferred by means of a parental order, discussed in Chapter 6.

## §2. WHO IS THE CHILD'S LEGAL PARENT?

*286.* The applicable rules differ according to the manner in which the child was conceived. Where the child was created as a result of assisted reproduction techniques provided by a licensed clinic, legal parenthood is determined by the Human Fertilization and Embryology Act 2008. Where a child is conceived through sexual intercourse, the common law rules will apply. Where the child is created through artificial insemination outside of a licensed clinic setting, parenthood may be determined by the Human Fertilization and Embryology Act 2008 or the common law rules depending on the mother's marital status.

## I. Parenthood at Common Law

*287.* The common law rule is that legal parenthood is governed by genetic parentage. This means that the mother of a child is the woman who provides the egg and gives birth to the child. It is obviously impossible to separate the two aspects of motherhood without medical intervention, but it is important to note that giving birth is regarded as proof of motherhood rather than the justification for ascribing motherhood.[677] Genetic testing has been used by the courts to ascertain legal motherhood.[678] The father is the man who provided the sperm. Where the mother is not married or in a civil partnership, the legal parentage of a child conceived by artificial insemination outside of a clinic setting will be determined by common law rules.

*288.* Before scientific methods of establishing paternity were developed, the courts applied various presumptions in an attempt to create certainty. Of these the

---

677. *The Ampthill Peerage* [1977] A.C. 547.
678. *Re P* [2012] 1 FLR 351.

most important – both in terms of the numbers affected and the consequences for the child – was that the mother's husband was the father of her child.[679] The presumption applies if the child was born or conceived within marriage, with the result that a child born a day after the marriage will be presumed to be the child of the husband, as will a child born nine months[680] after the husband's death or the dissolution or annulment of the marriage. In the past, the presumption was made difficult to rebut. Only if the evidence established 'beyond all reasonable doubt' that he was not the father would the presumption be rebutted.[681] The declining significance of legitimacy, together with the increased emphasis placed on learning the truth and the availability of the scientific means for doing so, mean that the evidential standard is now simply 'the balance of probabilities'.[682]

*289.* Two further presumptions should also be noted. The first is that the man named on the birth certificate is the child's father. This is not explicitly spelt out in the relevant legislation, but the courts have taken the view that an entry in the register is at least prima facie evidence of the details entered.[683] The possibility of a man who is not married to the mother being registered as the child's father without his knowledge[684] and consent is obviated by the rules on who can register the birth, which are examined elsewhere.

*290.* The second presumption is that if, in court proceedings (other than those involving an application for a declaration of parentage), a court decides that a particular man is the father, he will be presumed to be the father. Again, both presumptions may be rebutted by evidence to the contrary. As noted below, an incidental decision in court proceedings will only bind the parties to that decision, whereas a decision directly relating to parentage will be conclusive. The circumstances in which the courts will order tests to be carried out to provide the relevant evidence are considered further below.

## II. Parenthood under the Human Fertilization and Embryology Act 2008

*291.* With the introduction of assisted reproduction, the link between genetic and gestational motherhood may be broken, as may the link between genetic parentage and social parenthood. Recent changes to English law now allow for the creation of children with three genetic parents.[685] The law must therefore make a policy choice between a range of possible parents. It should, however, be borne in mind that in

---

679. The *Marriage (Same Sex Couples) Act* 2013 makes it clear that this presumption does not extend to same-sex marriages: *see* Sch. 4, para. 2.
680. Or possibly more: the House of Lords accepted in *Preston-Jones v. Preston-Jones* [1951] A.C. 391 that the gestation period may be longer, although on the facts it was decided that a child born 360 days after the husband had last had sex with his wife was not the child of the husband.
681. *See* discussion in *Serio v. Serio* [1983] FLR 756.
682. *The Family Law Reform Act 1969*, s26; *H v. A* [2002] EWCA Civ 383.
683. *Brierley v. Brierley* [1918] P. 257.
684. *Re R (Parental Responsibility)* [2011] 2 FLR 1132.
685. *Human Fertilisation and Embryology (Mitochondrial Donation) Regulations 2015.*

most cases, assisted reproduction replicates the 'traditional' family: often the parties' own genetic materials are used; surrogacy is relatively rare; few children are born as a result of egg donation and even fewer as a result of embryo donation.[686]

*292.* The Act prescribes that the person who gives birth to the child will be the child's legal mother,[687] thereby preferring gestation over either genetic parentage or social parenthood. This means that in a surrogacy arrangement the surrogate mother will be the legal mother – at least initially – even if she has no genetic link to the child that she is carrying and intends to give up the child after birth.

*293.* By contrast, more weight is attached to social fatherhood in deciding who should be the legal father of a child. The common law presumption that the husband of the mother is the child's father finds an echo in the statutory provision that the husband of the woman who gives birth to a child as a result of assisted reproduction (whether this takes place in a licensed clinic or not)[688] will be deemed to be the child's father unless he did not consent to the process.[689] Indeed, the position of the husband is stronger under the 2008 Act than under the common law. At common law, proof that he is not the father will displace the presumption in his favour, but under the Act his legal fatherhood is unassailable even if it is known that it is a fiction. The only situation in which the husband will not be the legal father is where it is shown that he did not consent, although the likelihood of such a finding has been increased by a decision that a general awareness that treatment is taking place is not sufficient; there must be a deliberate exercise of choice.[690]

*294.* The Act also provides that a man who is not married to the mother will be deemed to be the legal father where treatment is provided at a clinic and the 'agreed fatherhood conditions' are satisfied.[691] These require that both the mother and the man in question agreed to him being treated as the father and that such consent was not withdrawn prior to the embryo being placed in the mother. Although the Act requires that any consent to treatment is recorded in a specific format, non-compliance with standard paperwork will not invalidate an otherwise valid consent.[692] There has recently been a large number of cases taken to secure parental legal status following an audit by the HFEA, which showed that a large number of clinics had 'anomalies' in their records.[693]

---

686. *See,* HFEA, *Fertility Treatment 2014: Trends and Figures* (2016).
687. *Human Fertilization and Embryology Act* 2008, s. 33(1).
688. *See M v. F and H* [2013] EWHC 1901 (Fam) for an example of unlicensed arrangements.
689. *Human Fertilization and Embryology Act* 2008, s. 35(1). The *Marriage (Same Sex Couples) Act* 2013, Sch. 7, para. 38, has amended the 2008 Act to make it clear that this provision only operates where the mother is married to a man, separate provision being made for a same-sex spouse to acquire the status of a parent.
690. *Re G (Human Fertilisation and Embryology Act 2008)* [2016] EWHC 729 (Fam).
691. *Human Fertilization and Embryology Act* 2008, s. 37.
692. *Re A* [2015] EWHC 2602.
693. *B v. B (Fertility Treatment - Paperwork Error)* [2017] EWHC 599 (Fam); *In the Matter of the Human Fertilisation and Embryology Act 2008 (Cases P, Q, R, S, T, U, W and X)* [2017] EWHC

*295.* The 2008 Act also introduced the possibility of a child born as a result of assisted reproduction having two legal parents of the same sex. The precise provisions to be applied depend on whether the relationship has been formalized or not. A civil partner or same-sex spouse of the mother will be treated as the child's other parent where the child is conceived through assisted reproductive technology unless she did not consent to the treatment.[694] Where a child is created through treatment provided by a licensed clinic, a woman who satisfies 'agreed female parenthood conditions' will be the child's second parent.[695]

*296.* The fact that there may be a considerable lapse of time between starting the process and the birth of a child raises a further possibility, namely that the father, spouse or partner will have died before a child is conceived. Provision is now made for those who would have been entitled to be registered as the father or parent while they were alive to be recorded on the birth register after their death. Since the result of such registration is limited – the deceased will not be treated as the child's legal father or parent for any other purposes – it is more appropriate to consider the detailed rules in the context of birth registration.[696]

*297.* The net result of these rules is that genetic parentage has little significance under the 2008 Act. The legislation specifically states that a man who donates sperm in a licensed clinic will not be regarded as the legal father of any resulting child.[697] But genetic parentage does have a residual role in determining legal parenthood, as is illustrated by *Leeds Teaching Hospital Trust v. A.* In this case, the sperm of one man was used to inseminate another man's wife. The genetic father was not deemed to be a sperm donor as he had not consented to his sperm being used to treat anyone other than his wife. This meant that he was not within the exception excluding sperm donors from legal parenthood. All other options having been exhausted, the court fell back on genetics and held him to be the legal father. While known genetic donors have a much weaker legal position than legal parents, the fact of genetic parenthood may be considered where a known genetic donor applies for leave to apply for a child arrangements order[698] or as part of the welfare checklist when determining whether such an order will be granted.[699]

---

49 (Fam); *Re Human Fertilisation and Embryology Act 2008 (Case K)* [2017] EWHC 50; *Human Fertilisation And Embryology Act (Cases AD, AE, AF, AG and AH - No 2)* [2017] EWHC 1782 (Fam).

694. *Human Fertilization and Embryology Act* 2008, s. 42, as amended by the *Marriage (Same Sex Couples) Act* 2013, Sch. 7, para. 40. *See, Re G (Human Fertilisation and Embryology Act 2008)* [2016] EWHC 729 (Fam).

695. *Ibid.*, s. 43. These requirements must be strictly observed: *see Re: E & F (Assisted Reproduction: Parent)* [2013] EWHC 1418 (Fam).

696. *See* para. 107.

697. *Human Fertilization and Embryology Act* 2008, s. 41(1).

698. *Re G (A Minor); Re Z (A Minor)* [2013] EWHC 134.

699. *Re X* [2015] EWFC 84 where Theis J held that the child's need for information could be satisfied by indirect contact with her genetic father.

*298.* As the above discussion has shown, there may be more than one candidate for legal fatherhood. The Act sets out a clear order of priority in such cases, privileging marriage over partnership; social relationships over genetic ones; and subsisting relationships over past ones. Indeed in *B v. C*[700] the fact that the gestational mother was in an existing marriage thwarted the express goal of the undertaking which was for the genetic father to become a parent through surrogacy.[701] The result is that a child can never have more than two legal parents at any point in time, although the possibility of transferring parenthood at a later date means that the identity of these two may change. It is also possible that a child may only have one legal parent; a child will be legally fatherless if born as a result of sperm donation to a mother who is single or whose husband or partner does not qualify as the father or parent under the terms of the Act.

§3. How May Parenthood Be Determined?

*299.* The issue of legal parenthood may fall to be resolved by the court in proceedings relating to other issues, for example, maintenance or contact. Such a finding is only binding on the parties to the decision, although it does raise a presumption that legal parenthood is as determined by the court. It is also possible for any person to apply to a court for a declaration as to whether or not a particular person is or was the parent of another specified person.[702] A declaration made in such proceedings is binding for all purposes, and the birth certificate can be re-registered in accordance with the court's findings.[703] Such a declaration may be made even once the child in question has attained adulthood.[704]

## I. The Availability of Bodily Samples

*300.* While DNA tests can establish parentage with virtual certainty, such tests obviously require that samples of the parties' DNA be made available. The parties may undergo DNA testing willingly. The ability of the person whose parentage is to be established to consent to such tests may be an issue: a person aged 16 years or over can give a valid consent,[705] whereas in the case of younger children the consent of the adult with care and control of the child must be given.[706] The potential parent's ability to consent may also be vitiated by mental disorder. In such cases, the relevant consent is that of the person with care and control of the sufferer, but

---

700. *B v. C* [2015] EWFC 17.
701. However, in *Re G (Human Fertilisation and Embryology Act 2008)* [2016] EWHC 729 the fact that the mother was in a existing civil partnership did not prevent her new partner from being recognized as the child's other parent under the agreed parenthood conditions.
702. *Family Law Act* 1986, s. 55A.
703. *Ibid.*, s. 55A(7); *Births and Deaths Registration Act* 1953, s. 14A.
704. *M v. W (Declaration of Parentage)* [2006] EWHC 2341 (Fam).
705. *Family Law Reform Act* 1969, s. 21(2).
706. *Ibid.*, s. 21(3).

the sample cannot be taken unless the medical practitioner responsible for the sufferer's care has certified that the taking of a sample will not be prejudicial to his or her proper care and treatment.[707]

*301.* In cases of disagreement, the court can direct that scientific tests be used to establish a person's parentage in any civil proceedings where this is a matter of dispute.[708] The courts have adopted the approach that a direction will only be refused if it would be against the child's interests to make one.[709] Given the importance that is attached to ascertaining the truth – as opposed to maintaining the family unit by presuming that the mother's husband is the father – it is likely that tests will virtually always be directed if parentage in is issue.[710] The courts have taken the view that 'the paternity of any child is to be established by science and not by legal presumption or inference'.[711] It should be noted, however, that a direction that tests should be used is not the same as an order to undergo testing; still less it is an authorization to remove bodily samples against the consent of an adult who refuses to undergo such testing. Two further issues may thus fall to be decided: first, should the court authorize the taking of samples from a child; second, what inferences should be drawn from a refusal to undergo testing?

*302.* Given the rules governing consent to the taking of samples, it will only be necessary for the court to authorize the taking of a sample from the child where the parent with care and control of the child is opposed to the test being carried out. The legislation provides that a sample may be taken 'if the court considers that it would be in [the child's] best interests for the sample to be taken'.[712] While the wording is not identical to the test applied by the courts when deciding whether a direction should be made,[713] there are no cases in which a court has decided that the direction would not be against the child's interests but that it is not in the child's best interests for a sample to be taken. The importance of ascertaining the truth is likely to influence both considerations.[714] The opposition of an older child may lead the court to stay the order until such time as the child should prove willing to provide a sample, or simply to refuse to compel the child to provide a sample altogether.[715]

---

707. *Ibid.*, s. 21(4).
708. *Ibid.*, s. 20(1).
709. *S v. McC, W v. W* [1972] A.C. 24; *Re F (A Minor: Paternity Test)* [1993] 1 F.L.R. 598. *See* A. Bainham, *Landmarks in Family Law* (S. Gilmore, J. Herring & R. Probert, ed., Ch. 7, Hart, 2011).
710. *Re H (Paternity: Blood Test)* [1996] F.L.R. 65; *Re H and A (Paternity: Blood Tests)* [2002] EWCA Civ 383.
711. *Re H and A (Children)* [2002] EWCA Civ 383, *per* Thorpe L.J.
712. *Family Law Reform Act* 1969, s. 21(3).
713. N. Lowe & G. Douglas, *Bromley's Family Law* 329–330 (10th ed., Oxford U. Press 2007); *see also Re L (A Child)* [2009] EWCA Civ 1239.
714. *See,* e.g., *Blunkett v. Quinn* [2005] 1 F.L.R. 648.
715. *Re D (Paternity)* [2006] EWHC 3545 (Fam); *L v. P (Paternity Test: Child's Objection)* [2011] EWHC 3399 (Fam); *Re P* [2012] 1 FLR 351.

*303.* The legislation is clear that a sample cannot be taken from a competent person over the age of 16 without his or her consent.[716] It is therefore possible for a man to refuse to undergo testing. However, the fact that the court can draw adverse inferences from a refusal to undergo testing[717] means that there is nothing to be gained from such a refusal; a man who doubts whether he is the father would be well advised to submit to the tests and have the matter resolved one way or the other rather than refuse and thereby raise what has been described as a 'virtually inescapable' inference that he is the father.[718] This has been held to override both the presumption that the mother's husband is the father of her child and the presumption that the man registered on the birth certificate as the father is so in fact.[719] Similarly, if the mother refuses to undergo testing, adverse inferences may be made against her. Specific provision is made to ensure that a party cannot simply rely on the presumption of legitimacy and refuse to undergo testing; in a situation of this kind the court may dismiss a claim for relief by the person refusing to take the test even if there is no other evidence to rebut the presumption.[720]

*304.* There is also the possibility that a potential parent may have died. The possibility of retained DNA samples being used in such a case was considered in the case of *London Borough of Lambeth v. S, C and Others*,[721] which concerned the paternity of a young boy. The man with whom the boy's mother had been living at the time of conception had been killed by the man who subsequently married her. A sample of the former's DNA was available on a bloodstain card, and the local authority sought a direction that this information be released to try to determine who was the boy's biological father. The court refused on the basis that disclosure of this evidence for the purpose of ascertaining the paternity of a child was contrary to the clear wording of the Police and Criminal Evidence Act 1984, which stated that it could not be used for any purposes other than those for which it had been collected (i.e., the detection of crime). The decision runs counter to the general tendency to ascertain the paternity of a child wherever possible, but may be justified both on the basis of the express statutory prohibition on using evidence for purposes for which it was not collected, and by the impact that proving the man not to be the boy's father might have on the child, who was being cared for by his (supposedly) paternal grandmother. In *Re Z*,[722] the court granted an order requiring the police to provide DNA profiles generated from blood samples from a crime scene to the local authority. In this case the children's mother had been murdered by a man who purported to be the children's father but refused to submit to DNA testing. The court drew attention to the vitally important nature of ascertaining paternity for the ongoing care planning of the children. A distinction was drawn between providing the DNA samples themselves and DNA profiles generated from the samples.

---

716. *Family Law Reform Act* 1969, s. 21(1).
717. *Ibid.*, s. 23(1).
718. *Re A (A Minor) (Paternity: Refusal of Blood Test)* [1994] 2 F.L.R. 463, 473.
719. *Secretary of State for Work and Pensions v. Jones* [2004] 1 F.L.R. 282.
720. *Family Law Reform Act* 1969, s. 23(2).
721. [2006] EWHC 326 (Fam).
722. [2014] EWHC 1999 (Fam).

## II. The Value of Other Evidence

*305.* If scientific tests are not ordered, then the cogency of other evidence will need to be determined by the court. The standard of proof will be the normal civil standard of the balance of probabilities, even the presumption that the mother's husband is the child's father may now be rebutted on this basis.[723] It may be that the presumption that a particular man is the father will be rebutted on the basis that he did not have intercourse with the mother at the relevant time, or was infertile. Conversely, the outcome may be determined by one of the presumptions if there is no evidence to the contrary.

*306.* It should be noted that proceedings of this kind will not always clarify who is the child's father. The rebuttal of one of the presumptions may simply indicate who is not the child's father. In general proceedings, this may enable the true father to be established by inference (although not necessarily, if there is more than one candidate), but in proceedings under section 55A the court does not have the power to make a declaration other than that for which an application has been made.[724] This means that if the applicant sought a declaration that X was the father but the evidence suggests that Y is the father; the court will refuse the declaration that X is the father but cannot make a declaration that Y is the father.

### §4. THE STATUS OF THE CHILD

*307.* In the past, the law drew a sharp distinction between what were termed 'legitimate' and 'illegitimate' children. The disadvantages that attached to the status of illegitimacy were gradually reduced, and in 1987 legislation explicitly provided that for the future, any references in legislation or other instruments 'to any relationship between two persons shall, unless the contrary intention appears, be construed without regard to whether or not the father and mother of either of them, or the father and mother of any person through whom the relationship is deduced, have or had been married to each other at any time'.[725] The same rule was also stated to apply to certain specified statutes; although the wholesale reform of the law relating to children two years later, in the Children Act 1989, rendered this provision largely redundant. Wills and trusts made after the legislation came into force will also be construed in this way,[726] and explicit provision was also made in the context of succession upon intestacy regarding the rights of a child whose parents were not married to each other.[727] More recently, the basis on which a child may acquire British

---

723. *Family Law Reform Act* 1969, s. 26.
724. *Family Law Act* 1986, s. 58(3).
725. *Family Law Act* 1987, s. 1(1).
726. Although *Hand v. George* [2017] EWHC 533 (Ch) suggests that the sections precluding children from benefiting from wills made prior to that date may be read so as to uphold such children's rights not to be discriminated against.
727. *Ibid.*, s. 18.

citizenship has been changed so as to enable citizenship to be transferred through a father who was not married to the mother.[728]

Given these changes, and the shifts in social attitudes that both prompted and resulted from the reform, it is unsurprising that the use of the terms 'legitimate' and 'illegitimate' should also have declined. It would appear that no case has been reported with the term 'illegitimate' in the title since Hale L.J. expressed her disapproval of this practice,[729] although the term has not yet been completely expunged from judicial language.[730]

*308.* However, the concept of legitimacy does have some residual relevance. The right to take property under settlements made before the implementation of the 1987 Act is unaffected by the 1987 Act,[731] as is succession to the Crown and to hereditary peerages under which succession is limited to heirs 'lawfully begotten'.[732] For the sake of completeness, then, and because legitimacy is not a simple matter of being born to parents who are married to each other at the time, it is appropriate to set out the circumstances in which a child will be legitimate, or will be treated as such.

A child who wishes to confirm that he or she is legitimate or legitimated can apply to the court for a declaration to this effect.[733]

## I.  Child Born within Valid or Voidable Marriage

*309.*  A child born or conceived while his or her parents were validly married to each other will be legitimate. If the marriage was voidable, then any children born before it got annulled will be legitimate.[734]

## II.  Child Born within Marriage Believed to Be Valid

*310.*  If the marriage was void, then any children born to the parties after the ceremony will be treated as legitimate if both parties in fact reasonably believed the marriage to be valid at the time of conception (or at the time of the celebration of the marriage, if this occurred after the conception).[735] It is now statutorily presumed, in relation to children born after 4 April 1988, that at least one of the parties reasonably believed in the validity of the marriage unless the contrary is shown.[736]

---

728. *See supra* Part I, Ch. 5, para. 182.
729. *Re R. (Surname: Using Both Parents)* [2001] EWCA Civ 1344.
730. *See*, e.g., *Official Solicitor to the Senior Courts v. Yemoh and Others* [2010] EWHC 3727 (Ch).
731. *See*, e.g., *Upton v. National Westminster Bank* [2004] EWHC 1962.
732. *See*, e.g., *Re Moynihan* [2000] 1 F.L.R. 113.
733. *Family Law Act* 1986, s. 56.
734. *Matrimonial Causes Act* 1973, s. 16.
735. *Legitimacy Act* 1976, s. 1(1).
736. *Ibid.*, s. 1(4), as inserted by the *Family Law Reform Act* 1987.

However, 'a belief that the marriage was valid by reason of a ceremony not recognized as constituting a valid marriage is not sufficient'.[737]

## III. Subsequent Marriage of Parents

*311.* Even if the parents of the child were not married to each other at the time of the birth, the child will be legitimated if they subsequently marry each other.[738] This rule initially only applied if the parties were free to marry each other at the time of the birth[739] – thus excluding children born as a result of adultery from the possibility of later legitimation – but the law was relaxed in 1976. It remains the case, however, that a child will not be legitimated by the fact that the parents go through a void ceremony of marriage after the child's birth.[740]

## IV. Adopted Children and Children Subject to Parental Orders

*312.* An adopted child or a child subject to a parental order will be treated as legitimate, regardless of the marital status of the adopters or adopter.[741]

---

737. *AAA v. ASH,* The Registrar General for England and Wales, The Secretary of State for Justice, The Advocate to the Court provided by the Attorney [2009] EWHC 636 (Fam), para. 28.
738. *Legitimacy Act* 1976, s. 2.
739. *Legitimation Act* 1926, s. 1(2).
740. *Re Spence* [1990] Ch. 652.
741. *Adoption and Children Act* 2002, s. 67(2) as amended by *Human Fertilisation and Embryology (Parental Orders) Regulations 2010/985.*

# Chapter 6. Parental Responsibility

## §1. INTRODUCTION

*313.* The terminology of 'parental responsibility' was adopted in the Children Act 1989 to emphasize that parenthood involved responsibilities to one's child rather than rights over him or her. The relationship between legal parenthood and parental responsibility is not a straightforward one: not all parents will have parental responsibility, and some persons who have parental responsibility will not be legal parents.[742] Nor does the lack of parental responsibility mean complete freedom from legal rights and duties: some rights and responsibilities flow from parental responsibility, and some flow from legal parenthood alone. Matters are complicated still further by the absence of any statutory definition of parental responsibility – other than that it constitutes 'all the rights, duties, powers, responsibilities, and authority which by law a parent of a child has in relation to the child and his property'.[743] This might suggest that parental responsibility is an unvarying bundle of rights, but the terms under which some persons and institutions acquire it is rather more limited.

This chapter will consider who may acquire parental responsibility, how it is exercised (which includes a consideration of the rights and responsibilities it entails), and the circumstances in which it may be brought to an end.

## §2. ACQUIRING PARENTAL RESPONSIBILITY

*314.* A distinction must be made between those persons who have parental responsibility automatically from the moment of the child's birth, and those who need to take steps to acquire it. Into the first group fall all legal mothers, all fathers who are married to the mother (at the time of the conception, birth or even later) and those civil partners or female spouses of the mother who are deemed to be the child's other legal parent.[744] The second group can be further subdivided into persons who may have a relationship with the child without having parental responsibility (e.g., fathers who are not married to the mother, step-parents, co-parents, other family members, de facto care providers); persons whose status in relation to the child is itself a legal creation which automatically carries parental responsibility (such as guardians, special guardians, those adopting the child); and those who acquire parental responsibility as a result of child protection measures (e.g., the local authority or a person in whose favour an emergency protection order has been made). This section will focus on the means by which parental responsibility may be acquired, identifying who may make use of which mechanisms.

---

742. *See* generally S. Gilmore, J. Herring & R. Probert, *Introduction: Parental Responsibility – Law, Issues and Themes,* in *Responsible Parents and Parental Responsibility* Ch. 1 (R. Probert, S. Gilmore & J. Herring ed., Hart 2009).
743. *Children Act* 1989, s. 3(1).
744. *Children Act* 1989, s. 2(2A), as inserted by the *Human Fertilization and Embryology Act* 2008.

## I. Registration

*315.* Since 1 December 2003, a father who registers the birth jointly with the mother will thereby acquire parental responsibility.[745] The law was changed in the light of empirical evidence that many fathers believed that registration already conferred parental responsibility. The reform was not retrospective, so those whose children were registered before this date must seek other means of acquiring parental responsibility. The circumstances in which a father's name may be entered on the birth certificate have already been considered;[746] it should however be noted that if the father succeeds in having his name registered otherwise than in accordance with the prescribed rules, the mere fact that it appears on the child's birth certificate will not confer parental responsibility on him.[747] Re-registration of a birth following a declaration of paternity does not confer parental responsibility on a father.[748]

A mother's same-sex partner may also acquire parental responsibility by this means if she is the child's legal parent.[749]

## II. Private Ordering

*316.* There are three ways in which parental responsibility may be conferred by private arrangements: first, a parental responsibility agreement may be used to confer parental responsibility on certain persons; second, any person may be appointed as a guardian to act *in loco parentis* after the death of one or both parents, a role which automatically entails parental responsibility; and third, parental responsibility may be delegated.

### A. Parental Responsibility Agreement

*317.* The father of the child may acquire parental responsibility by entering into a formal agreement with the mother,[750] as may the child's other legal parent.[751] A step-parent (i.e., a non-parent who is married to or in a civil partnership with the child's legal parent) may also acquire parental responsibility by this means.[752] In this case, the agreement of both legal parents is required, but only if they both have parental responsibility.

---

745. *Children Act* 1989, s. 4(1)(a), as amended by the *Adoption and Children Act* 2002, s. 111.
746. *See* Part I, Ch. 2, para. 58.
747. *AAA v. ASH, The Registrar General for England and Wales, The Secretary of State for Justice, The Advocate to the Court provided by the Attorney* [2009] EWHC 636 (Fam).
748. *Re S (a child) (declaration of parentage)* [2012] EWCA Civ 1160; *M v. F and H (Legal Paternity)* [2013] EWHC 1901 (Fam); *JB v. KS(Contact: Parental Responsibility)* [2015] EWHC 180.
749. *Children Act* 1989, s. 4ZA(1)(a), as inserted by the *Human Fertilization and Embryology Act* 2008.
750. *Children Act* 1989, s. 4(1)(b). *See the Parental Responsibility Agreement (Amendment) Regulations* 1994, S.I. 1994/3157, for the required form.
751. *Ibid.*, s. 4ZA(1)(b), as inserted by the *Human Fertilization and Embryology Act* 2008.
752. *Ibid.*, s. 4A(1)(a), as inserted by the *Adoption and Children Act* 2002.

## B. Appointment of a Guardian

*318.* The role of a guardian is essentially to take over responsibility for a child where both parents are deceased or where the surviving parent does not have parental responsibility. It is possible for a parent to be appointed as a guardian, although – save in the case of an unmarried father who does not have parental responsibility – such a course would usually be unnecessary.

*319.* The appointment of a guardian must be made in writing and signed by the person making the appointment (or at that person's direction, in his or her presence and before witnesses).[753] Any parent who has parental responsibility may appoint a guardian,[754] as may a guardian or special guardian.[755] The appointment will only take effect after the death of the last parent with parental responsibility (or, if, the appointment was made by a guardian or special guardian, after that person's death).[756] This avoids the problem of a guardian appointed by one parent exercising parental responsibility concomitantly with another parent with parental responsibility. There is, however, a further provision that if a child arrangements order is in force naming a person with whom the child is to live, an appointment made by that person will have effect as soon as that person dies, even if there is another parent with parental responsibility.[757] The same rule applies to appointments made by the sole or last surviving special guardian.[758] In both cases, the fact that the deceased parent or special guardian has primary responsibility for the child during their lifetime justifies more weight being given to their choice of guardian after their death.

*320.* Since there is no requirement that the appointment should have been agreed with the intended guardian, the person appointed is entitled to disclaim the appointment within a reasonable period.[759] Such a disclaimer must be made in writing. There is, however, no provision that the appointment should be scrutinized by the court. The choice of the deceased parent will be left undisturbed unless the guardian's care of the child is so poor as to require state intervention. The appointment of a guardian does not, of course, prevent anyone else from applying for a child arrangements order to take over care for the child, and in a case of this kind the relative merits of the guardian and applicant will have to be weighed in deciding where the best interests of the child lie.

## C. Delegation

*321.* Although parental responsibility is not transferable, it is possible for a person with parental responsibility to 'arrange for some or all of it to be met by one or

---

753. *Children Act* 1989, s. 5(5).
754. *Ibid.*, s. 5(3).
755. *Ibid.*, s. 5(4).
756. *Ibid.*, s. 5(7).
757. *Ibid.*, s. 5(7)(b).
758. *Ibid.*, s. 5(7)(b), as amended by the *Adoption and Children Act* 2002.
759. *Children Act* 1989, s. 6(5).

more persons acting on his behalf'.[760] This is a flexible provision that would cover everything from the child being left in the temporary care of a nanny or au pair while the parents are away, to more permanent arrangements (e.g., if the child moves to live with relatives). Anyone delegating powers to another is encouraged to do so responsibly by the provision that he or she will remain liable for any failure to meet any part of parental responsibility for the child.[761]

322. It should also be noted that a person who has care of a child but lacks parental responsibility may 'do what is reasonable in all the circumstances of the case for the purpose of safeguarding or promoting the child's welfare'.[762] This means, e.g., that someone caring for the child in the absence of a person with parental responsibility may authorize emergency medical treatment.

## III. Court Orders

323. Parental responsibility may be conferred on a range of different persons and institutions by court order: in some cases the sole point of making the order is to confer parental responsibility, while in others the conferral of parental responsibility is a by-product of a more general order relating to the child. While the orders that confer parental responsibility are quite disparate – ranging from the permanence of an adoption order to a short-term emergency protection order – there is a unifying theme, namely the desire to ensure that those who are in a position of responsibility vis-à-vis a child are clothed with the legal powers to discharge their role appropriately.

### A. Orders Transferring Legal Parenthood

324. The making of an adoption order transfers both legal parenthood and parental responsibility to the adoptive parents. The same is true of a parental order made under the Human Fertilization and Embryology Act 2008, which is essentially an expedited form of adoption for use in surrogacy cases.[763] The fact that such orders also operate to extinguish the legal parenthood or parental responsibility of any other person reflects the way in which the child effectively becomes the child of the adopters or commissioning parents for all legal purposes.

Since a child will usually be living with the prospective adopters before the adoption order is made, provision is also made for them to acquire parental responsibility once the child is placed with them, either as a result of a placement order or with parental consent.[764] Until the adoption order is made, however, the prospective

---

760. *Children Act* 1989, s. 2(9).
761. *Ibid.*, s. 2(11).
762. *Children Act* 1989, s. 3(5).
763. *Human Fertilization and Embryology Act* 2008, s. 54.
764. *Adoption and Children Act* 2002, s. 25.

adopters will share parental responsibility with the adoption agency and any other persons who have retained parental responsibility.

## B. Appointment of a Guardian

325. In the event of there being no parent with parental responsibility – e.g., where the child has been abandoned and the parents are unknown or where the only parent with parental responsibility has died without having appointed a guardian – the court has the power to make such an appointment.[765] This is also the case if a child arrangements order was in place for the child to live with a parent, guardian or special guardian who died while the order was in force, or where the sole or last surviving special guardian has died. In deciding whether to make such an order, the welfare of the child will be the court's paramount consideration.

## C. Special Guardianship Orders

326. The concept of a special guardian was introduced by the Adoption and Children Act 2002, and was intended to provide an arrangement midway between a permanent adoption and more temporary arrangements. Certain persons are automatically entitled to apply for a special guardianship order to be made in their favour;[766] others may apply with the leave of the court.[767] The court also has the power to make a special guardianship order in any family proceedings in which a question arises with respect to the welfare of the child, even if no such application has been made. The only restrictions are that a parent cannot be a special guardian,[768] and that no such order can be made without a report from the local authority on the suitability of the applicant to be a special guardian.[769]

A special guardianship order will only be made if it is in the best interests of the child. Since the case law has focused on the relative merits of adoption versus special guardianship, it will be considered in the chapter on adoption.[770]

## D. Parental Responsibility Order

327. The orders described above are all ways of conferring a new status and consequent parental responsibility on non-parents. It is also possible for an order to be

---

765. *Children Act* 1989, s. 5(1).
766. *Children Act* 1989, s. 14A(5).
767. *Ibid.*, s. 14A(3)(b) and (5); *see infra* Part II, Ch. 7, para. 358.
768. *Ibid.*, s. 14A(2)(b), as inserted by the *Adoption and Children Act* 2002.
769. Changes to the Special Guardianship Regulations 2005 (as amended by the Special Guardianship (Amendment) Regulations 2016 now require the special guardian report to deal expressly with the risk of harm posed to the child and to consider their current and future needs.
770. Part II, Ch. 7, paras 358–364.

made specifically for the purpose of conferring parental responsibility on an existing parent. A parental responsibility order may be made in favour of the father,[771]
other parent[772] or a step-parent of the child.[773] The need for such an order to be
made in favour of a legal father has been greatly reduced since the reforms enacted
by the Adoption and Children Act 2002. As a result, it is likely that in time the only
fathers seeking an order from the court will be those who had no real relationship
with the mother at the time of the child's birth. Whether this will have any effect on
the court's willingness to make such orders remains to be seen.

*328.* In deciding whether or not to make a parental responsibility order, the
courts have applied the principle that the welfare of the child, rather than the wishes
of the parent, is the paramount consideration.[774] The factors to be taken into account
include the degree of the father's commitment and attachment to the child and his
reasons for seeking the order.[775] The court must also consider the new statutory presumption that involvement of both legal parents in the child's life will further the
child's welfare unless the contrary is proved.[776] The courts have generally taken the
view that it is for the benefit of the child to confer parental responsibility upon a
concerned father. Child welfare and parental wishes were conflated in *Re C and V
(Contact and Parental Responsibility)*,[777] in which Ward L.J. commented that:

> a child needs for its self-esteem to grow up, wherever it can, having a favour-
> able positive image of an absent parent; and it is important that, wherever pos-
> sible, the law should confer on a concerned father that stamp of approval
> because he has shown himself willing and anxious to pick up the responsibil-
> ity of fatherhood and not to deny or avoid it.

However, if it is apparent that the father is seeking parental responsibility for
improper reasons or to undermine the mother's care, then the court is likely to refuse
to grant the order.[778] The courts have also refused to grant unconstrained parental
responsibility to the biological father where this might undermine the family unit of
the mother and her same-sex partner[779]

---

771. *Children Act* 1989, s. 4(1)(c).
772. *Ibid.*, s. 4ZA(1)(c), as inserted by the *Human Fertilization and Embryology Act* 2008.
773. *Ibid.*, s. 4A(1)(b), as inserted by the *Adoption and Children Act* 2002, s. 112.
774. *Re H (A Minor) (Parental Responsibility)* [1998] 1 F.L.R. 855.
775. *Re H (Minors) (Local Authority: Parental Rights) (No. 3)* [1991] 2 All E.R. 185.
776. *Children Act 1989*, s. 1(2A) as inserted by the *Children and Families Act 2014*.
777. [1998] 1 F.L.R. 392, quoted with approval in *W (Children)* [2013] EWCA Civ 335.
778. *Re P. (Parental responsibility)* [1998] 2 F.L.R. 96; *Re M (Contact: Parental responsibility)* [2001]
     2 F.L.R. 342; *PM v. MB & Anor* [2013] EWCA Civ 969.
779. *B v. A, C and D (Acting By Her Guardian)* [2006] EWHC 2 (Fam) (parental responsibility granted
     subject to conditions); *Re B (Role of Biological Father)* [2007] EWHC 1952 (Fam) (parental
     responsibility refused); *R v. E (Female Parents: Known Father)* [2010] EWHC 417 (parental
     responsibility refused).

### E. Child Arrangement Orders

*329.* It may seem somewhat surprising that the range of persons in whose favour a parental responsibility order can be made is so narrow. What about other persons who may be caring for the child on a day-to-day basis? This contingency is covered by the possibility of making a child arrangements order in their favour. If a child arrangements order is made in favour of a father (or a second female parent as recognized by the Human Fertilization and Embryology Act 2008) who did not previously have parental responsibility, a specific parental responsibility order will be made to ensure that the parental responsibility does not terminate if and when the child arrangements order comes to an end.[780] Where a child arrangements order is made for a child to live with a person who is not already the parent or guardian of the child (formerly known as residence orders), the order will of itself confer parental responsibility.[781] Where the court makes a child arrangements order for an individual to spend time or otherwise have contact with a child the court may, at its discretion, provide for that person to have parental responsibility while the child arrangements order subsists.[782]

*330.* The courts have been willing to use residence orders for the very purpose of conferring parental responsibility on persons who would not otherwise be able to acquire it, e.g., the cohabitant of a parent, or a family member who is caring for the child.[783] The ability to grant parental responsibility through any type of child arrangements order means that there is no longer any requirement for the child to live with such an individual for parental responsibility to be conferred upon them.

### F. Care Orders

*331.* The making of a care order will confer parental responsibility on the local authority,[784] but does not extinguish the parental responsibility of the child's parents.

### G. Emergency Protection Orders

*332.* Any person may apply for an emergency protection order, and the grant of such an order confers parental responsibility on the applicant for the duration of the

---

780. *Ibid.*, s. 12(1).
781. *Children Act 1989*, s. 12(2).
782. *Children Act 1989*, s. 12(2A), as inserted by the *Children and Families Act 2014. See*, e.g. Re B (No2) [2017] EWHC 488 (Fam).
783. *Re G (Residence: Same-Sex Partner)* [2005] EWCA Civ 462; *T v. T* [2010] EWCA Civ 1366; *A v. B and C* [2012] EWCA Civ 285; *Re G* [2014] EWCA Civ 336.
784. *Children Act 1989*, s. 33(3)(a).

order.[785] Given that this is limited to a maximum of fifteen days, the scope for exercising parental responsibility will obviously be limited, but the conferral of parental responsibility in this context reflects the need for someone to have the right to care for the child in an emergency situation.

§3. EXERCISING PARENTAL RESPONSIBILITY

*333.* Parental responsibility involves a range of rights and duties, but not every person with parental responsibility will be entitled to exercise the full range, and the ability of a person to exercise parental responsibility in a particular way may be curtailed by the opposition of a mature child, by the standards set by the State in certain areas, or by the opposition of another person with parental responsibility. These points will be considered in turn.

## I. The Content of Parental Responsibility

*334.* As noted above, there is no statutory list of what is encompassed by the term 'parental responsibility', but there is a core of rights and duties that is generally agreed to fall within its scope.[786] These range from the practical – the right to name the child, the responsibility to make arrangements for the disposal of a child's body after death[787] – to the more abstract – the right to determine the child's religion, e.g., can be seen as allowing the person with parental responsibility to transmit his or her values to the child.[788]

*335.* Some involve elements of rights and duties: e.g., the right to determine a child's education is accompanied by a duty to ensure that the child receives an appropriate education; while the responsibility to provide a home for the child carries with it the corresponding right to decide where that home should be. It could also be argued that the right to withhold consent from a proposed marriage or civil partnership while the child is under the age of 18 years is matched by the responsibility not to force an unwilling child into such an arrangement.[789] It is the problem of forced marriage that has attracted more attention in recent years than parental unwillingness to consent to their minor children contracting a marriage. Similarly, the right to discipline the child is subject to a duty to ensure that such discipline is exercised within limits.[790]

---

785. *Children Act* 1989, s. 44(4)(c).
786. For lists *see* N. Lowe & G. Douglas, *Bromley's Family Law* 377 (Oxford U. Press 2006); R. Probert, *Cretney's Family Law* 243 (Sweet & Maxwell 2009). *See* generally R. Probert, S. Gilmore & J. Herring, *Responsible Parents and Parental Responsibility* (Hart 2009).
787. *See*, Re JS (Disposal of Body) [2016] EWHC 2859 (Fam).
788. *See* R. Taylor, *Responsible Parents and Parental Responsibility* Ch. 7 (R. Probert, S. Gilmore & J. Herring, eds., Hart 2009).
789. *See supra* Part II, Ch. 1, para. 197.
790. *Children Act* 2004, s. 58. *See* S. Choudhry, *Responsible Parents and Parental Responsibility* Ch. 9 (R. Probert, S. Gilmore & J. Herring, eds., Hart 2009).

*336.* Sometimes the right in question has relevance for third parties. Since a child cannot give a valid consent to medical treatment, it will be necessary for a doctor to obtain the consent of a person with parental responsibility to avoid committing an assault – although the legislation does make provision for actions to be taken in emergencies. Some rights and duties are administrative in nature, e.g., the right to administer any property owned by the child (who, as a minor, cannot be the legal owner of property, and thus cannot deal with it, but may be an equitable owner and enjoy the benefit of it); the right to enter into certain contracts on the child's behalf; and the right to act for the child in legal proceedings.

*337.* Some commentators include contact with the child as an aspect of parental responsibility. This, however, is problematic, since it is difficult to classify contact as either a duty or a right. While successive government documents have extolled the benefits of contact between the child and the non-resident parent in the wake of parental separation, there was no legal obligation on the latter to maintain contact even if a contact order has been made.[791] At the same time, the English courts have been reluctant to classify contact as a parent's right. The Children and Families Act 2014 introduced a legal presumption that involvement of both parents in the life of the child will further the child's welfare.[792] Child arrangements orders now name the person with whom the child is to have contact but it remains to be seen if the court will make an enforcement order against a parent who does not maintain such contact.[793] The European Court of Human Rights has stressed the importance of contact as 'a fundamental element of family life' and requires careful scrutiny of any decision to suspend contact, but acknowledges that the welfare of the child may justify contact being curtailed in appropriate cases. More fundamental for present purposes is the fact that contact is not tied to parental responsibility; a father without parental responsibility may still apply for a contact order, while the courts are likely to attach less importance to contact between the child and a non-parent with parental responsibility.

*338.* Similarly, although it could be said that parental responsibility entails a broad duty to provide for the child, the specific duty of paying child support is not linked to the possession of parental responsibility but rather to legal parenthood. Thus an unmarried father without parental responsibility will still be liable for child support if he is not living with the child, whereas a guardian will not.

## II. Limitations on Who May Exercise Particular Rights

*339.* It should be noted that not all persons who have parental responsibility have all the rights and duties that normally flow from that status. A person in whose favour a child arrangements order conferring parental responsibility has been made cannot appoint a guardian for the child, or withhold consent to the making of an

---

791. Compare the explicit provision in the *Children (Scotland) Act* 1995, s. 1(1)(c).
792. *Children Act 1989* s. 1(2A).
793. *Children Act 1989* s. 11J as amended by the *Children and Families Act* 2014.

adoption order. Similar constraints apply to a local authority that has acquired parental responsibility as a consequence of a care order, with the added restriction that it may not cause the child to be brought up in a different religious persuasion from that in which he or she would have been brought up had the order not been made.[794] Most limited of all are the powers of a person who has parental responsibility by virtue of an emergency protection order, who is warned that he or she 'shall take, and shall only take, such action in meeting his parental responsibility for the child as is reasonably required to safeguard or promote the welfare of the child (having regard in particular to the duration of the order)'.[795]

## III. Limitations on How Rights May Be Exercised

*340.* This chapter has so far focused on parental responsibility as a relationship between an adult and a child to whom certain responsibilities are owed. The exercise of parental responsibility will be affected by the age of the child: children will need to be looked after until they reach adulthood, but the ability to make choices for the child will wane once the child is able to exercise his or her own judgment on such matters.[796]

Parental responsibility does have a further connotation, namely that it is the role of the parent, rather than of the state, to care for the child.[797] As Baroness Hale put it in *R (Williamson) v. Secretary of State for Education and Employment*:

> Children have the right to be properly cared for and brought up so that they can fulfil their potential and play their part in society. Their parents have both the primary responsibility and the primary right to do this.[798]

Yet, as she went on to note, the state may step in 'to regulate the exercise of that responsibility in the interests of children and society as a whole'. The fact that a particular person has parental responsibility does not guarantee that he or she will be able to determine the upbringing of the child. If, e.g., legislation has stipulated that a child cannot participate in certain activities until he or she has reached a certain age, parental consent cannot override such stipulations. Parenting that falls below a certain threshold may necessitate the intervention of the local authority in order to protect the child. Parents who allow their children to engage in antisocial activities may find both their children and themselves subject to sanctions,[799] as may those who fail to ensure that their children receive a suitable education.[800] And, in *Wilkinson* itself, it was decided that the parents' rights had not been infringed by a legal

---

794. *Children Act* 1989, s. 33(6).
795. *Ibid.*, s. 44(5)(b).
796. *See*, e.g., *Gillick v. West Norfolk and Wisbech Area HA* [1986] A.C. 112 on the relationship between parental responsibility and children's autonomy.
797. *See* J. Eekelaar, *Parental Responsibility: State of Nature or Nature of the State?* 1 J. Social Welfare and Family Law 37 (1991).
798. [2005] UKHL 15, para. 72.
799. *Crime and Disorder Act* 1998; *Anti-social Behaviour Act* 2003.
800. *Education Act* 1996, s. 444; *Education Act* 2005, s. 116.

provision banning the use of physical discipline in schools, even though the parents wanted their children to be educated in a tradition that included such discipline.

In addition, if the exercise of parental responsibility is questioned in court, it will be the child's best interests, rather than the wishes of the person with parental responsibility, that determine the outcome.[801]

## IV. Sharing Parental Responsibility

*341.* Since more than one person or body may have parental responsibility for the same child at the same time, it is necessary to consider how any disputes will be resolved. Sometimes the legislation identifies who is to have the greater role. For example, if a care order has been made the local authority has the power to determine the extent to which the child's parents, guardian, special guardian, or stepparent with parental responsibility may meet their parental responsibility for the child.[802] Similarly, a special guardian is entitled to exercise parental responsibility 'to the exclusion of any other person with parental responsibility'.[803]

*342.* In the absence of an explicit provision of this kind, there are general provisions in the Act that set out how parental responsibility is to be shared. The basic rule is that each person with parental responsibility may act alone in meeting their responsibility to the child,[804] as long as their actions do not conflict with an existing court order.[805] This apparently clear provision has been modified by judicial decisions suggesting that some decisions should not be unilateral and require either the consent of all those with parental responsibility or the approval of the court. Into this category fall decisions to change a child's surname, to carry out medical operations such as circumcision or sterilization,[806] and to send a child to a particular school.[807]

If those with parental responsibility disagree, the matter may be referred to the court for resolution by means of a section 8 order.[808]

## §4. ENDING PARENTAL RESPONSIBILITY

*343.* In some cases, parental responsibility will come to an end when the order that conferred it ends: this is the case for emergency protection orders, care orders, and child arrangement orders. In other cases, a person's parental responsibility will continue during the child's minority unless brought to an end earlier.[809] Those who

---

801. *See*, e.g., *Re A (Minors) (Conjoined Twins: Medical Treatment)* [2001] 1 F.L.R. 1.
802. *Children Act* 1989, s. 33(3)(b).
803. *Ibid.*, s. 14C(1), as inserted by the *Adoption and Children Act* 2002.
804. *Children Act* 1989, s. 2(7).
805. *Ibid.*, s. 2(8).
806. *Re J (Specific Issue Orders: Child's Religious Upbringing and Circumcision)* [2000] 1 F.L.R. 571.
807. *Re G (Parental Responsibility: Education)* [1994] 2 F.L.R. 964.
808. *See infra* Part II, Ch. 8, para. 368.
809. *Children Act* 1989, s. 91(7), (8).

enjoyed parental responsibility from the moment of the child's birth will only lose parental responsibility if the child is adopted by third parties (and consenting to a child's adoption can be seen in itself as an exercise of parental responsibility). The same applies to those to whom legal parenthood has been transferred. Those who have acquired parental responsibility as a result of registration, a parental responsibility order or a parental responsibility agreement may lose it, but only by court order.[810] Guardianship may be brought to an end by the court, either upon the application of the child or any person with parental responsibility or of its own motion.[811] The court must be satisfied that this course is in the best interests of the child.

What all of these methods of terminating parental responsibility while the child is still a minor have in common is that they involve a court order: either the order that conferred parental responsibility comes to an end or an order is made that has the effect of terminating parental responsibility. Private transfers or surrenders of parental responsibility are specifically prohibited by the legislation.[812]

---

810. *Ibid.*, s. 4(2A); *See*, e.g., *Re P. (Terminating Parental Responsibility)* [1995] 1 F.L.R. 1048; *CW v. SG* [2013] EWHC 854 (Fam); *Re D (withdrawal of parental responsibility)* [2014] EWCA civ 315.
811. *Ibid.*, s. 6(7).
812. *Ibid.*, s. 2(9). *See* generally J. Scherpe, *Responsible Parents and Parental Responsibility* Ch. 3 (R. Probert, S. Gilmore & J. Herring eds., Hart 2009).

# Chapter 7. Adoption and Its Alternatives

§1. INTRODUCTION

*344.* Adoption may serve a number of purposes, each of which has been important at different times in the past century: it provides a permanent substitute home for children who are unable to live with their birth parents; it provides an option for women who, for whatever reason, are unable to care for their child; it enables young, unmarried women to conceal the fact that they have given birth, while ensuring that their child is cared for; it allows couples who are unable to have their own children to bring up a child; and it provides a means of conferring the legal status of parent upon the new partner of a parent. Today, it is the adoption of children from care that dominates the workload of adoption agencies. For such children, adoption is not the only option: a special guardianship order, child arrangements order or fostering may, in the circumstances of the case, be the preferred option to achieve permanence for a child.

§2. ADOPTION

*345.* The law relating to adoption was reformed by the Adoption and Children Act 2002, which came into force on 30 December 2005.

## I. Who May Be Adopted?

*346.* Under English law, an application for an adoption order may only be made in relation to a child under the age of 18 years[813] who has never been married or entered into a civil partnership;[814] an order, however, may be made in favour of a person who has reached the age of 18 years since the adoption process commenced,[815] but not in favour of a person who has attained the age of 19 years.[816] It is clear, therefore, that adoption is intended as a means for providing a family for a child; although, if a child is approaching the age of 18 years, the fact that the benefits of the order will largely accrue to the adoptee after reaching the age of 18 years is not a reason for refusing to make it.[817]

## II. Who May Adopt?

*347.* There are very few limits on who may apply to adopt a child. Statute imposes a residence requirement, stipulating that a sole applicant or at least one of

---

813. *Adoption and Children Act* 2002, s. 49(4).
814. *Ibid.*, s. 47(8) and (8A).
815. *Ibid.*, s. 49(5).
816. *Ibid.*, s. 47(9); *Re A* [2017] EWHC 1178 (Fam).
817. *See*, e.g., *Re D (A Minor) (Adoption Order: Validity)* [1991] 2 F.L.R. 66.

a couple wishing to adopt must either be domiciled in a part of the British Islands or have been habitually resident there for at least the preceding year.[818] It also sets a minimum age limit of 21 years,[819] except if one of a couple wishing to adopt is actually the parent of the child, in which case the order may be made if the birth parent is at least 18 years of age and the other applicant at least 21 years.[820]

*348.* An adoption order may be made in favour of a single person or a couple – who may be married,[821] in a civil partnership,[822] or simply 'two people (whether of different sexes or the same-sex) living as parties in an enduring family relationship'.[823] Related individuals – parents, grandparents, siblings, and aunts and uncles – are specifically excluded from the definition of a 'couple',[824] although there is nothing to prevent a person who is related to the child from applying to adopt as an individual.

Adoption orders in favour of a parent and his or her new spouse were common in the 1970s and were the only way in which a step-parent could acquire parental responsibility, although the desirability of such adoptions has been debated.[825] Two reforms in the Adoption and Children Act 2002 have rendered this option unnecessary. First, a step-parent may acquire parental responsibility by other means,[826] and second, adoption by the new partner of a birth parent[827] – whether a spouse, civil partner or other person with whom the parent has an 'enduring family relationship' – no longer eliminates the parental responsibility and status of that birth parent,[828] and so the birth parent no longer has to be a party to the adoption order to preserve his or her parental status.

*349.* There are restrictions on making an adoption order on the sole application of a person who is married or in a civil partnership. In cases of this kind, the court may make the adoption order if it is satisfied that the other spouse or civil partner either cannot be found, or is incapable of applying for an order by reason of ill health, or is living apart from the applicant and the separation is likely to be permanent.[829]

*350.* There are also restrictions on making an adoption order in favour of an existing parent who has not repartnered. The justification for the additional restrictions in this situation is that the adoption order will have the effect of terminating

---

818. *Adoption and Children Act* 2002, s. 49(2) and (3). *See further* Part I, Ch. 6.
819. *Ibid.*, ss 50(1), 51(1).
820. *Ibid.*, s. 50(2).
821. *Adoption and Children Act* 2002, s. 144(4)(a).
822. *Ibid.*, s. 144(4)(aa).
823. *Ibid.*, s. 144(4)(b). This requirement has been found to be satisfied even where the individuals concerned are living in separate households: *T and M v. OCC and C* [2010] EWHC 964 (Fam).
824. *Ibid.*, s. 144(5).
825. *Re P (Step-Parent Adoption)* [2014] EWCA Civ 1174.
826. *See supra* Part II, Ch. 6, para. 312.
827. *Adoption and Children Act* 2002, s. 51(2), and *see* s. 144(7).
828. *Ibid.*, s. 46(3)(b).
829. *Adoption and Children Act* 2002, s. 51(3) and (3A).

the legal relationship with the other existing parent without providing any substitute. The legislation accordingly provides that a court cannot make an adoption order in this situation unless the other parent is dead or cannot be found, or where there simply is no other legal parent (a possibility in cases of assisted reproduction)[830] or there is some other reason justifying the child being adopted by the applicant alone.[831]

*351.* These fairly minimal statutory restrictions on the ability of a person to apply for an adoption order are supplemented in practice by the policies adopted by local authorities. In addition, although placements across religious, racial or cultural boundaries are not prohibited, the legislation directs that the adoption agency in Wales 'give due consideration to the child's religious persuasion, racial origin and cultural and linguistic background'[832] in placing a child for adoption. This requirement has been removed by the Children and Family Act 2014 in relation to English adoption agencies.

## III. The Necessity of Consent

*352.* Before an adoption order can be made, the court must be satisfied either that the consent of the child's parent or guardian has been obtained, or that such consent should be dispensed with.[833]

### A. Whose Consent Is Required?

*353.* While the consent of any parent or guardian is required, 'parent', for these purposes, means only a legal parent with parental responsibility[834] (but does not include other persons, even step-parents, with parental responsibility). 'Guardian', in this context, includes both guardians and special guardians. This means that the consent of more than one person may be required. For example, if a guardian had been appointed by a person named as the person with whom the child should live in a child arrangements order, who then subsequently died, there might be another living parent with parental responsibility; similarly, a special guardian may be appointed even where there are two parents with parental responsibility.

*354.* It should be noted that the consent of the child is not a prerequisite for the making of an adoption order, although the legislation does require the court to take

---

830. *See supra* Part II, Ch. 5, para. 293.
831. *Adoption and Children Act* 2002, s. 51(4), and *see In re B (A minor) (Respondent)* [2001] UKHL 70.
832. *Adoption and Children Act* 2002, s. 1(5).
833. *Ibid.*, s. 47(2).
834. *Ibid.*, s. 52(6).

into account the ascertainable wishes and feelings of the child, 'considered in the light of the child's age and understanding'.[835]

## B. When Can Consent Be Given?

355. Adoption is a two-stage process: first, the child is placed with adoptive parents, and then, if appropriate, an adoption order will be made. A child may only be placed with potential adopters with the consent of those persons whose consent would be necessary to the making of an adoption order, unless the court decides that their consent should be dispensed with.

This two-stage process has a number of implications. First, while a mother cannot validly consent to an adoption order being made until the child is at least six weeks old,[836] she can consent to the child being placed for adoption in this period. Second, a father who did not have parental responsibility at the time that the child was placed with the potential adopters but who later acquires it will be deemed to have given consent in the same terms as those in which the first parent gave consent.[837] Third, advance consent to adoption may be given at the time that the child is placed for adoption;[838] however, if this is within six weeks of the birth it will not give the courts jurisdiction to make an adoption order.[839] Finally, even if such advance consent has not been given, an initial consent to the child being placed with potential adopters may not be withdrawn once an application has been made for an adoption order (or indeed a placement order).[840]

## C. When May Consent Be Dispensed With?

356. There are two situations in which the court may dispense with the otherwise requisite consents. The first is where a parent or guardian cannot be found or 'lacks capacity (within the meaning of the Mental Capacity Act 2005) to give consent'.[841] It must be shown that all reasonable steps have been taken to try to find the parent or guardian, or that there are no practical means of communication.[842] The second, and far broader provision, is that 'the welfare of the child requires the consent to be dispensed with'.[843] This provision of the 2002 Act replaced an earlier set of conditions which allowed parental consent to be dispensed with only in cases of

---

835. *Ibid.*, s. 1(4)(a).
836. *Ibid.*, s. 52(3).
837. *Ibid.*, s. 52(10).
838. *Ibid.*, s. 20(1).
839. *A Local Authority v. GC and Others* [2008] EWHC 2555 (Fam).
840. *Adoption and Children Act* 2002, s. 32(1) and (5).
841. *Adoption and Children Act* 2002, s. 52(1)(a), as amended by the *Mental Capacity Act* 2005, Sch. 6, para. 45.
842. *Re R (Adoption)* [1967] 1 W.L.R. 34 (parents resident in totalitarian country and attempts to contact them would be dangerous); *Re A (Adoption of a Russian Child)* [2000] 1 F.L.R. 539 (refusal of Russian court to contact child's mother on the basis that it was against the law to do so once an adoption order had been made in that country).
843. *Adoption and Children Act* 2002, s. 52(1)(b).

parental default or where consent was being unreasonably withheld, but given that it was the practice of the courts to hold that a reasonable parent would take the welfare of the child into account[844] – and so would consent to adoption where this was clearly in the child's best interests – this change has not had a significant impact.[845] It should, however, be noted that the 2002 Act also introduced a welfare checklist for consideration in adoption cases, which draws attention to such matters as 'the likely effect on the child (throughout his life) of having ceased to be a member of the original family and become an adopted person',[846] the value of existing family relationships to the child,[847] and the wishes and feelings of the child's relatives.[848] As Wall L.J. has noted, adoption has 'lifelong implications'[849] and such factors:

> are not boxes to be ticked so that this court can be satisfied that the judge has gone through the motions [but] important statutory provisions, bolstered by decisions of this court which require a judge fully and carefully to consider whether the welfare of the child concerned *throughout his life* ... requires adoption.[850]

In *Re B-S*,[851] Munby L.J. held that although the child's interests are paramount, when making the decision to override parental consent the court must be alert that these interests include being brought up by a birth family. In *Re W*[852] the Court of Appeal emphasized the right of the child to have decisions made which afford paramount concern to the child's welfare throughout her life, in a manner which is proportionate and compatible with the need to respect any Article 8 rights engaged.

## IV. Should an Adoption Order Be Made?

*357.* As noted above, adoption is a two-stage process, and a court cannot make an adoption order unless the child has been living with the potential adopters for a minimum period of time. The precise period required depends upon the status of the applicants: if the child has been placed with the adopter(s) by an adoption agency, or a placement order has been made, or the applicant is a parent of the child, an application for an adoption order cannot be made unless the child has been living with the applicant(s) for the ten weeks preceding the application.[853] If the applicant

---

844. *See*, e.g., *Re W (An Infant)* [1971] A.C. 682; *Re C (A Minor) (Adoption: Parental Agreement: Contact)* [1993] 2 F.L.R. 260.
845. Although note *Re S (Adoption Order or Special Guardianship Order)* [2007] EWCA Civ 54, para. 69, which notes that the new wording 'constitutes a major change'.
846. *Adoption and Children Act* 2002, s. 1(4)(c).
847. *Ibid.*, s. 1(4)(f)(i).
848. *Ibid.*, s. 1(4)(f)(iii).
849. *Re P (Placement Orders: Parental Consent)* [2008] EWCA Civ 535, para. 128.
850. *EH v. X London Borough Council, AA, REA & RHA (through their Children's Guardian), A (Children)* [2010] EWCA Civ 344, at para. 96.
851. *Re B-S (Children) (Adoption Order: Leave to Oppose)* [2013] EWCA Civ 1146, [26].
852. *Re W* [2016] All ER (D) 25 (Aug). [68]-[69].
853. *Adoption and Children Act* 2002, s. 42(2).

is the new partner of one of the child's parents, a six-month period is imposed.[854] This rises to one year in the case of local authority foster parents,[855] and any other applicants must show that the child has been living with them for at least three out of the past five years.[856] In relation to these last two cases, however, the court does have the power to grant leave to make an application for an adoption order even if the full period has not been satisfied.[857]

*358.* From this it will be clear that the point at which the child begins to live with the potential adopters is not automatically the subject of court control. A court may become involved at the placement stage if a parent or guardian is withholding consent, or where application is made for a placement order, but the task of selecting potential adopters and matching them with the child is left to the adoption agency. There is a clear policy that placements should be channelled through the appropriate official agencies; private placements – save with a relative of the child – are prohibited,[858] and may render the parties vulnerable to prosecution.

Thus when an application for an adoption order comes before the court, the issue may simply be whether an adoption order should be made in favour of this particular couple in relation to this particular child. Other arrangements might not be on offer. Even so, it is not simply the role of the court to give formal approval to existing arrangements: it must, as already discussed, determine whether the requisite consents have been given or can be dispensed with, and must be satisfied that making an adoption order is in the best interests of the child. The legislation directs the court to consider 'the whole range of powers available to it' and states that it should not make an order 'unless it considers that making the order would be better for the child than not doing so'.[859] In *Re B*,[860] the Supreme Court made clear that a duty lies on local authorities to explore and attempt alternative solutions. Adoption without the permission of the parents is permissible only where it is 'justified by an overriding requirement pertaining to the child's best interest,' where, 'nothing else will do'. Even if there are no other persons willing and able to care for the child, it may be that a lesser order – such as a child arrangements order or special guardianship order – will be more appropriate in the circumstances.[861]

## V.   What Are the Legal Implications of Adoption?

*359.* The effect of making an adoption order is one reason why adoption may not be the most appropriate solution in every case. An adoption order operates as a

---

854. *Ibid.*, s. 42(3).
855. *Ibid.*, s. 42(4).
856. *Ibid.*, s. 42(5).
857. *Ibid.*, s. 42(6); *ASB and KBS v. MQS* [2009] EWHC 2491 (Fam); *IH (A Child) (Permission to Apply for Adoption)* [2013] EWHC 1235 (Fam) (permission refused).
858. *Adoption and Children Act 2002*, s.93.
859. *Ibid.*, s. 1(6).
860. [2013] UKSC 33.
861. *See. Re T (A Child: Adoption or Special Guardianship)* [2017] EWCA Civ 1797, where the decision to make an adoption order was upheld.

'legal transplant'. The birth parents cease to be, and the adoptive parents become, the child's legal parents for virtually all purposes.[862] The order confers parental responsibility on the adoptive parents and extinguishes the parental responsibility of the birth parent(s),[863] except where the order is made in favour of the new partner of one of the birth parents.[864] An adoption order is permanent and cannot usually be revoked,[865] even at the request of an adoptee that has attained the age of 18 years,[866] although an adopted child may be re-adopted by new adoptive parents.[867]

*360.* The legislation directs that the adopted child is treated as if he or she had been born as the child of the adopter(s).[868] This is, however, subject to a number of modifications. One is a social fiction; an adopted child is always legitimate, whether adopted by a single person or an unmarried couple.[869] Another is intended to preserve the existing nationality of a child. Adoption may confer British citizenship but cannot deprive an adoptee of it. A third exception reflects the biological reality that has remained unaltered by the adoption: the prohibited degrees between the adopted child and his or her birth family remain unaffected by the adoption order for the purposes of marriage and civil partnership.[870]

*361.* This last exception presumes that the adoptee has the means of discovering the identity of his or her birth family before entering into a relationship of this kind. In general, an adoptee can only apply for access to his or her original birth records upon attaining the age of 18 years,[871] but a 16- or 17-year old who is intending to marry or form a civil partnership may apply to the Registrar General to ascertain whether there is any information on the register suggesting that the applicant and the intended spouse or civil partner are related within the prohibited degrees.[872]

§3. SPECIAL GUARDIANSHIP

*362.* It was long felt that 'legal transplant' model of adoption was not appropriate in all cases. As the Government White Paper that preceded the legislation noted:

> Adoption is not always appropriate for children who cannot return to their birth parents. Some older children do not wish to be legally separated from their birth parents. Adoption may not be best for some children being cared for on

---

862. Except the succession to peerages: *Adoption and Children Act* 2002, s. 71(1).
863. *Adoption and Children Act* 2002, s. 46(1) and (2).
864. *Ibid.*, s. 46(3)(b).
865. Unless the circumstances are exceptional: *See*, e.g., *PK v. Mr and Mrs K* [2015] EWHC 2316.
866. *Re B (Adoption: Jurisdiction to Set Aside)* [1995] Fam. 239.
867. *Adoption and Children Act* 2002, s. 46(5).
868. *Ibid.*, s. 67(1).
869. *Ibid.*, s. 67(2).
870. *See supra* Part II, Ch. 1, para. 145.
871. *Adoption and Children Act* 2002, s. 60(1). The right is not absolute, but access will only be denied in exceptional circumstances: *Adoption and Children Act* 2002, s. 60(3) and *See*, e.g., *R v. Registrar General, Ex p Smith* [1991] 1 F.L.R. 255.
872. *Adoption and Children Act* 2002, s. 79(7).

a permanent basis by members of their wider birth family. Some minority ethnic communities have religious and cultural difficulties with adoption as it is set out in law. Unaccompanied asylum-seeking children may also need secure, permanent homes, but have strong attachments to their families abroad.[873]

The concept of 'special guardianship' was introduced in the 2002 Act to provide an arrangement that offered security without severing the child's legal relationship with his or her birth family.

## I. Who May Be a Special Guardian?

*363.* A special guardian must be an adult and not a parent of the child in question.[874] A child can have more than one special guardian.[875] Certain persons are automatically entitled to apply for a special guardianship order: a guardian; any person named in a child arrangements order as person with whom the child should live; local authority foster parents with whom the child has been living for at least one year immediately prior to the application; any person with whom the child has lived for three out of the past five years; and any person who has the consent of all persons with parental responsibility or (if a child arrangements order is in force), of the person(s) in whose favour a child arrangements order conferring PR was made or (if a care order has been made) of the local authority.[876] Further restrictions apply if a placement order is in force. The leave of the court is required for an application to be made in such cases.[877] Other persons may apply with the leave of the court.[878]

## II. What Are the Legal Implications of an Order?

*364.* The making of a special guardianship order confers parental responsibility upon the special guardian(s), who may exercise it 'to the exclusion of any other person with parental responsibility for the child (apart from another special guardian)'.[879] It will bring any existing care order or child arrangements order to an end.[880]

Although a special guardian therefore enjoys a degree of exclusivity in exercising parental responsibility that is absent in other arrangements (e.g., a child arrangements order),[881] a special guardianship order does not offer complete security from parental intervention. In contrast to the position where an adoption order has been

---

873. *Adoption – A New Approach* (2000), para. 5.8.
874. *Children Act* 1989, s. 14A(2).
875. *Ibid.*, s. 14A(1).
876. *Ibid.*, s. 14A(5).
877. *Ibid.*, s. 14A(13).
878. *Ibid.*, s. 14A(3)(b). Section 9(3) of the Act will apply in determining whether leave should be granted: *see infra* Part II, Ch. 8, para. 378.
879. *Children Act* 1989, s. 14C(1).
880. *Ibid.*, s. 91(5A).
881. *See* the discussion in *Re L (A Child)* [2007] EWCA Civ 196.

made – in which case the birth parents are no longer the child's legal parents and must apply for leave if they wish to make an application for an order under section 8 of the Children Act – there are no automatic restrictions on applications by parents for specific issue orders, prohibited steps orders or contact orders while a special guardianship order is in force. Leave is required before an application for a child arrangements order relating to where a child should live is made,[882] and the court may impose a leave requirement on applications for other orders if it deems this appropriate.[883] The fact that the special guardian and the child do not have the same security of knowing that they are free from further litigation as if an adoption order had been made has been noted as a disadvantage of a special guardianship order.[884]

*365.* There are, moreover, certain restrictions on the exercise of parental responsibility by a special guardian that do not apply to adoptive parents. A special guardian may remove the child from the jurisdiction for up to three months, but longer absences require either the consent of every person with parental responsibility or the leave of the court.[885] A special guardian may not change the child's surname without either the consent of every person with parental responsibility or the leave of the court.[886]

*366.* Finally, unlike an adoption order, a special guardianship order is not permanent: it may be varied or discharged by the court,[887] and will come to an end when the child reaches the age of 18.[888] A special guardian is automatically entitled to apply to vary or discharge the special guardianship order, whereas the child, a parent, guardian, step-parent with parental responsibility, and any person who had parental responsibility up until the making of the special guardianship order must apply for leave before making such an application. Leave will not be granted to a child unless the court is satisfied that he or she has sufficient understanding to make the application, nor will it be granted to any other person unless the court is satisfied that there has been a significant change in circumstances since the making of the special guardianship order.[889]

### III. When Will a Special Guardianship Order Be Made?

*367.* A court cannot make a special guardianship order unless it has received a report from the local authority dealing with the applicant's suitability to be a special

---

882. *Children Act* 1989, s. 10(7A).
883. *See*, e.g., *K (Children) v. Sheffield City Council* [2011] EWCA Civ 635, in which an order restricting further applications by the parents was imposed by the court.
884. *Re S (Adoption Order or Special Guardianship Order)* [2007] EWCA Civ 54, para. 65.
885. *Children Act* 1989, s. 14C(3)(b).
886. *Ibid.*, s. 14C(3)(a).
887. *Children Act* 1989, s. 14D.
888. *Ibid.*, s. 91(13).
889. *Re G (A Child) (Special Guardianship Order: Application to Discharge)* [2010] EWCA Civ 300.

guardian.[890] This means that if an application for a special guardianship order is envisaged, the potential applicant(s) must notify the local authority at least three months before making the application so that the report can be prepared.[891] If the court decides of its own motion that a special guardianship order would be appropriate, it may ask the local authority to conduct the necessary investigation.[892]

368. The making of a special guardianship order is governed by the welfare principle. The courts have stressed that '[t]here can be no routine solutions' and that each case must be decided on its particular facts.[893] The lesser legal consequences of a special guardianship order – as opposed to an adoption order – have figured heavily in the cases that have considered the two options:[894] if the child needs long-term stability and the assurance that the security of the placement could not be disturbed, an adoption order is likely to be preferable to a special guardianship order.[895] Although, it was initially suggested that the special guardianship order might be an appropriate order where children are to be cared for on a long-term basis by members of their extended family, the courts have stressed that there is no assumption that a special guardianship order is the appropriate order in that type of case.[896] In each individual case, the question for the court is: 'which order will better serve the welfare of this particular child?'[897]

In one respect, the lesser legal consequences of a special guardianship order may prove to be an argument in favour of making such an order. The Court of Appeal has noted that '[i]t is a material feature of the special guardianship regime that it is "less intrusive" than adoption.' In an appropriate case, therefore, where the needs of the child can be equally well met by a special guardianship order as by an adoption order, 'the fact that the welfare objective can be achieved with less disruption of existing family relationships can properly be regarded as helping to tip the balance'.[898] However, there is no obligation on the court to choose 'the least interventionist option': the starting point must always be the child's welfare.[899]

---

890. *Children Act* 1989, s. 14A(11). Although if the order has been made, the breach could be rectified by requiring the local authority subsequently to produce such a report: *Re S (Adoption Order or Special Guardianship Order) (No. 2)* [2007] EWCA Civ 90.

891. *Children Act* 1989, s. 14A(7).

892. *Ibid.*, s. 14A(9). Although note *Birmingham City Council v. R* [2006] EWCA Civ 1748.

893. *Re S (Adoption Order or Special Guardianship Order)* [2007] EWCA Civ 54, paras 43, 47.

894. *See*, e.g., *Re S (Adoption Order or Special Guardianship Order)* [2007] EWCA Civ 54, para. 46.

895. *Re AJ (Adoption Order or Special Guardianship Order)* [2007] EWCA Civ 55, para. 45; *Re M-J (Adoption Order or Special Guardianship Order)* [2007] EWCA Civ 56; *Re S (Adoption Order or Special Guardianship Order)* [2007] EWCA Civ 54, para. 68.

896. *Re AJ (Adoption Order or Special Guardianship Order)* [2007] EWCA Civ 55, para. 44; *Re M-J (Adoption Order or Special Guardianship Order)* [2007] EWCA Civ 56, para. 17.

897. *Re S (Adoption Order or Special Guardianship Order)* [2007] EWCA Civ 54, para. 47. *See also N v. B & Ors* [2013] EWHC 820 (Fam), in which it was held that an adoption order, rather than a special guardianship, was needed to guarantee the long-term security of the children.

898. *Ibid.*, [2007] EWCA Civ 54, para. 49. *See also K (Children) v. Sheffield City Council* [2011] EWCA Civ 635.

899. *Re M-J (Adoption Order or Special Guardianship Order)* [2007] EWCA Civ 56, para. 19; *Re T (A Child: Adoption or Special Guardianship)* [2017] EWCA Civ 179.

# Chapter 8. Child Arrangements Orders

## §1. INTRODUCTION

*369.* One of the facets of parental responsibility is the responsibility to provide a home for the child and the right to determine where that home will be. Yet when parents separate, they may each want the child to live with them; in addition, there may be other persons who have been caring for the child who wish to continue doing so. The law of England and Wales operates a flexible regime when determining with whom the child should live. While there is a general assumption that, all things being equal, it is preferable for children to remain with their biological parents (or at least one of them), there a wide range of persons may apply for a child arrangements order to be made providing that the child will live with them. The old terminology of 'custody' and 'access' was swept away by the Children Act 1989 and replaced by the more neutral and child-focused terms 'residence' and 'contact'. In 2014, the distinction between a residence order and a contact order was abolished by the Children and Families Act on the basis that such terminology had been unhelpfully associated with ideas of winning and losing and heightens animosity between parents. This builds on a trend visible in the last five years to make 'shared residence' order rather than a residence order and a contact order. All such orders are now known as 'child arrangements orders'. The new label is intended to put the emphasis back on children's needs and practical arrangements made for their upbringing. Child arrangements orders may be used to regulate with whom the child is to live, spend time or otherwise have contact.

## §2. THE COURT'S JURISDICTION TO MAKE AN ORDER

*370.* Section 8 of the Children Act 1989 governs the making of child arrangements orders (as well as prohibited steps orders and specific issue orders, which are intended to deal with specific exercises of parental responsibility). A court will generally have jurisdiction to make an order under section 8 of the Children Act if certain specified family proceedings are before the court, or if an application for the order has been made either by a person who is entitled to apply for such an order or by a person who has obtained the leave of the court to apply for such an order.[900] There are, however, certain statutory restrictions on the court's jurisdiction, which are set out below.

## I. Family Proceedings

*371.* It may be that an issue relating to the welfare and upbringing of the child arises in the course of other family proceedings. If so, the court has jurisdiction to make an order under section 8 even if none of the parties have applied for such an

---

900. *Children Act* 1989, s. 10(1) and (2).

order.[901] Indeed, the court may make an order in favour of persons who would not themselves have been able to apply for an order.[902]

For this purpose 'family proceedings' are defined as proceedings under any of Parts I, II, and IV of the Children Act itself, the Matrimonial Causes Act 1973, Schedules 5 and 6 of the Civil Partnership Act 2004, the Adoption and Children Act 2002, the Domestic Proceedings and Magistrates' Courts Act 1978, Part III of the Matrimonial and Family Proceedings Act 1984, the Family Law Act 1996 or sections 11 and 12 of the Crime and Disorder Act 1998,[903] or any proceedings under the inherent jurisdiction of the court in relation to children.[904]

## II. Persons Entitled to Apply for an Order

372. Just as the range of persons who may acquire parental responsibility for a child extends far beyond the legal parents of a child, so too there is an extensive list of persons who may apply for child arrangements order to determine the child's residence or whether they should have contact with the child. The rules governing who may apply for an order are intended to strike a balance between ensuring that those who have a legitimate interest in the child's upbringing may apply without hindrance and protecting the family against unwarranted interference.

373. Certain persons are entitled to apply for any type of section 8 order: namely, a legal parent (whether or not possessing parental responsibility), a guardian (including a special guardian), a step-parent who has acquired parental responsibility and any person named in a child arrangements order that is in force as a person with whom the child should live.[905]

374. A second group of persons are entitled to apply only for a child arrangements order. These include any persons who are not the parents of the child but who are – or have at some point been – married to or in a civil partnership with a parent of the child and in relation to whom the child is a 'child of the family'.[906] This means that a step-parent is entitled to apply for a child arrangements order after the relationship with the child's parent has come to an end, even if he or she does not have parental responsibility for the child. A person who is simply cohabiting with the child's parent does not have this right, but may qualify under the next ground, as a person with whom the child has lived for three out of the past five years.[907] Certain persons may also apply if they have the requisite consents: if a child arrangements order is in place, this means the consent of persons named in a child arrangements order as persons with whom the child should live;[908] if a care order is

---

901. *Ibid.*, s. 10(1)(b).
902. *Gloucestershire CC v. P.* [1999] 2 F.L.R. 61.
903. *Children Act* 1989, s. 8(3)(b) and (4).
904. *Ibid.*, s. 8(3)(a).
905. *Children Act* 1989, s. 10(4)(a).
906. *Ibid.*, s. 10(5)(a) and (aa).
907. *Ibid.*, s. 10(5)(b) and (10).
908. *Ibid.*, s. 10(5)(c)(i).

in force, the consent of the local authority is necessary;[909] and in other cases the consent of everyone with parental responsibility for the child is required.[910] A person who has parental responsibility for the child under a child arrangements order which does not specify that the child is to live with them[911] may also apply for a child arrangements order.[912]

*375.* A third, more limited, group of persons are only entitled to apply for a child arrangements order relating to where the child should live, namely local authority foster parents, or a relative of the child with whom the child has been living for at least one year immediately prior to the application.[913]

*376.* Extensive though this list is, there are some obvious omissions. A grandparent, e.g., has no automatic right to apply for any of the section 8 orders unless he or she falls into one of the groups outlined above. Similarly, a parent whose child has been adopted – and who is therefore no longer the child's legal parent – would no longer be able to apply. Perhaps most surprisingly of all, a child has no automatic right to apply for a section 8 order either. However, a person who does not fall within any of the defined groups may still seek the leave of the court to apply for an order.

## III. Seeking Leave to Apply

*377.* The court has discretion whether or not to grant such leave. If the application is brought by the child concerned, the court may only grant leave if it is satisfied that he or she has sufficient understanding to make the proposed application.[914] The threshold of 'understanding' has been set at a high level,[915] and, since the legislation does not state the court must grant leave if the child does have sufficient understanding, it has been held that the court has discretion to refuse leave even if convinced of the child's competence.[916] Leave has been refused both on the basis that there is common ground between one of the parents and the child (and thus no need for the child to make a separate application) and on the basis that the court is worried about a child being drawn into an argument with the parents.[917]

*378.* If the application for leave is brought by someone other than the child, the court is directed to 'have particular regard' to the nature of the proposed application for the section 8 order; to the applicant's connection with the child; to any risk there might be of that proposed application disrupting the child's life to such an extent

---

909. *Ibid.*, s. 10(5)(c)(ii).
910. *Ibid.*, s. 10(5)(c)(iii).
911. That is, under the newly created *Children Act 1989* s. 12(2A).
912. *Children Act* 1989, s. 10(5)(d).
913. *Ibid.*, s. 10(5A) and (5B).
914. *Ibid.*, s. 10(8).
915. *See*, e.g., *Re S (A Minor) (Independent Representation)* [1993] Fam. 263.
916. *See*, e.g., *Re C (A Minor) (Leave to Seek s. 8 order)* [1994] 1 F.L.R. 26.
917. *Re H (Residence order; Child's Application for Leave)* [2000] 1 F.L.R. 780.

that he or she would be harmed by it; and – where the child is being looked after by a local authority – to the authority's plans for the child's future, and the wishes and feelings of the child's parents.[918] These specific guidelines must be applied in place of the general principle under the Children Act that the welfare of the child is the paramount consideration.[919] The question as to whether leave should be granted to a particular person is independent of the question as to whether the substantive application for a section 8 order is likely to succeed,[920] although the likelihood of success is a factor to be taken into account in deciding whether to grant leave.[921]

*379.* One group of persons is debarred even from seeking leave to apply for an order. Local authority foster carers are not entitled to apply for leave unless they have the consent of the local authority, or are related to the child, or the child has been living with them for at least one year preceding the application.[922] The rationale for this restriction is rooted in the often short-term nature of foster care. If the child has returned to his or her parents, then it is likely to be undesirable for the family to be disrupted by applications from a previous foster carer; if, on the other hand, the child has been placed with new carers by the local authority, this is a matter for the local authority to decide.

*380.* It should also be noted that a person who would normally be entitled to apply for an order automatically may be required to seek leave in certain circumstances. This may the case if, e.g., the child has been placed for adoption (or if a placement order has been made), or if a special guardianship order is in force. Furthermore, if there has already been extensive litigation regarding the child, the court may take the view that future applications should be restricted and make an order that certain persons should be prevented from making any further application without the leave of the court.[923]

## IV. Restrictions on Making an Order

*381.* There are a number of provisions in the Children Act 1989 limiting when certain orders can be made. First, if the child is in the care of a local authority, the court is not entitled to make any section 8 order, with the sole exception of a child arrangements order as to where and with whom the child should live.[924] The reason for this is that while a care order subsists the local authority has the power to determine the extent to which the child's parents, guardian, special guardian or stepparent with parental responsibility may meet their parental responsibility for the

---

918. *Children Act* 1989, s. 10(9); *see*, e.g., *Re B (Paternal Grandmother: Joinder as Party)* [2012] EWCA Civ 737, emphasizing that all the factors listed need to be taken into account.
919. *Re A (Minors) (Residence Orders: Leave to Apply)* [1992] Fam. 182; *Re G (A Minor); Re Z (A Minor)* [2013] EWHC 134 (Fam).
920. *Re H (Leave to Apply for Residence Order)* [2008] EWCA Civ 503.
921. *Re R (Adoption: Contact)* [2005] EWCA Civ 1128.
922. *Children Act* 1989, s. 9(3).
923. *Ibid.*, s. 91(14).
924. *Ibid.*, s. 9(1).

child:[925] to allow such persons to constrain the local authority's powers by means of a prohibited steps order or a specific issue order would be to subvert the local authority's statutory powers. Specific provision is also made under Part IV of the Children Act relating to contact between the child in care and certain specified persons.[926] The making of a child arrangements order as to where a child should live, by contrast, brings a care order to an end – a factor that would of course be taken into account by the court in deciding whether or not to make such an order.

*382.* The separation between 'private' and 'public' cases under the Children Act – i.e., those cases dealing with disputes between individuals and those instigated by the local authority exercising its powers to protect children – is also evident in the second restriction on the court's powers. A local authority may not apply for a child arrangements order, and no court may make such orders in favour of a local authority.[927] If a local authority wishes to take a child into care, it must satisfy the more stringent threshold criteria – which stipulate that a care order cannot be made unless the child is suffering or likely to suffer significant harm attributable to parental default or insufficient parental control[928] – rather than the simple welfare test required when making a child arrangements order.

*383.* Linked to this restriction is the provision that the court may not make a specific issue order or prohibited steps order with the aim of achieving a result which could be achieved by making a child arrangements order. The restriction on making the latter type of orders in favour of a local authority would be rendered ineffective if it could be circumvented simply by making an order with a different name.

*384.* The final restrictions relate to the age of the child who is the intended subject of the section 8 order. The legislation directs that, except in exceptional circumstances, the court should not make an order under section 8 once the child has reached the age of 16 years (although it may vary or discharge any existing order).[929] It further directs that the court should not make an order (except an order relating to with whom the child should live) that will continue after the child has reached the age of 16 years, again with the proviso that this may be done if the circumstances are exceptional.[930]

§3. GENERAL PRINCIPLES GOVERNING THE MAKING OF CHILD ARRANGEMENTS ORDERS

*385.* In private law proceedings, the basic principle is that the child's welfare is paramount. While this is assessed on a case-by-case basis, there are certain general trends in the exercise of court discretion that should be noted. Where the court is

---

925. *Ibid.*, s. 33(3)(b).
926. *Ibid.*, s. 34.
927. *Ibid.*, s. 9(2).
928. *Ibid.*, s. 31(2).
929. *Ibid.*, s. 9(7).
930. *Ibid.*, s. 9(6).

considering whether to make a section 8 order and the order is opposed by any party in the proceedings the court must presume, unless the contrary is shown, that involvement of each parent in the life of the child concerned will further the child's welfare.[931] The purpose of this amendment to the welfare principle is to reinforce the importance of children having an ongoing relationship with both parents. The amendment does not promote a solution of equal time with both parents. Section 1(2B) explicitly defines 'involvement' as 'involvement of some kind, either direct or indirect, but not any particular division of a child's time'.

## I. Orders as to Where and with Whom a Child Should Live

*386.* While the majority of orders are made for children to live with their mothers, there is no legal presumption to this effect. There is an assumption that it is generally in the best interests of the child to remain with his or her primary carer, but this may be either parent.[932] Indeed, there is no presumption that an order as to where the child should live should be made in favour of the child's biological parent – as opposed to, e.g., what might be termed a social or psychological parent or other person who has been caring for the child.[933] Two contrasting cases may be used to illustrate how fact-sensitive this is. In *In re G*,[934] a case involving a dispute between the biological mother and her (female) ex-partner, it was held that the primary residence of the children should continue to be with the biological mother, despite her attempts to exclude her ex-partner from the children's lives. The ex-partner's status as a psychological parent was accepted by the court, but, on the application of the welfare checklist, it was felt that the balance tipped in favour of the biological mother. By contrast, *In re B (A Child)*,[935] the Supreme Court upheld the making of a residence order in favour of a young boy's grandmother, with whom he had spent the entirety of his short life, rather than his father.

In *In re G*, there was a shared residence order in force – made during earlier proceedings in order to confer parental responsibility upon the mother's ex-partner[936] – but the division of time between the two households was markedly unequal. Earlier case law held that such orders should only be made in exceptional circumstances or where there was a positive benefit to the child in making such an order; more recently the courts have adopted the view that a shared residence order should be made where this would reflect the 'underlying reality' of the situation.[937] It has even been suggested that if children do divide their time between their parents'

931. *Children Act* 1989, s. 1(2A) as inserted by the *Children and Families Act* 2014.
932. *See*, e.g., *Re H (Agreed Joint Residence: Mediation)* [2005] 1 F.L.R. 8.
933. *Re H (a child) (residence)* [2001] EWCA Civ 742; *In re B (A Child)* [2009] UKSC 5; *Re E-R (A Child)* [2015] EWCA Civ 405.
934. *In re G* [2006] UKHL 43.
935. [2009] UKSC 5.
936. *Re G (Residence: Same-Sex Partner)* [2005] EWCA Civ 462.
937. *D v. D (Shared Residence order)* [2001] 1 F.L.R. 495; *Re R (Residence: Shared Care: Children's Views)* [2005] EWCA Civ 542.

homes then there must be good reasons *not* to make a shared residence order,[938] although the suggestion that such orders are 'nowadays the rule rather than the exception' is something of an exaggeration.[939]

Under the new child arrangements orders framework it is possible to replicate the symbolic labelling of a shared residence order by stating within the terms of the child arrangements order that the child should live with one parent at particular times and live with the other parent at other times.

Another feature of the House of Lords' decision in *In re G* was that the lower courts had transferred the primary residence of the children because of the biological mother's attempts to cut her ex-partner out of their lives. There have been a number of cases in which primary residence of the child has been transferred in similar circumstances:[940] the courts have, however, stressed that the transfer must be in the best interests of the child rather than simply being used as a means of punishing the recalcitrant parent. It is thus dependent on the suitability of the other parent as a primary carer for the child.[941]

## II. Order Relating to Contact with the Child

*387.* The new presumption of parental involvement reinforces a pre-existing assumption in case law that it is beneficial for a child to maintain a relationship with both parents in the wake of parental separation.[942] This is reinforced by the jurisprudence of the European Court of Human Rights, which has stressed the importance of contact as an element of 'family life' under Article 8,[943] and the obligations on the State to promote such contact.[944] The activities of fathers' rights groups have kept the issue of contact on the political agenda in recent years, and residential parents who frustrate contact without good reason are seen as acting contrary to the welfare of their children.[945] A number of mechanisms may be used to require the residential parent to comply with a section 8 order for contact, including a fine or

---

938. *Pengelly v. Enright-Redding* [2005] EWCA Civ 1639; *Re P (Shared Residence Order)* [2006] 2 F.L.R. 347, *per* Wall L.J. at para. 22.
939. *Re AR (A Child: Relocation)* [2010] EWHC 1346 (Fam).
940. *See*, e.g., *V v. V (Children) (Contact: Implacable Hostility)* [2004] 2 F.L.R. 851; *Re N (Sexual Abuse Allegations: Professionals Not Abiding by Findings of Fact)* [2005] 2 F.L.R. 340; *A v. A (Shared Residence)* [2004] 1 F.L.R. 1195; *Re R (A Child)* [2009] EWHC B38 (Fam); *Re S (Transfer of Residence)* [2010] EWHC 192 (Fam), although *see* the sequel in *Re S (Transfer of Residence)* [2011] 1 F.L.R. 1789, in which it was noted that the transfer had had to be abandoned due to the child's own opposition; *TB v. DB* [2013] EWHC 2275 (Fam).
941. *V v. V (Contact: Implacable Hostility)* [2004] 2 F.L.R. 851, *per* J. Bracewell, para. 10.
942. *Re L; Re V; Re M; Re H (Contact: Domestic Violence)* [2000] 2 F.L.R. 334.
943. *See*, e.g., *Kosmopoulou v. Greece* [2004] 1 F.L.R. 800, para. 26, and, in the domestic courts, *Re C (A Child) (Suspension of Contact)* [2011] EWCA Civ 521, at para. 47.
944. *Hokkanen v. Finland* [1996] 1 F.L.R. 289; *Sylvester v. Austria* (2003) 37 E.H.R.R. 417; [2003] 2 F.L.R. 210; *Zawadka v. Poland* [2005] 2 F.L.R. 897.
945. *See*, e.g., *Gibbs v. Gibbs* [2017] EWHC 1700; *Re C (A Child)* [2007] EWCA Civ 866; *Re S and Others (Residence)* [2008] EWCA Civ 653.

even prison.[946] Another option is for the court to transfer residence to the other parent.[947] The Children and Adoption Act 2006 also introduced the novel provision that '[i]f the court is satisfied beyond reasonable doubt that a person has failed to comply with the contact order, it may make an order … imposing on the person an unpaid work requirement.'[948] It should be noted that the duty of the residential parent is usually merely to allow contact, rather than to ensure that it takes place, and the intransigence of the child concerned may frustrate the court's best attempts to bring about contact.[949] Recently the Court of Appeal has emphasized the duty on parents to go further and actively encourage contact.[950] As child arrangements orders now name the person with whom the child will have contact, it is possible for the courts to take enforcement proceedings against a parent who does not comply with the order.[951]

## §4. Applying the Welfare Principle

*388.* It has been long established that the court will be guided by what it perceives as the child's best interests in making decisions about the future of that child,[952] and the very first provision of the Children Act 1989 directs that 'the child's welfare shall be the court's paramount consideration' when it is resolving any question with respect to that child's upbringing or the administration of the child's property.[953]

*389.* The form of this provision assumes that the case before the court will involve only one child. The interests of other children who may be affected by the court's decision are thereby excluded.[954] It is only the child who is the subject of proceedings whose welfare is paramount.[955] If, however, more than one child is the subject of the proceedings, it is the task of the court to balance the interests of both children and find the least detrimental alternative.[956]

---

946. *Gibbs v. Gibbs* [2017] EWHC 1700; *Re S (Contact Dispute: Committal)* [2005] 1 F.L.R. 812; *Re D (Intractable Contact Dispute: Publicity)* [2004] 1 F.L.R. 1226, *Williams v. Minnock* [2015] Official Transcript, 2015 WL 3875632; *Mukabi v. Warui* [2015] EWHC 2493 although note the caveats in, *V v. V (Contact: Implacable Hostility)* [2004] 2 F.L.R. 851, para. 10 and *Re L-W (Enforcement and Committal: Contact); CPL v. CH-W and Others* [2010] EWCA 1253.
947. *S (A Child)* [2014] EWCA Civ 1682.
948. *Children and Adoption Act 2006*, s. 4, inserting s. 11J into the *Children Act* 1989.
949. See, e.g., *Re S (Transfer of Residence)* [2011] 1 F.L.R. 1789; *Re L-W (Enforcement and Committal: Contact); CPL v. CH-W and Others* [2010] EWCA 1253.
950. Re M [2017] EWCA Civ 2164 [79]-[80]; *Re H-B (Contact)* [2015] EWCA Civ 389.
951. *Children Act 1989*, s. 11J.
952. *See*, e.g., *Guardianship of Infants Act 1925*, s. 1; *J v. C* [1970] A.C. 668.
953. *Children Act 1989*, s. 1(1).
954. Compare the recommendations of the Law Commission, *Family Law: Review of Child Law, Guardianship and Custody* Law Com. No. 172 para. 3.13 (HMSO 1988).
955. *Birmingham CC v. H (No. 3)* [1994] 1 F.L.R. 224.
956. *Re A (Conjoined Twins: Medical Treatment)* [2001] 1 F.L.R. 1.

*390.* It should be noted, however, that not every issue affecting a child will be deemed to be an issue directly[957] relating to that child's upbringing.[958] Children's interests are not the paramount consideration for the court when it is deciding how the assets of divorcing parents should be divided. Similarly, although the welfare principle applies when the court is considering the appropriate administration of the child's property, it does not apply when it is considering whether property should be settled for the benefit of a child; and 'upbringing' is defined by statute to exclude 'maintenance'.[959] In addition, the order must be one that the court can make; the court does not have an unfettered discretion to make whatever order is in the best interests of the child, as the above discussion about jurisdiction indicates.

*391.* Even in those contexts in which the welfare principle does apply, there are disputes as to how it should apply. Such debates are in part due to the fact that perceptions of welfare may differ between individuals and are liable to change in the light of new evidence or changing social norms. There is, in addition, a specific debate about the compatibility of the welfare principle with the European Convention on Human Rights. The English judiciary[960] has been more confident on this point than academic commentators have been.[961] It would seem, however, that the welfare principle is capable of incorporating the rights of all the parties concerned. The leading case on the interpretation of the welfare principle included a statement by Lord MacDermott to the effect that its application involves:

> a process whereby, when all of the relevant facts, relationships, claims and wishes of parents, risks, choices and other circumstances are taken into account and weighed, the course to be followed will be that which is most in the interests of the child's welfare as that term is now to be understood.[962]

The fact that the welfare of the child is to determine the outcome of the case would not render it incompatible with the European Convention, since the European Court of Human Rights has accepted that '[i]f any balancing of interests is necessary, the interests of the child must prevail' and has on occasion (although not consistently) suggested that the interests of the child are 'paramount.'[963]

There are four key aspects to the welfare principle.

---

957. As required by *S v. S, W v. Official Solicitor* [1972] A.C. 24; *Richards v. Richards* [1984] A.C. 174.
958. *ZH (Tanzania) v. Secretary of State for the Home Department* [2011] UKSC 4.
959. *Children Act* 1989, s. 105(1).
960. *See*, e.g., *Re KD (a minor) (ward: termination of access)* [1988] 1 All E.R. 577; *Re B* [2002] 1 F.L.R. 196; *Re B (Care Proceedings: Appeal)* [2013] UKSC 33.
961. For criticisms *see*, e.g., J. Herring, *The Human Rights Act and the Welfare Principle in Family Law – Conflicting or Complementary?* 11 Child & Fam. L. Q. 223 (1999); S. Choudhry & H. Fenwick, *Taking the Rights of Parents and Children Seriously: Confronting the Welfare Principle under the Human Rights Act*, 25 Oxford J. Leg. Stud. 453 (2005).
962. *J v. C* [1970] A.C. 668, 710–711.
963. *Yousef v. The Netherlands* [2003] 1 F.L.R. 210; *Zawadka v. Poland* [2005] 2 F.L.R. 897. For discussion *see ZH (Tanzania) v. Secretary of State for the Home Department* [2011] UKSC 4.

## I. The Presumption of Parental Involvement

*392.* Where the court is considering whether or not to make a parental responsibility order or a section 8 order in contested proceedings, the court must presume, unless the contrary is shown that involvement of each parent in the life of the child concerned will further the child's welfare.[964] A parent will benefit from this presumption if he/she can be involved in the child's life in a way that does not put the child at risk of suffering harm.[965] In recent cases, the Court of Appeal has emphasized that direct contact between parent and child should be stopped only as a last resort and only where it is not in the best interests of children to continue.[966]

## II. No Unnecessary Delay

*393.* The court is directed to have regard 'to the general principle that any delay in determining the question is likely to prejudice the welfare of the child'.[967] This does not mean that the speedy resolution of the case must be the top priority for the court; a short delay may be necessary to secure the information necessary in order for the court to make an informed decision. The concern is rather that the uncertainty generated by litigation may be damaging to the child and that if matters are not resolved expeditiously the passage of time may mean that the issue is effectively determined by default.

## III. No Unnecessary Orders

*394.* The court 'shall not make the order or any of the orders unless it considers that doing so would be better for the child than making no order at all'.[968] The intention behind the introduction of this provision was to prevent orders being made where there was no real dispute between the parties – e.g., as part of a package of orders made by consent upon divorce. It is clear, however, that there is no presumption against the making of an order,[969] nor does it have to be shown that the making of an order would confer a positive benefit on the child. While an order will obviously be needed if the parents are in dispute,[970] the courts have also held that the

---

964. *Children Act* 1989, s. 1(2A).
965. *Ibid.*, s. 6.
966. Re M [2017] EWCA Civ 2164.
967. *Children Act* 1989, s. 1(2).
968. *Ibid.*, s. 1(5).
969. *Re G (Children)* [2005] EWCA Civ 1237.
970. *Re P (Parental Dispute: Judicial Determination)* [2002] EWCA Civ 1627.

authority of a court order may be useful even if the parents have reached an agreement, since the security conferred by such an order would be reflected in increased stability for the children.[971] Moreover, an order may be desirable to clarify the position for third parties.[972]

## IV. The Welfare Checklist

395. In certain circumstances – if there is a contested application to make, vary or discharge a section 8 order, a special guardianship order, or an order under Part IV of the Children Act – the court is to have 'particular regard' to a checklist of factors:[973]

(a) the ascertainable wishes and feelings of the child concerned (considered in the light of his or her age and understanding);
(b) his or her physical, emotional and educational needs;
(c) the likely effect on him or her of any change in his or her circumstances;
(d) his or her age, sex, background and any characteristics of his or her which the court considers relevant;
(e) any harm which he or she has suffered or is at risk of suffering;
(f) how capable each of his or her parents, and any other person in relation to whom the court considers the question to be relevant, is of meeting his or her needs;
(g) the range of powers available to the court under this Act in the proceedings in question.

Some of the most important factors are considered in more detail below. However, it should be noted that the 'checklist' is not exhaustive and the court can take into account other factors as well which are not mentioned.[974]

## A. The Wishes and Feelings of the Child

396. If an older child expresses a clear preference for living with one parent rather than another, it is likely that the court will attach considerable weight to that preference. The court will often take the pragmatic view that children will simply 'vote with their feet' if the order of the court runs counter to their wishes.[975] Similarly, in the context of orders for the child to have contact, the court has recognized that making such an order in relation to young adults may be counterproductive.[976]

---

971. *Re G (Children)* [2005] EWCA Civ 1237.
972. *See* discussion in M Harding and A Newnham, *How Do County Courts Share Care of Children Between Parents?* (2015).
973. *Children Act* 1989, s. 1(4).
974. *Re G* [2006] UKHL 43, [40].
975. *Puxty v. Moore* [2005] EWCA Civ 1386.
976. *Re S (Contact: Children's Views)* [2002] EWHC 540; *Re L-W (Enforcement and Committal: Contact); CPL v. CH-W and Others* [2010] EWCA 1253.

The views of younger children may also be taken into account where appropriate; the reference to the child's 'feelings' means that the child does not actually have to articulate a preference for a particular course of action. The particular circumstances of the case may require more or less weight to be attached to the views of the child. For example, the distress caused to a young child by witnessing domestic violence between his or her parents has been held to justify the refusal of a contact order.[977]

The weight that is attached to the wishes and feelings of the child will vary not only according to the age of the child but also according to the court's perception of the child's level of understanding.[978] The court may take the view that the child's understanding has been 'corrupted' and that the child has effectively been 'brainwashed' by one of the adults involved. In such cases, attempts may be made to address the underlying issues through professional intervention.[979] More positively, the court may take the view that a relatively young child has a degree of maturity beyond his or her years.[980]

The courts have stressed, however, that the wishes and feelings of the child are only one factor to be taken into account, and that the ultimate decision lies with the court, not the child.[981]

## B. The Child's Needs

*397.* As with many of the factors listed in the checklist, the court's assessment of the child's needs will have both an objective and a subjective element. At a very basic level, it is necessary that the parent seeking an order for the child to live with them should have accommodation to offer the child.[982] Beyond this, more subjective considerations come into play. The emotional need of the child for a relationship with both parents, e.g., may dictate that the child is to live with the parent best able to foster a relationship with the absent parent,[983] while relationships between siblings may also be important in deciding where each is to live.[984]

---

977. *Re L, Re V, Re M, Re H (Contact: Domestic Violence)* [2000] 2 F.L.R. 334; *Re G (A Child) (Domestic Violence: Direct Contact)* [2001] 2 F.C.R. 134; *Re M and B (children) (Contact: Domestic Violence)* [2001] 1 F.C.R. 116.

978. *See*, e.g., *Re JS (Disposal of Body)* [2016] EWHC 2859 (Fam); *J v. S (Leave to Remove)* [2010] EWHC 2098 (Fam).

979. *In Re M (Children) (Contact: Long-Term Best Interests* [2005] EWCA Civ 1090.

980. *R (A Child)* [2009] EWCA Civ 445.

981. *Re K (Children)* [2004] EWCA Civ 1821; *Re R (A Child)* [2009] EWHC B38 (Fam); *M (Children)* [2012] EWHC 1948 (Fam), at para. [74]; *Re P-S* [2013] EWCA Civ 223; *Re D (A Child)* [2014] EWCA Civ 1057.

982. *See*, e.g., *Re M (Residence)* [2002] 2 F.L.R. 1059; *Re R (Children) (Care Proceedings: Maternal Grandmother's Application)* [2007] EWCA Civ 139; *Holmes-Moorhouse v. London Borough of Richmond-upon-Thames* [2009] UKHL 7.

983. *Re J (Children) (Residence: Expert Evidence)* [2001] 2 F.C.R. 44; *Re T (A Child)* [2005] EWCA 1397; *M v. M (Residence)* [2010] EWHC 3579 (Fam).

984. *Re R (Children) (Care Proceedings: Maternal Grandmother's Application)* [2007] EWCA Civ 139.

*C. The Status Quo*

*398.* The importance of stability in the child's life has been stressed in a number of cases, and if the status quo is satisfactory it is unlikely to be disturbed unless there are compelling reasons justifying an alternative arrangement.[985] The weight that is attached to the status quo may lead to preliminary skirmishes between parents on the assumption that the advantage lies with the parent who has the care of the child at the time of the court hearing. Self-help measures have, however, been discouraged by the courts: the Court of Appeal has stressed that if the children had been in the care of one parent under a court order and were then wrongfully retained by the other, the appropriate order of the court would be for the peremptory return of the children to the original carer.[986]

In some cases, however, other factors may outweigh the importance of maintaining the status quo: as ever, the court's perception of the best interests of the child may mean that a different arrangement is regarded as the better option.[987]

*D. The Child's Characteristics*

*399.* There is still a factual assumption that babies should remain with their mother,[988] and, as the House of Lords noted in *Brixey v. Lynas*, 'where a very young child has been with its mother since birth and there is no criticism of her ability to care for the child only the strongest competing advantages are likely to prevail'.[989] If, however, the mother's care is unsatisfactory and has been disrupted, then the fact that the child is very young will not prevent an order being made for the child to live with the father.[990] There is no general principle that a child would be better off with the parent of the same-sex as them.[991]

Relevant characteristics will include the child's cultural and religious background.[992] The weight that is given to a child's religious beliefs will depend on the age of the child.[993] There may be cases in which the child's background includes a number of competing elements, in which case the court will try to make an order that reflects these different elements.[994] The age of the child may also affect his or her ability to cope with an order for residence to be shared.[995]

---

985. *Re B (Residence Order: Status Quo)* [1998] 1 F.L.R. 368.
986. *Re H (Children)* [2007] EWCA Civ 529.
987. *Re M (Child's Upbringing)* [1996] 2 F.L.R. 441; *Re F (Shared Residence)* [2009] EWCA Civ 313; *M v. M (Residence)* [2010] EWHC 3579 (Fam); *TB v. DB* [2013] EWHC 2275 (Fam).
988. *Re W (A Minor) (Residence Order)* [1992] 2 F.L.R. 332.
989. [1996] 2 F.L.R. 499 at 505.
990. *Re D (A Child) (Residence: Ability to Parent)* [2001] 2 F.C.R. 751.
991. *Re N* [2009] EWHC 1807 (Fam).
992. *Re M (Child's Upbringing)* [1996] 2 F.L.R. 441.
993. *Re M* [2017] EWCA Civ 2164.
994. *Re S (Change of Names: Cultural Factors)* [2001] 2 F.L.R. 1005.
995. *Re W (A Child)* [2005] EWCA Civ 1276.

*E. Potential Harm*

*400.* If the child is at risk from his or her parents, then the case may be one requiring the intervention of the local authority. More subtle forms of harm, falling short of the threshold necessary for a care order, may also be taken into account in deciding upon matters of residence and contact. The harm caused to a child by witnessing domestic violence will be an important factor, as will emotional harm caused by one parent's hostility to the child maintaining a relationship with the other parent.[996]

*F. Capability of Potential Carers*

*401.* There is no presumption that a mother is more capable of meeting the needs of a child than is a father, although the fact that mothers continue to assume greater responsibility for their children's care during intact relationships does mean that they are often better able to demonstrate their capability for meeting the child's needs upon separation.

The fact that the checklist refers to 'any other person' raises the question as to whether – and, if so, when – such a person will be preferred to a parent. Again, much will depend on the circumstances of the case: in one case the status quo might suggest that the child should remain with unrelated carers;[997] in another, religious and cultural factors may outweigh such considerations.[998] As Thorpe L.J. noted in *Re H (a child: residence),*[999] a non-parent may become a child's 'psychological parent' if he or she assumes primary responsibility for that child's care, while the child might cease to regard the birth parent as the 'natural' parent. However, in contested cases, the court will now have to consider the presumption of parental involvement when deciding whether or not to make a child arrangements order for the child to live with a non-parent.

§5. Consequences of a Child Arrangements Order

*402.* The making of a child arrangements order naming the person with whom the child should live is an important step, since that person will have day-to-day responsibility for the child. It is therefore logical that such an order should confer parental responsibility if the person in whose favour it is made does not already have it.[1000] A child arrangements order naming a person which whom the child

---

996. *V v. V (Contact: Implacable Hostility)* [2004] 2 F.L.R. 851; *M v. M (Residence)* [2010] EWHC 3579 (Fam).
997. *J v. C* [1970] A.C. 668; *Re P. (s. 91(14) Guidelines) (Residence and Religious Heritage)* [1999] 2 F.L.R. 573.
998. *Re M (Child's Upbringing)* [1996] 2 F.L.R. 441.
999. [2002] 3 F.C.R. 277.
1000. *Children Act* 1989, s. 12(2).

should have contact may also confer parental responsibility at the court's discretion.[1001] Parental responsibility conferred by child arrangements order will last for the duration of the order.[1002] Since the court, in making a child arrangements order naming the person with whom the child should live, has decided that it is in the best interests of the child to live with the person named in the order, such an order also has the effect of bringing any existing care order to an end. One less obvious consequence of a child arrangements order naming with whom the child should live is that while it is in force, no one can change the child's surname without either the written consent of all those who have parental responsibility or the approval of the court.[1003]

403. In general, a person named in a child arrangements orders as the person with whom the child should live may choose where the family home is to be. But the making of such an order may be influenced by the place where the child is to reside as well as the person who is to be the primary carer. For example, the availability of schools within a particular locality may be an important factor to take into account, as may the ability of the child to maintain regular contact with the non-residential parent. So what happens if the residential parent wants to move to another part of the country? Although there are no specific statutory restrictions on moves within England and Wales, it is possible for the non-residential parent to seek to prevent such a move by means of a prohibited steps order.[1004] Historically, the courts were unwilling to impose such restrictions,[1005] except in exceptional cases where the relationship between the child and the other parent would be severely impaired,[1006] or where the move was specifically intended to frustrate the other parent's contact with the child.[1007] Internal relocation cases were thus approached quite differently to cases where the residential parent wished to move outside the jurisdiction. However, in *Re C (Internal relocation)*,[1008] the Court of Appeal found this distinction, which gave the resident parent more freedom to move within the UK than to relocate outside the UK to be without any satisfactory foundation. Lady Justice Black held that the governing principle in *any* relocation case was the welfare of the child concerned. The outcome would depend entirely on the facts of the case. The court is unlikely to impose restrictions on a move to the next village but where the move is likely to meaningfully impact the relationship of a child with one of his parents, the case will merit the same sort of careful consideration as external relocation cases.[1009]

---

1001. *Ibid.*, s. 12(2A); *See* for example, *Re B (No2)* [2017] EWHC 488 (Fam).
1002. *See supra*, para. 382.
1003. *Children Act* 1989, s. 13(1)(a).
1004. *Re F (Internal Relocation)* [2010] EWCA Civ 1428.
1005. *See*, e.g., *Re E (Minors) (Residence Orders)* [1997] 2 F.L.R. 638; *Re H (Residence Order: Placement Out of Jurisdiction)* [2004] EWHC 2935 (Fam).
1006. *Re S (a child)* [2002] EWCA Civ 1795; *Re H (Children) (Residence Order: Condition)* [2001] EWCA Civ 1338.
1007. *B v. B (Residence: Condition Limiting Geographic Area)* [2004] 2 F.L.R. 979.
1008. *Re C (Internal relocation)* [2015] EWCA Civ 1305.
1009. *Ibid.*, para. 54. *See also*, *Re R* [2016] EWCA Civ 1016.

§6. RESTRICTIONS ON REMOVAL OF CHILDREN FROM THE JURISDICTION

*404.* The issue of international relocation has become increasingly important in recent years, as people form relationships, move to new countries, split up and wish to return to their country and family of origin – or alternatively to follow a new partner to a new country. Employment opportunities may take a parent or a new partner to the other side of the world. Moves of this kind obviously have an impact on the child and on the relationship with the parent and wider family who are left behind. How, then, is the court to decide whether to authorize the move?

## I. Restrictions on Removal

*405.* The precise legal restrictions on the removal of a child from England and Wales depend on a number of factors. If only one person has parental responsibility for the child, then he or she is free to remove the child from the jurisdiction without consulting any other person or seeking authorization from the court. However, it is criminal offence for a parent who does not hold parental responsibility, or any other person, to remove a child from the jurisdiction without the consent of the parent with parental responsibility or leave of court. If more than one person has parental responsibility, then the consent of every such person, or the leave of the court, is required. And, where a child arrangements order naming the person with whom the child should live is in place, such consent must be in writing.[1010] No criminal offence is committed where the person who is named in a child arrangements order as a person with whom the child is to live, or a special guardian, removes the child from the UK for a period of less than 3 months.[1011] This parent is entitled to take the child out of the jurisdiction for up to one month without the consent of other persons with parental responsibility or the sanction of the court. This sensible exception means that the person who has day-to-day responsibility for the child under a child arrangements order can take the child abroad for short holidays without his or her plans being frustrated by the opposition of such other persons as possess parental responsibility.

## II. The Form of Application to the Court

*406.* The issue may come before the court in one of a number of ways. The person wishing to remove the child from the jurisdiction may make an application under section 13 of the Children Act 1989 if a child arrangements order is in force, or, alternatively, seek a specific issue order under section 8 of the Act.[1012] A person wishing to oppose the move may seek a prohibited steps order under section 8 with the aim of preventing it,[1013] assuming that he or she has standing to apply for such

---

1010. *Children Act* 1989, s. 13(1)(b).
1011. *Child Abduction Act 1984*, s. 1(4); *Children Act* 1989, s. 13(2).
1012. *See*, e.g., *AP v. TD (Relocation: Retention of Jurisdiction)* [2010] EWHC 2040 (Fam).
1013. *See*, e.g., *J v. S (Leave to Remove)* [2010] EWHC 2098 (Fam).

an order. In practice, it does not matter which of these approaches is adopted, as the court will apply the same principles in each case. Technically, the welfare checklist only has to be taken into account in assessing the welfare of the child in contested section 8 applications and proceedings under Part IV of the Children Act (which deals with the State's powers to intervene in a family on behalf of a child). The courts have, however, confirmed that although an application under section 13 is not technically subject to the welfare checklist, in cases concerning either external or internal relocation the only test that the court applies is the paramount principle as to the welfare of the child. The application of that test involves a holistic balancing exercise undertaken with the assistance, by analogy, of the welfare checklist, even where it is not statutorily applicable.[1014]

## III. Factors Taken into Account in Deciding Whether to Grant Leave

*407.* Statute dictates that the welfare of the child is the paramount consideration for the court in deciding any question relating to the child's upbringing.[1015] Historically, considerable weight was attached to the wishes of the primary care giver on the basis that frustrating the wishes of the primary carer might have an adverse effect on the care provided for the child.[1016] Thus judges have found, e.g., that there is a benefit to a child in the mother 'realizing or at least trying to realize her potential as a lawyer in Brazil',[1017] and – in granting leave to relocate to enable the primary carer's new partner to take up employment – that 'the welfare of the children cannot be achieved unless the new family has the ordinary opportunity to pursue its goals and to make its choices without unreasonable restriction'.[1018]

*408.* In the previously leading case of *Payne v. Payne,*[1019] the court outlined a number of express considerations for judges assessing whether or not the move was in the best interests of the child; whether the application to relocate was both genuine and realistic, whether opposition was motivated by genuine concern for the child or some ulterior motive, how far contact could be maintained with the parent left behind and the resulting detriment to relationship between parent and child, and finally the impact that refusing leave would have on the primary caregiving parent. In *Payne* itself the Court of Appeal reiterated the importance of the 'emotional and

---

1014. *Re C (Internal relocation)* [2015] EWCA Civ 1305, para. [82] *per* Vos LJ.
1015. *Children Act* 1989, s. 1(1). *See also Re TC and JC (Children: Relocation)* [2013] EWHC 292 (Fam), at para. 11, describing this as the 'only authentic principle to be applied when determining an application to relocate a child permanently overseas'.
1016. *See,* e.g., *Re B (Children) (Removal from the Jurisdiction)* [2001] 1 F.C.R. 108; *Re B (Removal from the Jurisdiction); Re S (Removal from the Jurisdiction)* [2003] EWCA Civ 1149.
1017. *Re MK (Relocation outside Jurisdiction)* [2006] EWCA Civ 1013, para. 44, per Arden L.J.
1018. *Re B (Removal from the Jurisdiction); Re S (Removal from the Jurisdiction)* [2003] EWCA Civ 1149.
1019. [2001] EWCA Civ 166.

psychological well-being of the primary carer' and directed that '[i]n any evaluation of the welfare of the child as the paramount consideration great weight must be given to this factor.'[1020]

*409.* In recent years, judges have distanced themselves from the idea that there is any presumption that the wishes of the primary care giver will receive the endorsement of the court and re-emphasized the centrality of the best interests of the child as the governing principle and the relevance of the welfare checklist. In *Re K,*[1021] the Court of Appeal emphasized that the only binding principle to come from *Payne v. Payne* is that the welfare of the child is paramount:

> the principle—the only authentic principle—that runs through the entire line of relocation authorities is that the welfare of the child is the court's paramount consideration. Everything that is considered by the court in reaching its determination is put into the balance with a view to measuring its impact on the child.

Black LJ further explained that the *Payne* guidance could be helpful in ensuring that all proper matters are considered in reaching the decision; however, the criteria should not dictate the outcome of the case.[1022]

*410.* In *Re F*, the Court of Appeal confirmed that the *Payne* criteria could be considered in cases where there was a more equal shared care arrangement in place if a judge considered it helpful and appropriate to do so.[1023] However, the Court emphasized the importance that the final decision is based on an investigation and evaluation of the child's best interests:

> The focus from beginning to end must be on the child's best interests. The child's welfare is paramount. Every case must be determined having regard to the 'welfare checklist', though of course also having regard, where relevant and helpful, to such guidance as may have been given by this court.[1024]

*411.* In the more recent case of *Re F,*[1025] the Court of Appeal overturned the decision of the trial judge on the basis that too much emphasis had been placed on the *Payne* guidance rather than considering the decision in welfare terms noting that:

> The questions identified in Payne may not be relevant on the facts of an individual case and the Court will be better placed if it concentrates not on assumptions or preconceptions but on the statutory welfare question which is before it.[1026]

---

1020. *Payne v. Payne* [2001] EWCA Civ 166, para. 41.
1021. *Re K (Children)* [2011] EWCA Civ 793,[141].
1022. *Ibid.*, [144].
1023. *Re F (A Child)* [2012] EWCA Civ 1364.
1024. *Ibid.*, [61].
1025. *Re F* [2015] EWCA Civ 882.
1026. *Ibid.*, para. 18 per Ryder LJ.

*412.* In *H v. C*,[1027] the Court of Appeal upheld a refusal to allow relocation from London to New York where the trial judge had reviewed the welfare checklist as well as number of other factors including those identified in *Payne,* stating that the court had engaged in a comprehensive holistic evaluation of the children's welfare as required by statute.

*413.* In *Re C*,[1028] Lord Justice Vos outlined the continued relevance of the *Payne* principles in both external and internal relocation cases as follows:

> In my judgment, one of the valid concerns about the *Payne* factors is that they do not adequately reflect the gender-neutral approach to these problems that the court will now adopt in every case. Whilst the *Payne* factors may still be of some utility in some cases, they are no part of the applicable test or the applicable principles. In some circumstances, the judge may find them useful. In others, the judge may not. If the judge finds them a useful guide to some of the factors that he should consider, he will be doing so only as part of the multi-factorial balancing exercise that is required.[1029]

## §7. Child Arrangements Order

*414.* The detailed criteria setting out who may apply for a child arrangements order, and the factors governing the making of such an order, are considered in Chapter 8. This section will simply note the circumstances in which a child arrangements order relating to persons with whom the child should live may be preferred to an adoption order. When making a child arrangements order the court must take account of a statutory presumption that the involvement of parents in a child's life is in the child's best interests unless the contrary is proved.[1030] If the child has a good relationship with the birth family, with extensive contact, a child arrangements order for the child to live with another person may be the more appropriate option.[1031] As with special guardianship orders, however, the lack of permanence offered by a child arrangements order may be a factor influencing the court's decision.[1032] As with the other orders considered in this chapter, each case will turn upon its own facts.

## §8. Foster Care

*415.* If a child is removed from his or her parents by virtue of a care order, or is voluntarily accommodated by the local authority at the request of the parents, it is

---

1027. *H v. C* [2015] EWCA Civ 1298.
1028. *Re C* [2015] EWCA Civ 1305.
1029. *Ibid.,* [83].
1030. *Children Act 1989*, s. 1(2A) as inserted by the *Children and Families Act 2014.*
1031. *Re B (Adoption Order)* [2001] EWCA Civ 347; *Re RA (Baby Relinquished for Adoption)* [2016] EWFC 47.
1032. *Re A (Placement of Child in Contravention of Adoption Act 1976, s. 11)* [2005] 2 F.L.R. 727.

common for the child to be looked after by local authority foster parents. Fostering is often a short-term option: the children may be able to return to their parents once matters at home have improved, or, if rehabilitation is not an option, may be placed with potential adopters. Foster parents do not acquire parental responsibility and thus their ability to do any more than provide day-to-day care is extremely limited. While longer-term foster care is not uncommon, the greater degree of commitment and security provided by adoption may tip the balance in favour of the latter where the choice lies between the two.[1033] Current Government policy is to minimize the time that children spend in foster care before adoption. Changes made by the Children and Families Act 2014 now require a local authority to consider placing children for whom adoption is a potential option with local authority foster parents who have been approved as prospective adopters.[1034]

*416.* Local authority fostering arrangements should be distinguished from private fostering arrangements. A child is defined as being privately fostered if he or she is under the age of 16 years and is provided with a home by someone who is not the child's parent or relative,[1035] who does not have parental responsibility for the child and who is not a local authority foster-parent.[1036] The fact that such arrangements are made privately, rather than at the instigation of the local authority, does not mean that they are unregulated.[1037] The local authority still has a duty to ensure that the welfare of the child is being satisfactorily safeguarded, and must visit the foster placement at regular intervals.[1038]

---

1033. *See*, e.g., the differences between the two identified in *Re V (Children)* [2013] EWCA Civ 913.
1034. *Children Act 1989*, s. 22C (9A–9B).
1035. As defined by *Children Act 1989*, s. 105(1), this means a grandparent, step-parent, sibling or aunt or uncle (whether of the full-blood or half-blood or by affinity).
1036. *Children Act 1989*, s. 66(1).
1037. Although some cases may not be so clear-cut. *See* Harding and Newnham, 'Section 8 orders on the public-private law divide,'(2017) 39(3) *Journal of Social Welfare and Family Law* pp. 83–101.
1038. *Ibid.*, s. 67(1); *Children (Private Arrangements for Fostering) Regulations* 2005, S.I. 2005/1533.

# Chapter 9. Kinship and Affinity

*417.* Family law in England and Wales tends to focus on the nuclear family of parent(s) and minor children. Relatively little attention is paid to the rights and responsibilities of wider kin. There are, however, a number of contexts in which wider family relationships are relevant.

*418.* First, as has been discussed, persons who are related to each other within the prohibited degrees are barred from entering into a marriage or civil partnership.[1039] In certain circumstances, restrictions are also placed on a step-parent marrying or entering into a civil partnership with a stepchild, but no other bars to marriage or civil partnership are created by affinity.

*419.* Second, certain relatives are encompassed within the concept of 'associated persons',[1040] which is central to the remedies that are available in cases of domestic violence and the occupation of the family home. For these purposes 'relatives' are defined as a person's parents, grandparents, children, grandchildren, stepparents and stepchildren, plus siblings, aunts, uncles, nieces, nephews, and first cousins.[1041] The latter group may be 'of the full-blood or of the half-blood or by marriage or civil partnership'. Indeed, the definition includes not only the relatives of a person's spouse or civil partner (current or former), but also the relatives of a person's cohabitant (whether of the same or opposite sex, and whether the relationship is continuing or not).

The breadth of this definition – possibly the widest definition of relationships deemed to be familial in English law – is justified by the context, the aim of the legislation being to improve the remedies available for victims of domestic violence. Any person may apply for a non-molestation order against another person with whom they are associated in order to prevent violence or harassment.[1042]

In the context of occupation orders relating to the family home, by contrast, eligibility to apply is more tightly constrained. Only associated persons may apply, but not all associated persons will be eligible to do so. First, the order sought must relate to a property that was, or was intended to be, the home of the applicant and an associated person.[1043] Second, and more significantly, a relative may only apply for an order if he or she has a right under the general law to occupy the home.[1044] This means that a relative who does not have a legal or beneficial interest in the home conferring a right of occupation will be unable to apply for an order (and a relative who does have such a right will in any case have the alternative option of making an application under the Trusts of Land and Appointment of Trustees Act 1996).[1045]

---

1039. *See supra* Part II, Ch. 1, para. 143.
1040. *Family Law Act* 1996, s. 62(3)(d).
1041. *Ibid.*, s. 63(1), as amended by the *Domestic Violence, Crimes and Victims Act* 2004.
1042. *Ibid.*, s. 42.
1043. *Ibid.*, s. 33(1)(b).
1044. *Ibid.*, s. 33(1).
1045. *See infra* Part III, Ch. 1, para. 440.

*420.* The third area in which wider kin may have significant rights is the law of intestacy. Legislation sets out a list of persons who are entitled to inherit the estate of a deceased person who died without making a will, and wider kin – down to the issue of aunts and uncles of the half-blood – may stand to inherit if there are no closer relatives.[1046]

*421.* The law also recognizes that relatives may provide substitute care for children who cannot live with their parents.[1047] Local authorities must give preference to placing a child with a relative in cases where the parents are unable to care for the child.[1048] The concept of a special guardianship order was devised in part with this situation in mind.[1049] While it is a criminal offence for anyone other than an adoption agency to place a child for adoption or make other arrangements for a child to be adopted,[1050] this bar does not extend to placements with relatives (defined in this context as grandparents, siblings, uncles and aunts, whether of the full-blood or half-blood, or by marriage or civil partnership).[1051] Of course, if a child is adopted by his or her relatives, a new nuclear family is created, in line with the 'legal transplant' model of adoption.[1052]

---

1046. *See infra* Part IV, Ch. 1, paras 497, 499.
1047. *See*, e.g., *Re A and B (One Parent Killed by Another)* [2011] 1 F.L.R. 783, although note that family members will not always be deemed suitable as carers (*A (a child) v. Leeds City Council* [2011] EWCA Civ 1365).
1048. *Children Act 1989* s. 22c.
1049. *See supra* Part II, Ch. 7, para. 357.
1050. *Adoption and Children Act* 2002, s. 93.
1051. *Ibid.*, s. 144(1). *See*, e.g., *B v. C* (Surrogacy: Adoption) [2015] EWFC 17.
1052. *See supra* Part II, Ch. 7, para. 354.

# Part III. Matrimonial Property Law

## Chapter 1. Rights and Obligations of Spouses

### §1. GENERAL PRINCIPLES

*422.* It is a matter of debate whether England and Wales actually have what could be termed a 'matrimonial property regime'. Certainly, there is no statutory code labelled as such, and Antokolskaia is justified in her suggestion that 'the concept of "matrimonial property regime", as understood in Continental Europe, is unknown in England and Wales'.[1053] The basic rule is that during the marriage each spouse retains ownership and control over his or her property, whether acquired before or during the marriage. On divorce, by contrast, little regard is paid to strict ownership rights when deciding how property should be allocated on the basis of need. Ownership of assets – particularly those acquired before the marriage – may, however, be taken into account when deciding how any surplus should be divided.[1054]

### §2. THE HOUSEHOLD EXPENSES

*423.* In keeping with the general reluctance of the legislature to lay down rules regarding the specific obligations of spouses during their marriage, there is no requirement that spouses share the household expenses equally, or even that each should make a fair contribution. While it is possible for one spouse to apply for maintenance from the other while the marriage is still subsisting, the relevant provisions clearly envisage that such applications will generally only be made where the parties have separated, since any periodical payments will come to an end after the spouses have been living together for six months.[1055]

*424.* The only specific provision relating to household expenses deals with the narrow question of the ownership of any surplus saved from a housekeeping allowance. At common law, any such surplus belonged to the person who had provided the allowance. This was subsequently amended by statute, and under the Married

---

1053. M. Antokolskaia, *Harmonization of Family Law in Europe: A Historical Perspective A Tale of Two Millennia* 467 (Intersentia 2006).
1054. *See* generally Part III, Ch. 2.
1055. *See infra*, para. 422.

Women's Property Act 1964 a wife became entitled (subject to any contrary agreement) to half of any savings she made out of a housekeeping allowance. However, it was not until 2010 that thrifty house-husbands were deemed worthy of recognition: the Equality Act of that year provided that any savings were to be shared between the spouses regardless of who had made the allowance, and the title of the 1964 legislation was accordingly recast to reflect the gender-neutral nature of the amended rule.[1056]

425. The general rule is that a spouse retains ownership of his or her income, and any purchases belong to the person who pays for them. If the spouses operate a joint bank account into which both make payments, then the money in the account will be regarded as joint property.[1057] Purchases made with money from a joint bank account are not, however, necessarily owned jointly: items intended for joint use will be, but items intended for individual use will be owned by the person who made the purchase.

§3. MAINTENANCE DURING THE MARRIAGE

426. Although the basic principle is that each spouse retains ownership of his or her own financial resources, the law does recognize that spouses have obligations to each other, and a spouse who fails to support the other can, in certain circumstances, be required to do so. It should be noted that the rules grew out of the need to ensure that a deserted spouse, or one who had left because of the other's conduct, was properly provided for: the ability of the state to dictate the contributions of the parties where they remain under the same roof is more limited.

427. Under the Domestic Proceedings and Magistrates' Courts Act 1978, the Family Court has powers to make financial orders (periodical payments or a lump sum of up to GBP 1,000) if the respondent has failed to provide reasonable maintenance for the applicant; has failed to provide, or to make a proper contribution towards, reasonable maintenance for any child of the family; has behaved in such a way that the other cannot reasonably be expected to live with him or her; or has deserted the applicant.[1058] In considering whether to make such an order, the court is referred to a range of factors and directed that first consideration is to be given to the welfare while a minor of any child of the family.[1059] An order for periodical payments may be time limited; if not, it may be cancelled during any subsequent divorce proceedings, and will end when the person receiving it remarries, or on the death of either party, or if the spouses subsequently live together for a continuous period of six months.[1060]

---

1056. *Matrimonial Property Act* 1964, s. 1, as amended by the *Equality Act* 2010, s. 200. As with other provisions of the Equality Act in this context, this has yet to be brought into force.
1057. *Jones v. Maynard* [1951] Ch. 572.
1058. *Domestic Proceedings and Magistrates' Courts Act* 1978, s. 1.
1059. *Ibid.*, s. 3.
1060. *Ibid.*, s. 25.

If the spouses separated by consent and have been living apart for at least three months, during which time one has been making periodical payments to the other, the recipient may apply for a periodical payments order.[1061]

The Family Court also has the power to make a consent order,[1062] if it is satisfied that the provision set out in the order has been agreed by the spouses and that it would not be contrary to the interests of justice to make the order.

*428.*   Finally, a spouse may apply for periodical payments and/or a lump sum on the ground that the other spouse has failed to provide reasonable maintenance for the applicant or has failed to provide, or make proper contribution towards, reasonable maintenance for a child of the family.[1063] Again, in considering whether to make such an order, first consideration is to be given to the welfare while a minor of any child of the family, and a range of factors, similar to those that apply when the court is considering the division of assets on divorce, must be taken into account.

§4. THE MATRIMONIAL HOME

*429.*   One leading comparativist has suggested that a 'special regime for the matrimonial home has been created at law and in equity over the course of the last decades'.[1064] This, however, is something of a moot point. There are no statutory provisions that apply only to spouses, although spouses do have certain advantages over other home-sharers. And there is no statutory code to determine the ownership or regulate the disposition of the matrimonial home. Every spouse will have a right to occupy the family home, but ownership is largely governed by the law of trusts, and the judiciary is divided on the extent to which the relationship of the parties should be relevant in the determination of their property rights. There are steps that one spouse can take to protect the other from disposing of the matrimonial home without his or her consent, but such protection is not automatic and may simply delay the sale. A spouse who is the sole legal and beneficial owner of the matrimonial home may therefore be free to dispose of it as he or she chooses, without even the requirement of consulting the other spouse. The matrimonial home is afforded some protection against third parties in the context of bankruptcy, but otherwise is not treated as a special form of property in such disputes.

These four areas – the determination of ownership, the rights of occupation, the regulation of dispositions and the protection afforded against third parties – will now be considered in turn.

---

1061. *Ibid.*, s. 7.
1062. *Ibid.*, s. 6.
1063. *Matrimonial Causes Act* 1973, s. 27.
1064. M. Antokolskaia, *Harmonization of Family Law in Europe: A Historical Perspective A Tale of Two Millennia* 469 (Intersentia 2006).

## I. Ownership

*430.* Ownership of the matrimonial home – like ownership of the non-matrimonial home – is governed by the law of trusts rather than by any special rules. The House of Lords has, however, indicated that the law of trusts should take into account the nature of the parties' relationship when drawing inferences about their intentions: as Baroness Hale of Richmond stated, 'to put it at its lowest, the interpretation to be put on the behaviour of people living together in an intimate relationship may be different from the interpretation to be put upon similar behaviour between commercial men'.[1065]

*431.* The distinction between legal and beneficial ownership is fundamental to the law of property in England and Wales. The legal owners have the right to deal with and control the property: i.e., to sell or mortgage it and to decide who occupies it. The beneficial owners have the right to occupy the property – subject to the decision of the legal owners – and a right to a share of the proceeds, commensurate with their respective beneficial interests, if the property is sold. The legal and beneficial owners will often be the same person; a married couple, e.g., may be both owners at law and owners in equity. They may be different: one spouse may hold the title on trust for both of them, or indeed for third parties who have contributed to the purchase of the property.

*432.* Ascertaining who the legal owners of the matrimonial home are is easy; they are the persons to whom the property has been conveyed, or, increasingly, the persons in whose names the property is registered at the Land Registry. The conveyance or registration will be conclusive save in cases of fraud or mistake.

*433.* Ascertaining who the beneficial owners of the matrimonial home are is rather more difficult. The starting point is to ask whether there is any written evidence of a declaration of trust.[1066] When most properties were unregistered, it was common for the conveyance to declare the purchasers' beneficial interests. By contrast, in registered land, it was an official policy to keep details of such trusts off the official register. It gradually came to be appreciated that this led to later disputes between the parties as to the extent of their beneficial interest in the property. Since 1997, therefore, it has been the practice that when two or more persons purchase a property together, they are directed to complete a declaration as to their beneficial interests in the property.[1067] A declaration of this kind is conclusive in the absence of fraud or mistake.[1068]

*434.* What of those couples who purchased their home in joint names before 1997, or who have failed to complete a declaration? The decision of the House of

---

1065. *Stack v. Dowden* [2007] UKHL 17, para. 42. This does not apply if the property has been bought by the spouses as an investment: *Gaspar v. Zaleski* [2017] EWHC 1770 (Ch).
1066. *Law of Property Act 1925*, s. 53(1)(b).
1067. *Land Registration Rules 2003.*
1068. *Goodman v. Gallant* [1986] 1 F.L.R. 513; *Pankhania v. Chandegra* [2012] EWCA Civ 1438. It may, however, be varied by later agreement or proprietary estoppel.

Lords in *Stack v. Dowden*[1069] addressed this issue: although that case dealt with a cohabiting relationship, their reasoning is equally applicable to married couples. All members of the House agreed that the starting point would be to assume that the joint legal owners were also joint beneficial owners: 'at least in the domestic consumer context, a conveyance into joint names indicates both legal and beneficial joint tenancy, unless and until the contrary is proved'.[1070] The majority held that it should be difficult to establish the contrary: the burden would be on the person seeking to establish that the parties did intend their beneficial interests to be different from their legal interests. Such an intention could be inferred from a wide range of factors – discussions between the parties, who paid for what, whether they had children, how far they pooled their finances – but it was emphasized that '[a]t the end of the day, having taken all this into account, cases in which the joint legal owners are to be taken to have intended that their beneficial interests should be different from their legal interests will be very unusual.'[1071]

435. Not all matrimonial homes are owned in joint names, however. Just as joint beneficial ownership is to be inferred from joint legal ownership, so the starting point in cases of sole legal ownership is sole beneficial ownership. The burden will lie on the spouse claiming an interest in the home to establish that such an interest has arisen. It should be borne in mind that the need for one spouse to establish an interest in the matrimonial home will generally arise only where the legal owner of the property has died and it is necessary to determine the extent of the estate or if there is a dispute with a third party. In the former context, evidence of discussions between the parties may be difficult to produce; in the latter the courts tend to be suspicious of claims by couples about their unevidenced intentions. Fox L.J. warned in *Midland Bank Plc v. Dobson* that:

> assertions made by a husband and wife as to a common intention formed thirty years ago regarding joint ownership, of which there is no contemporary evidence and which happens to accommodate their current need to defeat the claims of a creditor, must be received by the Courts with caution.[1072]

436. In determining whether one spouse has an interest in the matrimonial home that is registered in the sole name of the other, the starting point is, once again, to ask whether there has been a declaration of trust. If there is written evidence of this, as required by section 53(1)(b) of the Law of Property Act 1925, then this is conclusive as to the parties' respective interests. If the promise of an interest was merely oral, it may give rise to an interest under a constructive trust if the promisee relied on it to his or her detriment.[1073] A claimant who wishes to establish 'detrimental reliance' must show that he or she did something as a result of the promise of an

---

1069. [2007] UKHL 17.
1070. At para. 58.
1071. At para. 69. Intentions may, however, change over time: *see*, e.g., *Jones v. Kernott* [2011] UKSC 53.
1072. [1986] 1 F.L.R. 171, 174. *See also The Crown Prosecution Service v. Piper* [2011] EWHC 3570 (Admin).
1073. *Lloyds Bank v. Rosset* [1991] A.C. 107.

interest – i.e., something he or she would not have done but for that promise. This may be making a financial contribution to the mortgage repayments or household expenses, making substantial improvements to the property,[1074] or unpaid work in a partner's business.[1075] Everyday contributions such as housework, decorating[1076] or looking after the children of the relationship are, by themselves, given little weight, since the courts have taken the view that such contributions to the relationship are made out of love and affection and not in the expectation of an interest in the property.[1077]

*437.* If there have been no conversations about the ownership of the property, then the next question is whether there is any evidence from which a common intention to share the beneficial interest can be inferred.[1078] It remains a moot point as to exactly what types of contributions will be taken to indicate such an intention. A direct financial contribution to the purchase price will usually be sufficient to justify such an inference.[1079] It seems likely that indirect contributions to the purchase price – e.g., where one party pays household bills, enabling the other to make the mortgage repayments – will also suffice. This had been a matter of debate for some time due to conflicting authorities. The House of Lords in *Gissing v. Gissing*[1080] seemed to be of the view that indirect contributions would suffice, but in the leading case of *Lloyds Bank v. Rosset* Lord Bridge suggested – *obiter* – that as he understood the authorities it was 'extremely doubtful' whether anything sort of a direct contribution would do. When the issue came back before the House of Lords again, in *Stack v. Dowden*, Lord Walker doubted whether Lord Bridge's view was in line with the earlier authorities. Since this statement was itself *obiter*, the point still lacks resolution at the highest level, but there is a High Court decision on point in which indirect contributions were accepted as justifying an inference that the beneficial interest was to be shared.[1081] Recently, paying for improvements to the property has also been held to generate an interest.[1082] As yet, however, non-financial contributions (whether making improvements to the property, working unpaid in a partner's business, or performing domestic chores) have not, by themselves, been seen as sufficient.[1083]

*438.* Once it has been established that a spouse has an interest in the matrimonial home, the next question is how that interest should be quantified. In quantifying the shares of the parties, the court will seek to ascertain what their intentions

---

1074. *Eves v. Eves* [1975] 1 W.L.R. 1338; *Cox v. Jones* [2004] EWHC 1486.
1075. *H v. M (Property: Beneficial Interest)* [1992] 2 F.L.R. 229.
1076. *Lloyds Bank v. Rosset* [1991] A.C. 107.
1077. *See*, e.g., *Curran v. Collins* [2015] EWCA Civ 404.
1078. *Lloyds Bank v. Rosset* [1991] A.C. 107; *Jones v. Kernott* [2011] UKSC 53; *Capehorn v. Harris and Another* [2015] EWCA Civ 955.
1079. *Lloyds Bank v. Rosset* [1991] A.C. 107; *The Crown Prosecution Service v. Piper* [2011] EWHC 3570 (Admin); although *see Lightfoot v. Lightfoot-Brown* [2005] EWCA Civ 201.
1080. [1971] A.C. 886.
1081. *Le Foe v. Le Foe* [2001] 2 F.L.R. 97.
1082. *Aspden v. Elvy* [2012] EWHC 1387 (Ch).
1083. *See* respectively *James v. Thomas* [2007] EWCA Civ 1212; *Geary v. Rankine* [2012] EWCA Civ 555; *Burns v. Burns* [1984] F.L.R. 216.

were. Its task is to undertake 'a survey of the whole course of dealing between the parties … [and take] account of all conduct which throws light on the question what shares were intended'.[1084] In the absence of any evidence as to what the parties' intentions were, the court may be 'driven to impute an intention to the parties which they may never have had',[1085] in which case 'the answer is that each is entitled to that share which the court considers fair having regard to the whole course of dealing between them in relation to the property'.[1086] At this stage, non-financial contributions can be taken into account in quantifying what is fair.[1087]

439.   There is, in addition, a specific statutory provision that substantial improvements to the family home made by a spouse, civil partner, fiancé(e), or a person who has agreed to enter into a civil partnership will confer a share (or enlarged share) in that property, unless there is an agreement to the contrary.[1088] The contribution of the claimant may take the form of money or money's worth, and it is for the court to quantify the claimant's share according to what it perceives to be just. Section 37 has generated little case law, largely because it was enacted at the same time as the importance of property rights to spouses diminished. The courts acquired sweeping powers to reallocate assets on divorce and judges therefore preferred to bypass considerations of who owned what at the end of the marriage.[1089] The few cases that there are do give some guidance on what will be deemed 'substantial': installing central heating was held to be sufficient,[1090] as was the expenditure of GBP 227 on a property worth GBP 9,000,[1091] but contributions to looking after the house – as opposed to repairing, altering or improving it – do not count for these purposes.[1092] Even making a 'substantial' contribution does not guarantee a substantial share: in *Re Nicholson* the wife's interest was raised from 1/2 to 21/41ths and in *Daubney v. Daubney*[1093] the husband's share was increased from 1/2 to 7/12ths. And in *Hosking v. Michaelides*,[1094] contributing GBP 20,000 to the cost of a swimming pool did not lead to the contributor obtaining any interest in the property, as there was no evidence that it had increased the value of the property.

---

1084. *Stack v. Dowden* [2007] UKHL 17, para. 61, quoting from Law Commission, *Sharing Homes: A Discussion Paper* para. 4.27 (2002).
1085. *Jones v. Kernott* [2011] UKSC 53.
1086. *Oxley v. Hiscock* [2004] EWCA Civ 546, para. 69, per Chadwick LJ; *Jones v. Kernott* [2011] UKSC 53, para. [51](4), per Lord Walker and Lady Hale.
1087. *See*, e.g., *Graham-York v. York* [2015] EWCA Civ 72.
1088. *Matrimonial Proceedings and Property Act* 1970, s. 37 (spouses); *Civil Partnership Act* 2004, s. 65 (civil partners) and s. 74 (persons who have agreed to enter into a civil partnership); *Law Reform (Miscellaneous Provisions) Act* 1970, s. 2(1) (engaged couples).
1089. *Kowalczuk v. Kowalczuk* [1973] 1 W.L.R. 930; *Griffiths v. Griffiths* [1974] 1 W.L.R. 1350.
1090. *Re Nicholson* [1974] 1 W.L.R. 476.
1091. *Samuels (WA)'s Trustee v. Samuels* (1973) 233 E.G. 149.
1092. *Kowalczuk v. Kowalczuk* [1973] 1 W.L.R. 930.
1093. [1976] 2 W.L.R. 959.
1094. [2004] All E.R. (D) 147.

## II. Occupation

*440.* If the spouses are joint beneficial owners of the matrimonial home, each will have a right to occupy it as a consequence. Yet even a spouse who has no interest in a property belonging to the other still has the right to occupy it by virtue of statutory 'home rights'.[1095] This means that he or she cannot be excluded from the home by the other party, unless such removal has been sanctioned by the court.[1096] A court may also make an order granting a spouse who is not currently in occupation of the home the right to enter and occupy it, even against the wishes of the other spouse.[1097]

Such rights were first conferred upon spouses by the Matrimonial Homes Act 1967, which was enacted to protect the position of the deserted wife whose husband had sold or mortgaged the property to a third party. Provision was thus made for the spouse's right to occupy the matrimonial home to be protected against a third party – such as a purchaser or mortgagee – by registration. Such registration does not guarantee that the spouse will be able to remain in occupation once the property has been sold to a third party. In such a case, the court still has the power to make an occupation order regulating the occupation of the property[1098] and is entitled to take account of the circumstances of the purchaser as well as those of the spouse.[1099]

Home rights will generally come to an end when the marriage ends – whether by death, divorce or annulment – but given the extensive powers of the courts in these three contexts this is unlikely to cause hardship to the occupying spouse.

## III. Disposition

*441.* If one spouse is the sole legal and beneficial owner of the home, then he or she can deal with it without regard to the other spouse's wishes, and the only option for the non-owning spouse is to register his or her home rights.

If one spouse is the sole legal owner, but the other has a beneficial interest in the property, then the former is directed by statute to consult the latter about any dealings with the property.[1100] This requirement applies to all trustee-beneficiary relationships, rather than simply to spouses, but is directory rather than mandatory.

If the spouse who is the sole legal owner sells the property, entitlement to the proceeds of the sale is dictated by the parties' respective beneficial interests.

*442.* Problems have arisen where one spouse mortgages the matrimonial home and then defaults on the payments. Although the mortgagee is not entitled to that

---

1095. *Family Law Act* 1996, s. 30.
1096. For examples of such removal *see*, e.g., *Grubb v. Grubb* [2009] EWCA Civ 976; *L (Children)* [2012] EWCA Civ 721.
1097. *Ibid.*, s. 33(3).
1098. *Ibid.*, s. 34(2).
1099. *Kashmir Kaur v. Gill* [1988] Fam. 110.
1100. *Trusts of Land and Appointment of Trustees Act* 1996, s. 11. The protection afforded by home rights appears to have been downplayed in the recent case of *Fred Perry (Holdings) Ltd v. Genis* [2015] 1 P. & C.R. DG5.

part of the equity that belongs to the other spouse, if the debt exceeds the equity it will be important to ascertain whose interest has priority. The law in this area is highly complex, but can be summarized by saying that case law has established that a spouse with only a beneficial interest in the property will have to cede priority to the mortgagee if the mortgage was used to purchase the property,[1101] if the spouse consented to or knew of the mortgage,[1102] or if the mortgage was executed by two or more legal owners.[1103] Even if none of these factors are present, the beneficial interest of the spouse will only be given priority over the mortgage if the mortgagee knew or could have known of that interest.[1104]

## IV. Protection

*443.* The legal protection afforded to the matrimonial home in the context of disputes with third parties depends on the precise nature of the dispute.

### A. Bankruptcy

*444.* If a spouse becomes bankrupt, and the trustee in bankruptcy applies for the sale of the matrimonial home, the court is directed to consider a range of factors in deciding whether or not to order sale. The interests of the creditors are one of the factors to be considered, and, one year after the bankrupt's property has vested in the trustee in bankruptcy, it will be assumed that their interests are paramount, in the absence of exceptional circumstances.[1105] The legislation thus ensures some delay for the family before the home has to be sold; the reported cases have all focused on whether there are sufficiently exceptional circumstances to justify a delay beyond a year. In general, a restrictive approach has been adopted: the illness of the bankrupt's spouse may justify a short respite,[1106] while a terminal illness may justify an indefinite postponement.[1107] Occasionally, however, a more family-sensitive approach may be taken, with the caring needs of the bankrupt's wife being taken into account in *Re Haghighat (A Bankrupt)*,[1108] and the network of neighbourly support for two teenage girls leading to a refusal of sale in *Martin-Sklan v. White*.[1109]

---

1101. *Abbey National Building Society v. Cann* [1991] A.C. 56.
1102. *Bristol and West Building Society v. Henning* [1985] 1 W.L.R. 778.
1103. *City of London Building Society v. Flegg* [1988] A.C. 54.
1104. *Law of Property Act* 1925, s. 199 (unregistered land); *Land Registration Act* 2002, Sch. 3 para. 2 (registered land).
1105. *Insolvency Act* 1986, s. 335A (where the property is co-owned), and s. 336 (where a spouse or civil partner has home rights).
1106. *Re Raval (A bankrupt)* [1998] 1 F.L.R. 718, but note the more generous approach in *Claughton v. Charalambas* [1999] 1 F.L.R. 740.
1107. *See*, e.g., *Judd v. Brown* [1998] 2 F.L.R. 360.
1108. [2009] 1 F.L.R. 1271.
1109. [2006] EWHC 3313 (Ch).

## B. Claims by Other Creditors

445.  If the matrimonial home is co-owned, any application for sale by a creditor must be made under section 14 of the Trusts of Land and Appointment of Trustees Act 1996. Under section 15, the courts are required to have regard to a number of factors in considering whether sale should be ordered at the instigation of a creditor: the intentions of the person or persons who created the trust; the purposes for which the property subject to the trust is held; the welfare of any minor who occupies or might reasonably be expected to occupy any land subject to the trust as his or her home; and the interests of any secured creditor of any beneficiary. The wishes of the debtor's spouse do not figure in this list, and the departure of the debtor has been held to signal that the purpose of providing a matrimonial or family home has come to an end.[1110] Childless spouses may therefore be worse off than under the insolvency regime. Their rights and needs are not a special consideration for the court; if the other party has left and there are no children then under the current approach none of the factors listed in section 15(1) will apply. This lack of specific protection is exacerbated by the fact that the general tendency of the courts has been to favour the interests of the creditors.[1111]

If the matrimonial home is not co-owned, it is a moot point whether the court is entitled to set any factors against the creditor's application for sale.[1112]

---

1110. *Bank of Ireland v. Bell* [2001] 2 F.L.R. 809.
1111. *Pritchard Englefield (A Firm) v. Steinberg* [2004] EWHC 1908 (Ch); *Bank of Ireland v. Bell* [2001] 2 F.L.R. 809; *First National Bank v. Achampong* [2003] EWCA Civ 487; *Fred Perry (Holdings) Ltd v. Genis & Anr* [2015] 1 P & C.R. DG5.
1112. *Pickering v. Wells* [2002] 2 F.L.R. 798; contrast *Close Invoice Finance Ltd v. Pile* [2008] EWHC 1580 (Ch).

# Chapter 2. Division of Assets on Divorce, Dissolution or Annulment

## §1. Introduction

*446.* Across Europe, the property consequences of divorce – as distinct from maintenance – are determined by the marital property regime applicable to or chosen by the spouses. This is not the case in England and Wales. As the then President of the Family Division, Sir Mark Potter, pointed out:

> [a]lmost uniquely our jurisdiction does not have a marital property regime and it is scarcely appropriate to classify our jurisdiction as having a marital regime of separation of property. More correctly we have no regime, simply accepting that each spouse owns his or her own separate property during the marriage but subject to the court's wide distributive powers in prospect upon a decree of judicial separation, nullity or divorce.[1113]

The same rules now apply to civil partners,[1114] but for the sake of convenience, this chapter will focus on the treatment of spouses. Since the principles applied by the courts in exercising these wide distributive powers have fluctuated over the years, a brief historical explanation is necessary in order to show how the law has developed.

*447.* When judicial divorce was first introduced in the nineteenth century, the court could order that a man pay maintenance to his former wife, or that a wife's property be settled for the benefit of the husband and children, but otherwise had no power to reallocate assets between the parties.[1115] A claim by a non-owner spouse to a share in the former matrimonial home had to be determined by the law of trusts.[1116] The powers of the courts were gradually extended,[1117] but it was not until the Matrimonial Proceedings and Property Act 1970 (later consolidated in the Matrimonial Causes Act 1973) that the courts acquired their current extensive powers to reallocate assets. As Lord Denning M.R. explained:

> The law takes the rights and obligations of the parties all together and puts the pieces into a mixed bag. Such pieces are the right to occupy the matrimonial home or to have a share in it, the obligation to maintain the … children and so on. The court than takes out the pieces and hands them to the two parties … so that each can provide for the future with the pieces allotted to him or to

---

1113. *Charman v. Charman* [2007] EWCA Civ 503, para. 124.
1114. *Civil Partnership Act* 2004, s. 72 and Sch. 5, and *see Lawrence v. Gallagher* [2012] EWCA Civ 394, in which it was noted that the fact that the parties were civil partners was of little significance.
1115. *See supra*, para. 12.
1116. *See supra* Part III, Ch. 1.
1117. S. Cretney, *Family Law in the Twentieth Century: A History* Ch. 10 (Oxford U. Press 2003).

her … without paying any too nice a regard to their legal or equitable rights but simply according to what is the fairest provision for the future.[1118]

The courts now have the power to make a range of financial orders (including orders for secured or unsecured periodical payments or a lump sum),[1119] property adjustment orders (order for the transfer or settlement of property or for the variation of an existing settlement),[1120] pension sharing orders[1121] and order for sale of any property belonging to the parties.[1122]

*448.* The range of orders that can be made is matched only by the width of the discretion conferred upon the courts. Under the original terms of the legislation, judges were directed to exercise their powers so as 'to place the parties, so far as is practicable and, having regard to their conduct, just to do so, in the financial position in which they would have been if the marriage had not broken down and each had properly discharged his or her financial obligations towards each other'.[1123] However, the application of the 'minimal loss' principle, as it was known, did pose certain problems. First, there was the practical problem that the resources that had maintained the intact family at a certain standard of living would often not provide the same standard of living for the parties once they had established separate households.[1124] Second, the very concept of ongoing obligations to a former spouse was inconsistent with the motivating factor behind the 1969 divorce reforms, namely the idea that a marriage that had in fact ended should be legally terminated and the spouses freed to form new unions.[1125] In response to these problems, and in the wake of pressure for reform from a campaign group representing divorced husbands and second wives, the Matrimonial and Family Proceedings Act 1984 removed the minimal loss principle and gave greater weight to the importance of each party doing everything possible to become self-sufficient.

*449.* The removal of the minimal loss principle meant that there was no longer any statutory direction setting out what the objective of courts should be. The law as it now stands provides that 'first consideration' is to be given 'to the welfare while a minor of any child of the family who has not attained the age of 18',[1126] but it was quickly established that 'first' did not mean 'paramount'.[1127] Judges are referred to a list of specified factors to which they are to have particular regard, namely:[1128]

---

1118. *Hanlon v. The Law Society* [1981] A.C. 124, 147.
1119. *Matrimonial Causes Act* 1973, s. 23.
1120. *Ibid.*, s. 24.
1121. *Ibid.*, s. 24B.
1122. *Ibid.*, s. 24A.
1123. *Matrimonial Causes Act* 1973, s. 25(1).
1124. *See*, e.g., *Gojkovic v. Gojkovic* [1990] 2 All E.R. 84.
1125. *See*, e.g., *Minton v. Minton* [1979] A.C. 593.
1126. *Matrimonial Causes Act* 1973, s. 25(1).
1127. *Suter v. Suter* [1987] 2 F.L.R. 232.
1128. *Matrimonial Causes Act* 1973, s. 25(2).

(a) the income, earning capacity, property and other financial resources which each of the parties to the marriage has or is likely to have in the foreseeable future, including in the case of earning capacity any increase in that capacity which it would in the opinion of the court be reasonable to expect a party to the marriage to take steps to acquire;

(b) the financial needs, obligations and responsibilities which each of the parties to the marriage has or is likely to have in the foreseeable future;

(c) the standard of living enjoyed by the family before the breakdown of the marriage;

(d) the age of each party to the marriage and the duration of the marriage;

(e) any physical or mental disability of either of the parties to the marriage;

(f) the contributions which each of the parties has made or is likely in the foreseeable future to make to the welfare of the family, including any contribution by looking after the home or caring for the family;

(g) the conduct of each of the parties, if that conduct is such that it would in the opinion of the court be inequitable to disregard it;

(h) in the case of proceedings for divorce or nullity of marriage, the value to each of the parties to the marriage of any benefit which, by reason of the dissolution or annulment of the marriage, that party will lose the chance of acquiring.

Yet, comprehensive though this list is, it is not exhaustive. Judges are also instructed 'to have regard to all the circumstances of the case'.[1129] Finally, the court is required to consider whether a clean break would be appropriate,[1130] but it has been emphasized that it is not the function of the court to strive to achieve a clean break regardless of the circumstances of the individual case.[1131]

*450.* Successive attempts by individual members of the judiciary to introduce a more formulaic approach met with disapprobation and the reassertion of the primacy of the statutory guidelines.[1132] In practice, the courts tended to focus on the needs of the parties and any children of the family. This had two main consequences. In cases involving couples with modest assets, this approach might well result in the primary carer receiving more than half of the assets.[1133] In 'big-money' cases, by contrast, a focus on needs – even when construed as what would be 'reasonable requirements' in the light of the parties' standard of living during the marriage – meant that the party who had not personally generated the assets – usually the wife – tended to receive significantly less than half of the assets.[1134]

---

1129. *Ibid.,* s. 25(1).
1130. *Ibid.,* s. 25A.
1131. *Clutton v. Clutton* [1991] 1 F.L.R. 242.
1132. For attempts to introduce a more formulaic approach, *see Wachtel v. Wachtel* [1973] 2 W.L.R. 366 and *Duxbury v. Duxbury* [1991] 3 W.L.R. 639. For rejections of such approaches, *see Gojkovic v. Gojkovic* [1990] 2 All E.R. 84; *Vicary v. Vicary* [1992] 2 F.L.R. 27; and *Burgess v. Burgess* [1996] 2 F.L.R. 34.
1133. *See,* e.g., *Scott v. Scott* [1978] 1 W.L.R. 723.
1134. *See,* e.g., *O'D v. O'D* [1976] Fam. 83; *Page v. Page* (1981) 2 F.L.R. 198; *F v. F (Ancillary Relief: Substantial Assets)* [1995] 2 F.L.R. 45; *Dart v. Dart* [1996] 2 F.L.R. 286; *Conran v. Conran* [1997] 2 F.L.R. 615.

*451.* The decision of the House of Lords in *White v. White*[1135] signalled a new approach to the allocation of assets on divorce. Lord Nicholls of Birkenhead, delivering the main judgment in the case, identified that the objective of the court in applying the statute 'must be to achieve a fair outcome'.[1136] He recognized, however, that 'fairness' is a concept that means different things to different people, and so attempted to set out principles to structure the discretion of the court.

Central to his judgment was the 'principle of universal application', that in seeking to achieve a fair outcome, there should be no place for discrimination between husband and wife and their respective roles; no bias against the homemaker in favour of the one who built up the assets.[1137] To ensure that no such discrimination occurred, he suggested that:

> [A] judge would always be well advised to check his tentative view against the yardstick of equality of division. As a general guide, equality should be departed from only if, and to the extent that, there is good reason for doing so. The need to consider and articulate reasons for departing from equality would help the parties and the court to focus on the need to ensure the absence of discrimination.[1138]

He did emphasize, however, that there was no presumption of equal division; to introduce such a presumption would go beyond the permissible bounds of interpretation. In fact, far from approving any automatic equal division of assets, Lord Nicholls was keen to assert that all the factors listed in section 25 of the Matrimonial Causes Act should be taken into account. He disapproved of the practice whereby requirements limited the amount of the award, holding that there was nothing in the legislation to indicate that the 'reasonable requirements' of the claimant should determine the amount awarded:

> Why ever should they? If a husband and wife by their joint efforts over many years, his directly in the business and hers indirectly at home, have built up a valuable business from scratch, why should the claimant wife be confined to the court's assessment of her reasonable requirements, and the husband left with a much larger share? Or, to put the question differently, in such a case, where the assets exceed the financial needs of both parties, why should the surplus belong solely to the husband?[1139]

*452.* In the wake of *White v. White*, the courts began to award wives a larger share of the assets in big-money cases, although there was considerable debate as to whether equal division was appropriate in shorter marriages as well as in those that had – like the marriage in *White v. White* – subsisted for a considerable period of

---

1135. [2000] 2 F.L.R. 981.
1136. *Ibid.*, at 989.
1137. *Ibid.*
1138. *Ibid.*
1139. *Ibid.*, at 992.

time.[1140] In addition, a new argument began to be heard in the courts: namely that the contribution of one spouse had been so significant that a departure from equality was justified.[1141] There were, however, two problems with this line of argument. First, it required the court to analyze the respective contributions of the parties over the course of the marriage.[1142] Second, as recognized by the Court of Appeal in *Lambert v. Lambert*,[1143] if amassing or inheriting substantial assets is regarded as a special contribution justifying a departure from equal division in and of itself, then equal division will never be regarded as appropriate in big-money cases. In that case, the court held that this line of argument discriminated against the homemaker and awarded Mrs Lambert 50% of the GBP 20 million fortune that her husband had built up during their marriage. It did, however, accept that it would, albeit only in exceptional circumstances, still be possible for one spouse to argue that he or she had made a 'special contribution' justifying a departure from equality.[1144]

453. The implications of the decision in *White v. White* were still being worked out by the lower courts when the issue of the allocation of assets on divorce came back before the House of Lords in the conjoined appeals of *Miller v. Miller* and *McFarlane v. McFarlane*.[1145] The two cases were very different. In *Miller v. Miller*, the parties had only been married for two years and nine months (after which Mr Miller left his wife for another woman), but during that period the value of shares held by Mr Miller had increased substantially in value (between GBP 12 million and GBP 18 million). The issue in this case was the level of capital provision that should be made for Mrs Miller. By contrast, *McFarlane v. McFarlane* involved a successful professional couple who had been married for sixteen years. Mrs McFarlane had, however, given up her career as a City Solicitor to look after their three children. They had agreed to divide their assets equally and the only issue in dispute was how much maintenance should be paid to Mrs McFarlane.

The House of Lords identified three key principles: need, compensation and sharing. The reference to needs was a reminder that Lord Nicholls' discussion of the 'yardstick of equality' in *White v. White* had been intended to apply only to those cases in which there were surplus assets, not to those cases in which the primary carer needed a greater share of the assets to house the children.[1146] The new principle of 'compensation' was intended to address cases like those of Mrs McFarlane, who had sacrificed a career for the sake of the family. The third principle of 'sharing' at first sight appeared to build upon the idea of marriage as a partnership that had been introduced in *White v. White*. Yet there was a division of opinion between the judges as to precisely what property should be shared. All agreed that there was

---

1140. *See*, e.g., *Foster v. Foster* [2003] EWCA Civ 565; *GW v. RW (Financial Provision: Departure from Equality)* [2003] 2 F.L.R. 108. For discussion, *see* J. Eekelaar, *Asset Distribution on Divorce – Time and Property*, 33 Fam. L. 828 (2003).
1141. *Cowan v. Cowan* [2001] 3 W.L.R. 684; *Dharamshi v. Dharamshi* [2001] 1 F.L.R. 736.
1142. *See*, e.g., *H v. H (Financial Provision: Special Contribution)* [2002] 2 F.L.R. 1021.
1143. [2002] EWCA Civ 1685.
1144. *See*, e.g., *Sorrell v. Sorrell* [2005] EWHC (Fam) 1717, and *see* further ** below.
1145. [2006] UKHL 24.
1146. *See*, e.g., L. Fisher, *The Unexpected Impact of White – Taking 'Equality' Too Far?* 32 Fam. L. 108 (2002).

a difference between 'matrimonial property' – namely property acquired by the joint efforts of the parties during the marriage – and other property, such as that acquired before the marriage or by gift or inheritance during the marriage. The former should be shared, the latter need not. Lord Nicholls, however, maintained that the business assets built up by one spouse during the marriage could be regarded as having been generated by the joint efforts of the parties, while the majority held that those assets should be regarded as assets generated by the efforts of one of the spouses alone. Even so, this did not mean that such assets should not be shared, merely that sharing would not be automatic.

Despite these differences, the five judges agreed on the outcome; the award of GBP 5 million to Mrs Miller (less than one-sixth of Mr Miller's assets, reflecting the shortness of the marriage), and the payment of GBP 250,000 per year to Mrs McFarlane without any time limit being specified (to recognize the career sacrifice that she had made).

*454.* The decision in *Miller v. Miller* and *McFarlane v. McFarlane* posed as many questions as it answered, not least because of the division of opinion between the five judges. The focus of the courts shifted again, this time to the question as to which assets of the parties could be said to be 'matrimonial' and therefore within the 'sharing principle'.[1147] It fell to the Court of Appeal in *Charman v. Charman*[1148] to try to provide some guidance for the lower courts.

It identified the new starting point as being the financial resources of the parties, since the principles of need, compensation and sharing set out in *Miller v. Miller* and *McFarlane v. McFarlane* 'must be applied in the light of the size and nature of all the computed resources, which are usually heavily circumscribing factors'.[1149] It reasserted the importance of the statutory list of factors set out in section 25(2) of the Matrimonial Causes Act, linking each of those three principles to factors on that list. It resolved the potential conflict between the three principles: holding that if the needs of one party required that they should receive more than half of the assets, then the needs principle would prevail, whereas if the needs of the parties did not exhaust the assets of the parties, then the sharing principle would apply. (The scope of the compensation principle, which had been little used by the courts, was left to be determined on another occasion.)

It defined the sharing principle as being that 'property should be shared in equal proportions unless there is good reason to depart from such proportions', a formulation that made it clear that 'departure [from equality] is not from the principle but takes place within the principle'.[1150] It built upon the concept of 'matrimonial property', holding that although the sharing principle applied to all property 'to the extent that their property is non-matrimonial, there is likely to be better reason for departure from equality'.[1151] It also noted that the suggestion in *Miller v. Miller* and

---

1147. *See*, e.g., *S v. S* [2006] EWHC 2339 (Fam); *S v. S (Non-Matrimonial Property: Conduct)* [2006] EWHC 2793; *Rossi v. Rossi* [2006] EWHC 1482 (Fam); *H v. H* [2007] EWHC 459 (Fam).
1148. [2007] EWCA Civ 503.
1149. At para. 68.
1150. At para. 65.
1151. At para. 66.

*McFarlane v. McFarlane* that business assets might fall outside the sharing principle was formulated in the context of short marriages, and expressed a preference for the 'more logical' reasoning of Lord Nicholls.[1152] It did, however, accept that the fact that one party had made a 'special contribution' might, in exceptional cases, justify a departure from equal division.

*455.* A decade on, however, the Court of Appeal revisited the issue of 'unilateral assets' in *Sharp v. Sharp*.[1153] During their six-year relationship, the wife had been awarded bonuses totalling EUR 10.5 million. In the light of the speeches of the majority in *Miller*, the view was taken that these were not 'family' assets and that in the context of a short, childless marriage, where both spouses had been in full-time employment and had not pooled all of their assets, some departure from 50% would be appropriate. The court emphasized that there were no hard-and-fast rules in this area and that a nuanced decision had to be made on the facts of the individual case, so it cannot be assumed that the same approach will be taken in all short dual-career marriages.

*456.* To sum up: the key principles that emerge from the case law are that if the resources of the parties are insufficient to meet their needs, then the court will focus primarily on meeting the needs of the children of the family and their primary carer;[1154] while if the parties have more than sufficient resources to meet their needs then those resources may be shared, depending on the source of the resources, the contributions of the parties and all the circumstances of the case.[1155] The courts have, however, been unwilling to extend the principle of compensation beyond the facts of *McFarlane v. McFarlane*; so far, it has been held to be inapplicable where no career was sacrificed,[1156] where the career sacrificed was not a high-earning one[1157] or was coming to an end anyway,[1158] or where giving up work was deemed to be a 'lifestyle choice' rather than a sacrifice for the family.[1159] The principle itself was heavily criticized in the recent case of *SA v. PA (Pre-marital agreement: Compensation)*,[1160] and it was predicted that it would be 'a very rare and exceptional case where the principle will be capable of being successfully invoked'.[1161]

*457.* The uncertainty engendered by the shifting focus of the courts over the past few years has raised the question as to whether parties should be able to determine for themselves how any assets should be allocated in the event of divorce. The

1152. At para. 86.
1153. [2017] EWCA Civ 408.
1154. *See*, e.g., *B v. B (Financial Provision: Welfare of Child and Conduct)* [2002] 1 F.L.R. 555; *Tattersall v. Tattersall* [2013] EWCA Civ 774 (70:30 split).
1155. *See*, e.g., *Young v. Young* [2013] EWHC 3637 (Fam).
1156. *NA v. MA* [2006] EWHC 2900 (Fam).
1157. *H v. H* [2007] EWHC 459 (Fam).
1158. *Hvorostovsky v. Hvorostovsky* [2009] EWCA Civ 791.
1159. *S v. S (Non-matrimonial Property: Conduct)* [2006] EWHC 2793.
1160. [2014] EWHC 392 (Fam).
1161. At para. 36. *See also P v. P* [2007] EWHC 779 (Fam).

weight given to different types of private arrangements is considered in the next section. This chapter will then go on to consider in more detail the way in which the specific statutory criteria have been interpreted by the courts and the circumstances in which a court will deem a clean break appropriate. It will close with a brief note on the implications of the current system for the claimant whose former spouse becomes insolvent.

## §2. PRIVATE ARRANGEMENTS

*458.* It is open to the parties to agree between themselves – either before the marriage or after the parties have separated – how their assets should be divided upon divorce. There is no requirement that a court should approve the arrangements made by the parties, and it would appear that a significant proportion of divorcing spouses choose to separate without bringing either their agreement or their disagreement before a court. To this extent, private ordering is possible under the law of England and Wales. However, if one party wishes to resile from such a private agreement, matters are rather different: such an agreement is not binding on the parties.

This section considers the weight that will be given to prenuptial, postnuptial and separation agreements, and outlines the other options for resolving the dispute that fall short of adjudication by the court.

## I. Prenuptial Agreements

*459.* Traditionally, the law of England and Wales held that prenuptial agreements were contrary to public policy, on the basis that they envisaged a divorce between the parties before the marriage had even begun. Over the last decade or so, however, there emerged a feeling that this objection is thought to be 'of less importance now that divorce is so commonplace'[1162] and in 2010 the Supreme Court confirmed that prenuptial agreements were no longer vulnerable to being struck down on that basis.[1163]

This does not mean, however, that such agreements are now binding on the parties. Married couples do not have the power to exclude the jurisdiction of the court by means of private agreement,[1164] and the weight to be given to any such agreement will therefore depend upon the circumstances of the individual case. *Radmacher* does, nonetheless, mark a significant landmark in the law relating to prenuptial agreements, as, although the Supreme Court reiterated that the role of the court was to achieve a fair outcome, it also held that the existence of a prenuptial agreement 'is capable of altering what is fair'.[1165] The approach approved by the majority was that a court 'should give effect to a nuptial agreement that is freely entered into by

---

1162. *M v. M (Prenuptial agreement)* [2002] 1 F.L.R. 654, *per* Connell J.
1163. *Radmacher v. Granatino* [2010] UKSC 42 at para. 52.
1164. *Ibid.*, para. 7.
1165. *Ibid.*, para. 75. *See also Z v. Z (No. 2)* [2011] EWHC 2878 (Fam).

each party with a full appreciation of its implications unless in the circumstances prevailing it would not be fair to hold the parties to their agreement'.[1166] The factors to be taken into account by the court in deciding whether or not it is fair to hold the parties to their agreement can be divided into two groups: those that relate to the procedural fairness of the agreement, and those that relate to its substantive fairness.

460. It is clearly important that procedural fairness be observed in the making of the agreement. The basic question for the court is whether each of the parties has made a free and informed decision to enter into the agreement.[1167] Although there are no hard-and-fast rules,[1168] it can be said that an agreement will carry more weight if both parties received independent legal advice prior to entering into the agreement;[1169] if there was full disclosure by each party of his or her assets;[1170] and if the process was free of duress or undue pressure. Even 'undue pressure (falling short of duress) will also be likely to eliminate the weight to be attached to the agreement, and other unworthy conduct, such as exploitation of a dominant position to secure an unfair advantage, would reduce or eliminate it'.[1171] However, the absence of independent legal advice will not necessarily lead to an agreement being set aside. In *Radmacher v. Granatino,*[1172] the wealthy investment banker husband had the opportunity to take independent legal advice before his marriage to an even wealthier German heiress, but chose not to avail himself of this option. As Moor J subsequently noted in *AH v. PH,*[1173] 'even where it is not fair to hold a party to an agreement, it may be that it is right to pay some regard to the agreement'.[1174]

In considering the substantive fairness of the agreement the court will take into account what property is excluded from division. An agreement that excludes inherited or preacquired property will generally be regarded as more reasonable than one seeking to exclude assets built up during the marriage.[1175] Moreover, as the Supreme Court emphasized in *Radmacher v. Granatino*, respect for individual autonomy has its limits and a nuptial agreement 'cannot be allowed to prejudice the reasonable requirements of any children of the family'.[1176] The circumstances of the

---

1166. *Ibid.*

1167. *See*, e.g., *L v. M* [2014] EWHC 2220 (Fam), discussing the broader impact of *Radmacher*; *SA v. PA (Pre-marital agreement: Compensation)* [2014] EWHC 392 (Fam), para. 63.

1168. And, as the Supreme Court pointed out in *Radmacher v. Granatino* [2010] UKSC 42 at para. 69, no need for such rules in the current state of the law.

1169. *See*, e.g., *K v. K (Ancillary Relief: Prenuptial Agreement)* [2003] 1 F.L.R. 120; cf. *J v. V (Disclosure: Offshore Corporations)* [2003] EWHC 3110 (Fam); *Kremen v. Agrest (No. 11) (Financial Remedy: Non-Disclosure: Post-Nuptial Agreement)* [2012] EWHC 45 (Fam), para. 74; *GS v. L* [2011] EWHC 1759 (Fam), para. 77; *B v. S (Financial Remedy: Marital Property Regime)* [2012] EWHC 265 (Fam), para. 20; *AC v. DC (No. 2)* [2012] EWHC 2420 (Fam); *Hopkins v. Hopkins* [2015] EWHC 812 (Fam).

1170. Or at least sufficient 'to enable a free decision to be made': *BN v. MA* [2013] EWHC 4250 (Fam), para. 30.

1171. *Radmacher v. Granatino* [2010] UKSC 42, at para. 71.

1172. [2009] EWCA Civ 649.

1173. [2013] EWHC 3873 (Fam).

1174. *Ibid.*, para. 54.

1175. *See*, e.g., *BN v MA* [2013] EWHC 4250; *WW v HW* [2015] EWHC 1844 (Fam).

1176. [2010] UKSC 42, para. 77.

parties may change over the course of their relationship, and the needs of one party, or the sacrifices he or she has made for the sake of the marriage, might well 'render it unfair to hold the parties to an ante-nuptial agreement'.[1177] The mere fact that one party has enjoyed unexpected success will not, however, necessarily make it unfair to hold the parties to the terms of the agreement.

*461.* Over the last few years there have been many calls for reform of the law in this area by academics, practitioners, government advisers and judges.[1178] Indeed, there was a powerful argument from Lady Hale in *Radmacher* that reforms should be left to law reform agencies such as the Law Commission rather than the judiciary.[1179] In the wake of *Radmacher*, the Law Commission recommended legislation introducing 'qualifying nuptial agreements' which would, assuming certain procedural safeguards had been met, be binding on the parties save to the extent that they precluded provision for needs.[1180] As yet, however, the government has not evinced any intention to introduce legislation on this issue.

## II. Postnuptial Agreements

*462.* Even prior to the decision in *Radmacher v. Granatino*, the Privy Council had held that a postnuptial agreement – i.e., one entered into after the marriage has taken place but while the parties are still living together – would be enforceable, even if it was not capable of binding the court.[1181] The argument in *Radmacher* that there was no material distinction between prenuptial and postnuptial agreements[1182] may well lead to the terms of postnuptial agreements carrying more weight than they would previously have done.

## III. Separation Agreements

*463.* The policy towards agreements reached upon separation has always been rather different, such agreements being positively encouraged by the courts.[1183] Since such agreements are only entered into upon separation, they are not subject to the objection that the parties are anticipating the end of the marriage before it has even started; moreover, the parties will know where they stand and will not be speculating about future assets and responsibilities. Thus, although it remains the case that an agreement reached between the parties on separation is not binding – since the parties cannot agree to exclude the court's jurisdiction to make orders in

---

1177. *Ibid.*, para. 81. *See*, e.g., *Luckwell v. Limata* [2014] EWHC 502 (Fam), where the agreement would have left the husband in real need.
1178. *See*, e.g., S.Thompson, *Prenuptial Agreements and the Presumption of Free Choice: Issues of Power in Theory and Practice* (Hart 2015).
1179. *Radmacher v. Granatino* [2010] UKSC 42.
1180. Law Commission, *Matrimonial Property, Needs, and Agreements* (2014) Law Com. No. 343.
1181. *Macleod v. Macleod* [2008] UKPC 68.
1182. *See Radmacher v. Granatino* [2010] UKSC 42, at para. 60.
1183. *X (Y and Z intervening)* [2002] 1 F.L.R. 508.

the exercise of its divorce jurisdiction[1184] – the courts are likely to uphold such an agreement unless there is very good reason to depart from its terms.[1185] In addition, where a considerable period of time has elapsed since the agreement was entered into, the court may decline to investigate the current position of the parties.[1186]

There will be good reason to depart from the terms of a separation agreement if it was entered into as a result of fraud, duress or undue influence,[1187] or if one of the parties did not have competent legal advice. The emphasis is on procedural rather than substantive fairness: the fact that one party has agreed to accept a lesser sum than that which might have been ordered by the court is not a ground for reopening the agreement.

## IV. Consent Orders

*464.* If the parties have agreed between themselves how their assets are to be divided, they may ask the court to make a consent order in the terms agreed.[1188] The significance of this is that a consent order is an order of the court[1189] and as a result is more difficult to challenge than even a formal agreement. A consent order will not be vitiated by the fact that one party was given inadequate legal advice.[1190] The court may make the order in the terms agreed on the basis of the information supplied by the parties 'unless it has reason to think that there are other circumstances into which it ought to inquire'.[1191] Recent research has indicated that judges do in fact play a more interventionist role in this respect than had previously been appreciated.[1192]

## V. Financial Dispute Resolution

*465.* A further option short of actual adjudication was introduced in 2000. Financial dispute resolution is intended to lead the parties towards settlement. It entails strong judicial case management and an 'early neutral evaluation' by a judge of what order a court would be likely to make if the parties went to court.[1193] An agreement reached by the parties in the course of financial dispute resolution is deemed to be an order of the court and therefore binding.[1194]

---

1184. *Matrimonial Causes Act* 1973, s. 34.
1185. *Edgar v. Edgar* [1980] 1 W.L.R 1410.
1186. *T v. T* [2013] EWHC B3 (Fam).
1187. *See*, e.g., *NA v. MI* [2006] EWHC 2900 (Fam).
1188. *Matrimonial Causes Act* 1973, s. 33A.
1189. *De Lasala v. De Lasala* [1980] A.C. 546.
1190. *Harris v. Manahan* [1997] 1 F.L.R. 205.
1191. *Matrimonial Causes Act* 1973, s. 33A(1).
1192. E. Hitchings, J. Miles and H. Woodward, *Assembling the Jigsaw Puzzle: Understanding Financial Settlement on Divorce* (University of Bristol, 2013).
1193. *Rose v. Rose* [2002] 1 F.L.R. 978.
1194. *Ibid.*

§3. ADJUDICATION BY THE COURT

*466.* As discussed above, the court is required to have regard to all the circumstances of the case in deciding how the assets of the parties should be reallocated on divorce. Although broad principles have been developed by the courts in *White v. White, Miller v. Miller* and *McFarlane v. McFarlane* and *Charman v. Charman*, the factors set out in section 25(2) of the Matrimonial Causes Act 1973 remain relevant to the court's deliberations, and the meaning of these factors must therefore be considered. The court is also required to consider the desirability of a clean break.

## I. The Statutory Factors

### A. Resources

*467.* The importance of ascertaining the resources of the parties has fluctuated over the years. Before the courts acquired their current extensive powers to reallocate property on divorce, who owned what determined how the parties' property would be divided. When the emphasis shifted to meeting the 'reasonable requirements' of the spouse claiming ancillary relief, it became unnecessary to ascertain the exact extent of the other spouse's wealth, wealthy spouses could raise the 'millionaire's defence' by stating that they had sufficient resources to meet whatever award the court might make.[1195] Now that equal sharing has become a firm principle – albeit one that allows for a departure from equality where appropriate – it is once again necessary to start by determining the assets of each of the parties.[1196]

*468.* The legislation is drafted in broad terms, requiring the court to have regard not only to existing income and assets but also to earning capacity (including any increase in that capacity that 'it would in the opinion of the court be reasonable to expect a party to the marriage to take steps to acquire')[1197] and resources that are likely to accrue in the foreseeable future. The way in which the courts have interpreted this provision has been equally expansive. Assets acquired before the marriage fall within its scope, as do those acquired after divorce.[1198] Property inherited from a third party may be taken into account, as may one party's expectation of an

---

1195. *See*, e.g., *Attar v. Attar (No. 1)* [1985] F.L.R. 649; *B v. B (Discovery: Financial Provision)* [1990] 2 F.L.R. 180; *Van G v. Van G (Financial Provision: Millionaire's Defence)* [1995] 1 F.L.R. 328. This remains a possibility where the case is being decided on the basis of needs: *see*, e.g., *AH v. PH* [2013] EWHC 3873 (Fam).

1196. *Charman v. Charman* [2007] EWCA Civ 503, para. 68. Although *see Cooper-Hohn v. Hohn* [2014] EWCA Civ 896, rejecting the need for expert evaluation of a particular resource.

1197. *Matrimonial Causes Act* 1973, s. 25(2)(a). *See*, e.g., *Q v. Q (Ancillary Relief: Periodical Payments)* [2005] EWHC 402 (Fam); *Tattersall v. Tattersall* [2013] EWCA Civ 774; *MF v. SF* [2015] EWHC 1273 (Fam).

1198. *See*, e.g., *H v. H (Financial Provision)* [2009] EWHC 494 (Fam); *H v. W (Cap on Wife's Share of Bonus Payments)* [2014] EWHC 4105 (Fam). The length of time that has elapsed between the divorce and the claim for financial provision will however be relevant to the division of the assets: *Vince v. Wyatt* [2015] UKSC 14.

inheritance from a person as yet living.[1199] The courts have even taken into account the damages that one spouse has received on account of personal injury.[1200]

*469.* The best summary of the breadth of the concept of a 'financial resource' was provided by Coleridge J. in *J v. V. (Disclosure Offshore Corporations):*[1201]

> It covers far more than merely property that is in the direct legal ownership of possession of one or other of the parties. Any arrangement that provides financial benefit to a party falls to be considered, evaluated and ultimately included as an asset. Mere voluntary and unenforceable arrangements can sometimes fall into this net especially if they arise out of a family arrangement or moral obligation of one kind or another.[1202]

This makes it clear that the court may take into account the fact that one spouse may have access to resources that he or she does not own directly. There is obviously a balance to be struck between respecting the rights of the third party who owns or controls the resources in question and being realistic about the resources available to each of the spouses.[1203] The basic rule is that the court will not act in direct invasion of the rights of a third party, or put a third party under pressure to act in a certain way, but may take into account the potential availability of wealth from sources owned or administered by others.[1204] The court may even pierce the corporate veil where one spouse has attempted to defeat the claims of the other by placing the assets under the nominal ownership of a company under his or her control.[1205]

*470.* While many of the cases were decided before the changes effected by *White v. White* and *Miller v. Miller* and *McFarlane v. McFarlane*, it has been confirmed that assets held in trust can still be taken into account and shared between the parties.[1206] In ascertaining the financial resources of the parties, the Court of Appeal has advocated 'a judicious mixture of worldly realism and of respect for the legal effects of trusts, the legal duties of trustees and, in the case of offshore trusts, the jurisdictions of offshore courts'.[1207]

---

1199. *Re G (Financial Provision: Liberty to Restore Application for Lump Sum)* [2004] EWHC 88 (Fam).
1200. *Mansfield v. Mansfield* [2011] EWCA Civ 1056.
1201. [2003] EWHC 3110 (Fam).
1202. At para. 43.
1203. *See*, e.g., *Quan v. Bray* [2014] EWHC 3340 (Fam).
1204. *Thomas v. Thomas* [1995] 2 F.L.R. 668. *See*, e.g., *M v. M (Maintenance Pending Suit)* [2002] EWHC 317; *C v. C (Ancillary Relief: Trust Fund)* [2009] EWHC 1491 (Fam).
1205. *Prest v. Petrodel Resources Limited and others* [2013] UKSC 34, para. 35. *See also AAZ v. BBZ* [2016] EWHC 3234 (Fam).
1206. *Charman v. Charman* [2007] EWCA Civ 503. *See also Whaley v. Whaley* [2011] EWCA Civ 617.
1207. *Ibid.*, para. 57. *See also DR v. GR and Others (Financial Remedy: Variation of Overseas Trust)* [2013] 1196 (Fam).

*471.* The fact that a particular asset is to be counted as a financial resource for the purposes of the statute does not mean that it must be shared.[1208] The fact that certain assets can be classified as non-matrimonial – i.e., they are 'not the financial product of or generated by the parties' endeavours during the marriage'[1209] – may well justify a departure from equality. Thus the courts have, in recent years, held that a departure from equality has been justified in cases involving inherited property,[1210] assets acquired before the marriage[1211] and those acquired or likely to be acquired after the end of the relationship.[1212] As ever, the precise application of the statutory factors will depend on all the circumstances of the case.

## B. Needs

*472.* The 'needs' of the parties may encompass everything from the bare necessities to the kind of provision ensuring that a spouse will 'never be in want'.[1213] This reflects the fact that while the application of the needs *principle* will lead to an award greater than 50% of the assets, the courts may also take the needs of the parties into account as a benchmark for an award when departing from sharing, for example, where there are significant non-matrimonial assets and sharing is not deemed appropriate. 'Need' is thus a flexible concept that reflects the resources available and the standard of living enjoyed by the parties.[1214] In lower-income cases, the needs of the parties may require the distinction between matrimonial and non-matrimonial property to be ignored: any of the parties' resources may be applied to meet the needs of either party.[1215]

## C. Standard of Living

*473.* The standard of living enjoyed by the parties will inevitably be entwined with the question of the assets available to them. The fact that the parties accepted a modest standard of living while building up a business will not count against a claimant,[1216] although a different approach has been deemed appropriate where one

---

1208. *See supra*, para. 449.
1209. *Hart v. Hart* [2017] EWCA Civ 1306, para. 2.
1210. *P v. P (Inherited Property)* [2004] EWHC 1364 (Fam); *NA v. MA* [2006] EWHC 2900 (Fam); *B v. B (Ancillary Relief)* [2008] EWCA Civ 543; *Robson v. Robson* [2010] EWCA Civ 1171; *K v. L (Ancillary Relief: Inherited Wealth)* [2011] EWCA Civ 550.
1211. *McCartney v. Mills-McCartney* [2008] EWHC 401 (Fam); *Jones v. Jones* [2011] EWCA Civ 41; *N v. F* [2011] EWHC 586 (Fam); *AC v. DC (No. 2)* [2012] EWHC 2420 (Fam).
1212. *M v. M (Financial Relief: Substantial Earning Capacity)* [2004] EWHC 688 (Fam); *B v. B* [2013] EWHC 1232 (Fam); *Evans v. Evans* [2013] EWHC 506 (Fam); *JB v. MB* [2015] EWHC 1846 (Fam).
1213. *Y v. Y* [2012] EWHC 2063 (Fam).
1214. *Rupp v. Sarre* [2016] EWCA Civ 93.
1215. *See*, e.g., *S v. S (Non-matrimonial Property: Conduct)* [2006] EWHC 2793; *K v. L (Ancillary Relief: Inherited Wealth)* [2011] EWCA Civ 550; *GS v. L* [2011] EWHC 1759 (Fam).
1216. *Preston v. Preston* [1981] 3 W.L.R. 619.

party's wealth was largely inherited.[1217] Conversely, there are cases where the parties have lived beyond their means during the marriage and there are no longer sufficient assets to maintain the standard of living they once enjoyed.[1218] In lower-income cases, both parties may need to accept a lower standard of living, given the difficulty in providing for two households out of the resources that previously supported one.[1219]

## D. Age of Parties and the Duration of the Marriage

*474.* The age of the parties will affect the court's assessment of their earning capacity[1220] and needs.[1221] The longer the marriage, the more appropriate it may be to divide surplus assets equally, regardless of their source. However, all of the factors must be considered together, with the result that a short childless marriage in which both spouses worked[1222] will yield very different results from a short marriage that has produced children, because of the necessity of securing adequate provision for the children and their primary carer.[1223] Nor does the mere length of the marriage justify the sharing of non-matrimonial property. In many cases, of course, the source of the assets will have become less important over the course of the marriage, as those assets are mingled with matrimonial assets, or invested in the family home. However, in cases where the non-matrimonial assets were kept separate throughout the marriage it is unlikely that they will be shared upon divorce.[1224]

Although the statute refers specifically to the duration of the marriage, the courts have in recent years been willing to take the entire duration of the parties' relationship – including periods of premarital cohabitation – into account as part of all the circumstances of the case.[1225]

## E. Disability

*475.* The fact that one of the parties suffers from a disability may have an impact on their income, earning capacity and needs. The courts have, however, emphasized that the disability of one of the parties should not be treated as the paramount factor,[1226] and that the needs of both parties must be considered.[1227]

---

1217. *K v. L (Ancillary Relief: Inherited Wealth)* [2011] EWCA Civ 550.
1218. *See,* e.g., *Fields v. Fields* [2015] EWHC 1670 (Fam).
1219. *MD v. D* [2008] EWHC 1929 (Fam); *MF v. SF* [2015] EWHC 1273 (Fam).
1220. *See,* e.g., *MF v. SF* [2015] EWHC 1273 (Fam); *Fields v. Fields* [2015] EWHC 1670 (Fam).
1221. *See,* e.g., *Tattersall v. Tattersall* [2013] EWCA Civ 744.
1222. *See,* e.g. *Sharp v. Sharp* [2017] EWCA Civ 408.
1223. *S v. B (Ancillary Relief: Costs)* [2004] EWHC 2089 (Fam) and *H v. H (Financial Provision)* [2009] EWHC 494 (Fam) *cf. Re G (Financial Provision: Liberty to Restore Application for Lump Sum)* [2004] EWHC 88 (Fam).
1224. *K v. L (Ancillary Relief: Inherited Wealth)* [2011] EWCA Civ 550.
1225. *Day v. Day* [1988] 1 F.L.R. 278; *CO v. CO (Ancillary Relief: Pre-Marriage Cohabitation)* [2004] EWHC 287 (Fam).
1226. *Wagstaff v. Wagstaff* [1992] 1 All E.R. 275.
1227. *Chadwick v. Chadwick* [1985] F.L.R. 606; *Seaton v. Seaton* [1986] 2 F.L.R. 398.

## F. Contributions

476. In sharp contrast to the position under the law of trusts,[1228] domestic contributions were accorded a positive value under the Matrimonial Causes Act as contributions 'to the welfare of the family', and the courts were swift to praise the contributions made by wives and mothers.[1229] In a number of recent cases the courts have emphasized that marriage is a partnership within which financial and domestic contributions should be regarded as equally valuable.[1230] Arguments that one spouse made a 'special contribution' that should be recognized by an award of more than 50% of the assets are unlikely to succeed unless that contribution derives from the 'exceptional and individual' ability of that spouse: the generation of significant wealth is not, in itself, sufficient.[1231]

## G. Conduct

477. At a time, when it was only possible to obtain a divorce on the basis of the other spouse's fault, considerations of guilt and blame would also influence the provision of maintenance. When the law was reformed in 1969, the idea that a marriage could break down through the fault of both, or neither, of the spouses was reflected in the approach taken to fault when deciding on the division of assets. As Lord Denning MR noted in the early 1970s:

> There will no doubt be a residue of cases where the conduct of one of the parties is ... 'both obvious and gross', so much so that to order one party to support another whose conduct falls into this category is repugnant to anyone's sense of justice ... But, short of cases falling into this category, the court should not reduce its order for financial provision merely because of what was formerly regarded as guilt or blame.[1232]

This approach was reinforced by a subsequent amendment to the legislation, which provided that the conduct of the parties would only be taken into account if the court was of the view that it would be 'inequitable' to disregard it.[1233]

478. Cases in which a spouse's conduct has been considered such that it would be inequitable to disregard it include *Evans v. Evans*,[1234] in which a wife hired

---

1228. *See supra* Part III, Ch. 1, para. 432.
1229. *See*, e.g., *Wachtel v. Wachtel* [1973] 2 W.L.R. 366; *Trippas v. Trippas* [1973] 2 All E.R. 1; *Hanlon v. Hanlon* [1978] 2 All E.R. 899.
1230. *JS v. RS* [2015] EWHC 2921 (Fam); *Fields v. Fields* [2015] EWHC 1670 (Fam); *Robertson v. Robertson* [2016] EWHC 613 (Fam).
1231. *Evans v. Evans* [2013] EWHC 506 (Fam); *X v. X (application for a financial remedies order)* [2016] EWHC 1995 (Fam); *AAZ v. BBZ* [2016] EWHC 3234 (Fam); *Work v. Gray* [2017] EWCA Civ 270.
1232. *Wachtel v. Wachtel* [1973] Fam. 72.
1233. *Matrimonial Causes Act* 1973, s. 25(2)(g).
1234. [1989] 1 F.L.R. 351.

someone to kill her ex-husband and *Clark v. Clark*,[1235] in which a wife kept her much older husband a virtual prisoner in one part of the house and lived in the main part with her lover, driving her husband to attempt to commit suicide. Wantonly dissipating matrimonial assets to reduce the other's claim has also been taken into account, although in one recent case the husband's spending on cocaine and prostitutes was regarded as being simply part of his flawed character rather than deliberate dissipation.[1236]

## H. Loss of Future Assets

479. The final paragraph of section 25(2) was inserted to deal with the situation where divorce would lead to the loss of valuable rights – e.g., under the pension of the other spouse. The courts now have extensive powers to make attachment or pension sharing orders to mitigate such hardship, although there is no requirement that pension assets should be shared.[1237] The court may also decide to take the simpler option of offsetting other assets against pension assets.[1238]

## II. The Clean Break

480. The legislation contains a number of provisions designed to promote a clean break between the parties. The court must, e.g., consider whether it would be appropriate to exercise its powers in a way that ensures 'that the financial obligations of each party towards the other will be terminated as soon after the grant of the decree as the court considers just and reasonable'.[1239] It is, however, only obliged to consider this possibility.[1240]

The desirability of a clean break may influence the form of provision (i.e., whether provision is made by way of lump sum or periodical payments),[1241] but it cannot affect the actual amount deemed appropriate. In *Miller; McFarlane*, it was confirmed that the different orders are merely different means for achieving a desired outcome: the role of periodical payments is not confined to meeting the needs of the economically weaker party but may be used for the purpose of compensation. In such cases, a clean break will be inapposite.

If periodical payments are ordered, then the court must consider whether it would be appropriate to specify the period for which the order should last,[1242] and it may

---

1235. [1999] 2 F.L.R. 498.
1236. *MAP v. MFP* [2015] EWHC 627 (Fam).
1237. *See,* e.g., *T v. T (Financial Relief: Pensions)* [1998] 1 F.L.R. 1072.
1238. *JS v. RS* [2015] EWHC 2921 (Fam).
1239. *Matrimonial Causes Act* 1973, s. 25A(1).
1240. *See,* e.g., *H v. H (Financial Provision)* [2009] EWHC 494 (Fam), in which a clean break was deemed inappropriate because the wife would not be able to adjust to the termination of her financial dependence upon her husband without undue hardship, cf. *L v. L* [2011] EWHC 2207 (Fam).
1241. *See,* e.g., *Robson v. Robson* [2010] EWCA Civ 1171.
1242. *Matrimonial Causes Act* 1973, s. 25A(2). *See,* e.g., *GS v. L* [2011] EWHC 1759 (Fam).

also direct that no application should be made in the future to increase that term.[1243] Periodical payments will automatically terminate if the recipient remarries or enters into a civil partnership;[1244] if the recipient begins to cohabit with another, however, the court has a discretion whether or not such payment should cease,[1245] since cohabitation – unlike a marriage or civil partnership – does not give rise to support obligations between the adults.

*481.* If it is later discovered that the order of the court was based on some factor such as misrepresentation, mistake, or material non-disclosure,[1246] or if there has been a subsequent fundamental and unforeseen change of circumstances,[1247] then the order may be set aside. This applies to consent orders and orders made in FDR proceedings as well as those made after a full hearing.

## §4. Divorce and Bankruptcy

*482.* In the wake of the decisions in *White v. White* and *Lambert v. Lambert*, it was suggested by some commentators that English law had effectively adopted a system of deferred community of property.[1248] Yet, as others pointed out, there were fundamental differences between the English system and a system of community of property, in that it could not be said that either spouse had any specific entitlement to the property of the other in advance of an agreement or adjudication to this effect.[1249]

The importance of the distinction is perhaps most obvious if one spouse becomes insolvent. The other spouse may be able to establish that he or she has an equitable interest in assets to which the bankrupt spouse is legally entitled: if so, such assets will not form part of the bankrupt's estate.

If, however, the bankrupt spouse transferred assets to the other as part of a divorce settlement, the transaction is vulnerable to being set aside as a transaction at an undervalue.[1250] In this context, it makes no difference whether the transfer occurred as a result of an agreement between the parties, a consent order or an order of the court.[1251]

---

1243. *Ibid.*, s. 28(1A).
1244. *Matrimonial Causes Act* 1973, s. 28(1)(a).
1245. *Fleming v. Fleming* [2003] EWCA Civ, para. 9; *Grey v. Grey* [2009] EWCA Civ 1424.
1246. *See Jenkins v. Livesey (formerly Jenkins)<r>* [1985] A.C. 424. For recent high-profile examples see *Sharland v. Sharland* [2015] UKSC 60; *Gohil v. Gohil* [2015] UKSC 61.
1247. *See Barder v. Barder (Caluori intervening)* [1987] 2 All E.R. 440. For recent applications of the principles in that case *see WA v. Executors of the Estate of HA & Others* [2015] EWHC 2233 (Fam); *Critchell v Critchell* [2015] EWCA Civ 436; *Nasim v. Nasim* [2015] EWHC 2620 (Fam).
1248. S. Cretney, *Community of Property Imposed By Judicial Decision*, 119 L. Q. Rev. 349 (2003).
1249. J. Eekelaar, *Asset Distribution on Divorce – Time and Property*, 33 Fam. L. 828 (2003).
1250. *Insolvency Act* 1986, s. 339(1); *see also Matrimonial Causes Act* 1973, s. 39.
1251. *Hill v. Haines* [2007] EWHC 1012 (Ch).

# Part IV. Succession Law

## Chapter 1. Intestate Succession

### §1. The Opening of the Succession

*483.* The rules that govern the devolution of property on death are of fundamental, if often overlooked, relevance to the family. Despite the increase in family breakdown, it remains the case that more marriages are ended by death than by divorce. With over 525,000 deaths registered in England and Wales in 2016,[1252] the law of succession affects more families than any of the topics considered so far. The death of a partner is also one of the areas in which cohabitants are entitled to some legal recognition.

Any adult of sound mind may make a will disposing of his or her property. The term 'will' encompasses two elements: it is both the physical document and the expression of the testator's wishes. An individual's will reflects their own perception of who is important to them – their own definition of 'family'.

A person who fails to make a will, or who makes a will that is not valid (whether because of lack of capacity or a failure to comply with the formalities), is said to die intestate. Intestacy may also be partial – e.g., if the will deals with only part of the deceased's assets. The intestacy rules are based to an extent on assumptions about the way in which the intestate would have wanted the estate to be divided, although convenience also plays a part in confining the categories of those entitled to inherit on intestacy to those related by blood or legal ties. The potential harshness of such rules is, however, mitigated by the ability of the court to make provision for certain specified persons under the Inheritance (Provision for Family and Dependants) Act 1975.[1253]

The transmission of property on death also offers an opportunity for the state to raise revenue through the medium of inheritance tax. The details of tax law lie outside the scope of this work, but the preference for the surviving spouse or civil partner that is enshrined in the intestacy laws is also evident in this area: no inheritance tax is payable on any part of the estate that passes to the surviving spouse or civil partner.[1254]

---

1252. ONS, 'Deaths Registered in England and Wales, 2016' (July 2017).
1253. *See* Part IV, Ch. 3.
1254. *Inheritance Act* 1984, s. 18, as amended by the *Tax and Civil Partnership Regulations* 2005, S.I. 2005/3229.

## I. Death

*484.* The rules governing the registration of deaths have been set out in Part I, Chapter 2.

## II. Missing Persons and Absentees

*485.* There has long been a legal presumption at common law that a person who has not been heard of for seven years has died. The complex mix of common law and statutory rules that developed has now been swept away by the Presumption of Death Act 2013, which came into force on 1 October 2014. The court may now make a declaration if it is satisfied either that the missing individual has died or that they have not been known to be alive for a period of at least seven years.[1255] This will then permit the estate to be distributed on the basis that the individual in question has died.

The Ministry of Justice has recently consulted on whether there should be a new legal mechanism by which a guardian could be appointed to act on behalf and in the best interests of a person who has gone missing, and, if so, what the process and terms of such an appointment should be.[1256] Its conclusion was that a new legal role should be created to deal with such matters.

§2. Entitlement to Succeed

## I. Capacity to Succeed

*486.* If persons who stand to inherit under the intestacy rules lack the legal capacity to hold property – e.g., on account of their youth or mental disability – then the property will be held on trust for them until they acquire such capacity.

## II. Commorientes

*487.* Specific legislative provision is made for the contingency that two or more persons who would stand to inherit from each other might die in circumstances rendering it uncertain who died first. It is directed that 'such deaths shall … for all purposes affecting the title to property, be presumed to have occurred in order of seniority and accordingly the younger shall be deemed to have survived the elder'.[1257] This rule operates even if their deaths must have been simultaneous (e.g., as a result of a plane crash or explosion).[1258]

---

1255. *See* eg *EA v. NA* [2018] EWHC 583 (Fam).
1256. MoJ, *Guardianship of the Property and Affairs of Missing Persons* (2014).
1257. *Law of Property Act* 1925, s. 184.
1258. *See*, e.g., *Hickman v. Peacey* [1945] A.C. 304; *Re Bate* [1947] 2 All E.R. 412.

*488.* The above rule applies whether the persons concerned died intestate or not, subject to any contrary intention expressed in their wills. The rule does not, however, apply to spouses or civil partners who die intestate. If a husband and wife, or two civil partners, die in circumstances rendering it uncertain who died first, the intestacy rules will be applied as if neither was survived by the other. Indeed, even if it is clear that one survived the other for a short interval (e.g., if both die of natural causes within a few days of each other), the intestacy rules will operate as if this was not the case unless the survivor died twenty-eight days after the day on which the intestate died.[1259] This rule is of particular importance now that many spouses may have children from previous relationships. It would be harsh if the children of the first spouse to die received a reduced entitlement under the intestacy rules in such circumstances.

## III. Unworthiness to Succeed

*489.* There is a general rule of public policy which states that a person should not profit from his or her own crime. In the law of succession, this has been applied to prevent those who are convicted of the murder or manslaughter of the deceased from benefiting from the death of the deceased. The rule only applies if a crime has been committed: a person who is not guilty by reason of insanity will be allowed to benefit from the death of the deceased (although a lack of legal capacity to hold property will mean that any property inherited will have to be held in trust for him or her), but a person who is guilty of aiding and abetting the suicide of another may not. The rule applies equally to potential benefits under a will or upon intestacy.

*490.* There had been debate as to how far the moral culpability of the killer should be taken into account. This issue has now been resolved by statute – the Forfeiture Act 1982 – and by subsequent case law interpreting its provisions. It is now clear that the application of the rule will differ according to the level of moral culpability of the killer. A person who is convicted of murder is never entitled to inherit,[1260] but a person convicted of manslaughter may be able to. The Forfeiture Act 1982 allowed the court to modify the rule that the killer should forfeit all benefits under the estate of the deceased, but directs that it should not do so unless satisfied that 'having regard to the conduct of the offender and of the deceased and to such other circumstances as appear to the court to be material, the justice of the case requires the effect of the rule to be modified in that case'.[1261] In *Dunbar v. Plant*,[1262] the Court of Appeal confirmed that the forfeiture rule applies to all cases of manslaughter,[1263] as well as the crime of aiding or abetting the suicide of another,

---

1259. *Ibid.*, s. 46(2A), as inserted by the *Law Reform (Succession) Act* 1995, s. 1, and amended by the *Civil Partnership Act* 2004.
1260. *Forfeiture Act* 1982, s. 5.
1261. *Ibid.*, s. 2(2).
1262. [1998] Ch. 412.
1263. *See also Land v. Land (Deceased)* [2006] EWHC 2069 (Ch) (manslaughter by gross negligence); *Dalton v. Latham* [2003] EWHC 796 (manslaughter by virtue of diminished responsibility).

but that the degree of culpability attending the potential beneficiary's criminal conduct should be taken into account by the court when exercising its discretion under the 1982 Act. In that case – which involved a suicide pact that resulted in the death of only one of the parties – full relief against forfeiture was granted by the court. The factors which the courts have taken into account in deciding whether or not to grant relief from forfeiture include the relationship between the parties; the conditions at the time of the event causing death; whether the level of provision is appropriate; whether there are any other claims and whether the operation of the forfeiture rule would result in a third party obtaining an unjustified windfall.[1264]

*491.* If any individuals are held to have forfeited their rights to inherit, to whom does the estate then pass? Until recently the law has been that the killer's share will pass to the person next entitled under the intestacy rules: so, e.g., in *Re DWS (Deceased)* the share of a man who had killed his parents passed to his sister rather than to his son.[1265] The Law Commission recommended that the law should be reformed, and that in such cases the estate should be distributed as if the killer had died before the deceased.[1266] Legislation was subsequently passed to give effect to this recommendation.[1267]

§3. THE SYSTEM OF DESCENT

*492.* The intestacy rules operate on a strict basis of priority and substitution. Section 46 of the Administration of Estates Act 1925 sets out a comprehensive list of who is entitled to succeed and in what order.

## I. The Classes of Beneficiaries

### A. *Surviving Spouse or Civil Partner*

*493.* The intestacy rules privilege the surviving spouse or civil partner. It is important to note that only an existing spouse or civil partner will be entitled; once the marriage or civil partnership has been legally terminated – through divorce, dissolution, or annulment – any entitlement comes to an end. A similar rule applies if the parties were living apart subject to a judicial separation or separation order: if one of the parties dies, the intestacy rules are applied as if the other were already dead.[1268] If the marriage or civil partnership is voidable, but has not been annulled,

---

1264. *See*, e.g., *Re K (deceased)* [1986] Ch. 180; *Re H (Deceased)* [1990] 1 F.L.R. 441; *Re S (Deceased) (Forfeiture Rule)* [1996] 1 F.L.R. 910; *Mack v. Lockwood* [2009] EWHC 1524 (Ch); *Chadwick v. Collinson* [2014] EWHC 3055 (Ch).
1265. [2001] Ch. 568.
1266. Law Commission, *The Forfeiture Rule and the Law of Succession*, Law Com. No. 295 (TSO 2005).
1267. *Estates of Deceased Persons (Forfeiture Rule and Law of Succession) Act* 2011, s. 1, inserting *Administration of Estates Act* 1925, s. 46A.
1268. *Matrimonial Causes Act* 1973, s. 18(2); *Civil Partnership Act* 2004, s. 57.

then it cannot be challenged after the death of either party and the survivor is entitled to inherit as any other spouse or civil partner would do. If, by contrast, the marriage or civil partnership is void, then the survivor has no entitlement.

*494.* The rules were drawn up at the time English law did not recognize polygamous marriages in any circumstances. Now, however, the law does recognize as valid those marriages celebrated overseas by individuals domiciled in a jurisdiction that permits polygamy. It was therefore inevitable that before long the courts would have to grapple with the question of how the estate should be divided where the deceased is survived by more than one legal spouse. In *Official Solicitor to the Senior Courts v. Yemoh* it was held that:

> a spouse lawfully married in accordance with the law of his domicile to someone dying intestate, is entitled to be recognized in this country in relation to property, including real property, of the intestate being administered here, as a surviving spouse for the purpose of section 46 of the 1925 Act.[1269]

*495.* If the deceased left issue – children, grandchildren or remoter descendants, whether born within a formalized relationship or not – the surviving spouse or civil partner will be entitled to all of the personal chattels,[1270] the first GBP 250,000 of the estate (the 'statutory legacy') and one-half of the balance (if any).[1271] If the deceased left more than one legal spouse, the statutory legacy will be divided between the surviving spouses. It was pointed out in *Official Solicitor to the Senior Courts v. Yemoh* – in which the deceased left no fewer than eight wives whom he had validly married under the customary law of Ghana – that otherwise the estate might be 'wholly exhausted by statutory legacies', which risked defeating the division intended by Parliament between the surviving spouse and issue.[1272]

Whether the deceased was survived by one spouse or several, the remaining half of the balance is held on the statutory trusts for the issue of the deceased.[1273] These prescribe that the balance is to be divided equally between those children of the intestate who are living at the time of his or her death, and who attain the age of 18 years or marry (or form a civil partnership) under that age.[1274] Thus if all of the children are adults they are entitled to the property immediately and absolutely, while if any are still minors the property will be held on trust for them until they reach adulthood. The share of a child who predeceased the intestate will pass to that child's children, again in equal shares, although this is no longer contingent on the predeceased child reaching the age of 18 years or formalizing a relationship under

---

1269. [2010] EWHC 3727 (Ch), at para. 20.
1270. These are defined by *Administration of Estates Act* 1925, s. 55(1)(x), as amended by *Inheritance and Trustees' Powers Act* 2014, s. 3.
1271. *Administration of Estates Act* 1925, s. 46, as amended by *Inheritance and Trustees' Powers Act* 2014, s. 1.
1272. [2010] EWHC 3727 (Ch), at para. 21.
1273. *Administration of Estates Act* 1925, s. 46(1)(i).
1274. *Ibid.*, s. 47(1)(i), as amended by *Civil Partnership Act* 2004, s. 71, Sch. 4, Pt. 2, para. 8(1), (2).

that age.[1275] If no child or other issue of the intestate attains an absolutely vested interest, the residuary estate will be divided as if the intestate had died without leaving issue.[1276]

*496.* If the deceased left no issue then the surviving spouse or civil partner will be entitled to the entire estate.[1277]

*497.* It should be noted that the sums prescribed as the 'statutory legacy' were intended to be set at a level to ensure that the surviving spouse would be able to remain in the matrimonial home. In furtherance of this policy, the surviving spouse or civil partner has the right to require that his or her share of the intestate's estate should be satisfied by the intestate's interest in the home.[1278] The level at which the statutory legacy is now set means that the surviving spouse will inherit the entire estate in the majority of cases.[1279]

*498.* At present, cohabitants have no rights under the intestacy laws, however long their relationship. Their legal rights have improved over the past decade or so, but this has been achieved by improving their rights under the discretionary regime rather than by conferring automatic rights.[1280] However, the Law Commission has proposed that those who have been living together for at least five years before the death of either partner should be treated in the same way as spouses under the intestacy rules, with those who have been living together for between two and five years being entitled to half of what a spouse would have received in the circumstances.[1281] While research indicates strong public support for the extension of such rights to cohabitants,[1282] the private member's bill proposing the implementation of this reform failed to proceed beyond a second reading.[1283]

---

1275. *Administration of Estates Act* 1925, s. 47(4B),(4C) and (4D), as inserted by the *Estates of Deceased Persons (Forfeiture Rule and Law of Succession) Act* 2011, s. 3.

1276. *Ibid.,* s. 47(2)(a).

1277. *Administration of Estates Act* 1925, s. 46(1)(i), as amended by *Inheritance and Trustees' Powers Act* 2014, s. 1.

1278. *Intestates' Estates Act* 1952, Sch. 2, para. 1(1), as amended by *Civil Partnership Act* 2004, Sch. 4, para. 13.

1279. *See also Administration of Estates Act 1925,* Sch. 1A as inserted by *Inheritance and Trustees' Powers Act* 2014, Sch. 1, for the provisions governing how the level will be updated.

1280. *See* Part IV, Ch. 3, para. 562.

1281. Law Commission, *Intestacy and Family Provision Claims on Death,* Law Com. No. 331 (2011), part 8.

1282. A. Humphrey et al., *Inheritance and the family: Attitudes to Will-making and Intestacy* (NatCen 2010).

1283. This was the *Inheritance (Cohabitants) Bill* 2012, introduced by Lord Lester; *see also* the *Cohabitation Rights Bill* 2014, which also proposes provision for cohabitants on intestacy and only progressed to a second reading, and the *Cohabitation Rights Bill* 2015.

## B. Descendants

*499.* As noted above, the descendants of the deceased – otherwise referred to as 'issue' – are entitled to a proportion of the estate if the deceased left a spouse or civil partner. If the deceased died single, they stand to inherit the entire estate. The rules provide for equal division among the deceased's children, with remoter issue only becoming entitled if their parent predeceased the deceased, and only to the share to which that parent would have been entitled.

*500.* As previous chapters have shown, the meaning of 'child' is not always straightforward. For the purposes of intestacy rules, it is legal parentage that is important. Thus, adopted children lose the right to inherit from their biological parents (although there would be nothing to prevent provision being made in a will) and acquire the right to inherit from their adoptive parents.[1284] Since 1988, no distinction has been made between children born within marriage and those born outside it.[1285]

*501.* Stepchildren have no entitlement under the intestacy rules. The concept of a 'child of the family' has not found its way into the intestacy rules, although such a person may claim provision under the Inheritance (Provision for Family and Dependants) Act 1975.

## C. Ascendants

*502.* The policy of the intestacy rules is to pass wealth down the generations rather than up,[1286] but if the deceased died single and without issue, his or her assets will pass – in order of priority – to parents, siblings (or their issue), grandparents, or uncles and aunts (or their issue). Within each category, relationships of the full-blood will be preferred to relationships of the half-blood, so if the deceased had two full siblings and one half-sibling (and no other closer relatives), the former will share the estate between them and the latter will not be entitled to anything. Similarly, if the deceased had one surviving sibling of the half-blood and one full sibling who predeceased him or her but left children, the latter will be entitled to the estate in preference to the half-sibling.

*503.* One specific rule applies to fathers who were not married to the mother of the person who has died. The presumption has been that the deceased was not survived by his or her father, or by any person related to him or her only through his

---

1284. *Adoption and Children Act* 2002, s. 67. *See* however the amendments made to s. 69 of the 2002 Act by the *Inheritance and Trustees' Powers Act* 2014, s. 4, to protect the contingent interests of children adopted after the death of their parents.

1285. *Family Law Reform Act* 1987, s. 1. *See*, e.g., *Official Solicitor to the Senior Courts v. Yemoh* [2010] EWHC 3727 (Ch).

1286. Although this policy may cause tension within families where a child benefits to the exclusion of a parent: *see*, e.g., *Cowderoy v. Cranfield* [2011] EWHC 1616 (Ch).

or her father, unless the contrary is shown.[1287] The rule was intended to deal with the problem that the father of the child may be unknown: since around 7% of births are registered without the father's name being included, this is a real possibility but one that no longer reflects the experience of the majority. Under the Inheritance and Trustees' Powers Act 2014, it is accordingly provided that this rule will not apply where someone has been registered as the father.[1288]

### D. Collaterals

*504.* Before the reforms to the intestacy rules carried out in 1925, there was no restriction on remoter kin inheriting, and the plot device of the long-lost relative turning up to claim the estate formed the basis of many Victorian novels. After 1925, the most remote relative who may – in default of other claimants – be entitled to inherit is a descendant of an aunt or uncle of the half-blood. If there are no relatives within the prescribed degrees, then the estate will pass to the Crown (or to the Duchy of Lancaster or Cornwall, if the intestate was resident there) as *bona vacantia.*[1289]

## II. Representation

*505.* Prior to 1996, gifts made to a child 'by way of advancement' would be taken into account under the 'hotchpotch' rules as part of that child's share of the intestate's estate, subject to any contrary intention. Similarly, in cases of partial intestacy, any interests taken by the surviving spouse or children under the will of the deceased would also be taken into account in determining how much each should be entitled to under the intestacy rules. Both provisions have now been abolished.[1290]

## III. Adoption

*506.* As noted above, an adopted child is the legal child of the adoptive parents, and will be treated as such for the purposes of the intestacy rules. Unlike the position in certain jurisdictions, there is no possibility of adopting an adult in order to confer legal rights.

---

1287. *Family Law Reform Act* 1987, s. 18(2).
1288. *Ibid.,* 18(2ZA), as inserted by *Inheritance and Trustees' Powers Act* 2014, s. 5. The same rule applies to someone who is the second legal parent under the *Human Fertilisation and Embryology Act* 2008: *see* further Part II, Ch. 5.
1289. *Administration of Estates Act* 1925, s. 46(1)(vi).
1290. By the *Law Reform (Succession) Act* 1995, s. 1(2).

§4. *Bona Vacantia*

*507.* As of January 2016, there were over 14,000 entries in the list of unclaimed estates held by the *Bona Vacantia* Division of the Government Legal Department. Many of these will, however, eventually be claimed by family members who belatedly discover their entitlement.

# Chapter 2. Testamentary Succession

## §1. INTRODUCTION

*508.* A will may be defined as a revocable ambulatory disposition of the maker's property which is intended to take effect upon death.[1291] As long as the maker intends to make such a disposition, it matters not that he or she did not actually know that he or she was making a will that would be admissible to probate.[1292] There is no need for the document to declare that it is the maker's 'last will and testament', although such labels do raise a presumption that the maker had the necessary testamentary intention. If it is clear from the will that it was only to come into effect if a certain condition was satisfied, then its validity is conditional upon that event occurring.[1293]

The terms of the will may also state the testator's preferred funeral arrangements, and make various appointments (including the appointment of a guardian for a minor child).[1294] Its main importance lies, of course, in the directions for the disposition of the testator's property. Since the making of a will is an important legal action, it is hedged around with formalities, as is its subsequent alteration or revocation. First of all, though, the maker must have the necessary capacity to make a will.

## §2. THE CAPACITY TO MAKE A WILL

*509.* The capacity to make a valid will encompasses a number of factors. First, the would-be testator must have attained adulthood – the age of which has been set at 18 years since 1969,[1295] although there are exceptions for those serving in the armed forces.[1296] Second, he or she must be mentally capable of making a will, and his or her choices must not have been brought about by duress or undue influence. The very context of the will's making may raise problems in relation to both an individual's general capacity, and his or her capacity in relation to that specific transaction, since illness and old age may have an impact on a person's cognitive capacity and can increase an individual's vulnerability to duress or undue influence. However, if the will has been drafted with professional assistance, this may be a factor suggesting that the deceased did have capacity: as was noted in *Hawes v. Burgess*, '[i]f, as here, an experienced lawyer has been instructed and has formed the opinion from a meeting or meetings that the testatrix understands what she is doing, the will so drafted and executed should only be set aside on the clearest evidence of lack of mental capacity.'[1297]

---

1291. *See,* e.g., *Re Berger* [1990] Ch. 118.
1292. *Re Servoz-Gavin (Deceased)* [2009] EWHC 3168 (Ch).
1293. *Roberts v. Roberts* (1862) 164 E.R. 1026; *In the Estate of Vines* [1910] P. 147; *Re Rowland* [1963] Ch. 1; *Corbett v. Newey* [1996] 2 All E.R. 914.
1294. *See* Part II, Ch. 6, paras 314–316.
1295. *Wills Act 1837,* s. 7, as amended by the *Family Law Reform Act 1969,* s. 1.
1296. *Wills (Soldiers and Sailors) Act 1918,* s. 1.
1297. *Hawes v. Burgess* [2013] EWCA Civ 94, at para. 60.

## I. Mental Capacity

*510.* At common law, there was no general test of capacity in the law of England and Wales, but rather what one might term 'transactional capacity', an individual's capacity to enter into a particular arrangement would depend on the nature and complexity of the particular arrangement. Thus a person may have capacity to enter into a valid marriage, but not to make a valid will; while a person who has the capacity to make a simple will may not have the requisite understanding to make a more complex one.[1298] This idea of 'transactional capacity' is preserved by the Mental Capacity Act 2005,[1299] and the courts have continued to apply the common law test in determining whether a person has the capacity to make a will.[1300]

*511.* According to the leading case of *Banks v. Goodfellow*, a testator:

> shall understand the nature of the act and its effects; shall understand the extent of the property of which he is disposing; shall be able to comprehend and appreciate the claims to which he ought to give effect; and, with a view to the latter object, that no disorder of the mind shall poison his affections, pervert his sense of right, or prevent the exercise of his natural faculties – that no insane delusion shall influence his will in disposing of his property and bring about a disposal of it which, if the mind had been sound, would not have been made.[1301]

In short, the testator must understand what he or she is doing, how much property he or she has, and which persons should be considered as possible beneficiaries.

*512.* It will be sufficient if the testator understands the substance of the transaction – namely that the wishes he or she is expressing will take effect upon his or her death and that up until that point he or she is free to change his or her mind. Similarly, a testator is not required to have a detailed knowledge of his or her assets, but the fact that a testator over- or underestimates his or her assets by some considerable margin may be evidence that he or she does not have the necessary capacity to make a will.[1302]

*513.* It is the condition that the testator should understand to whom he or she intends to leave his or her assets that raises more difficult questions. The law of England and Wales adopts the view that a testator is entitled to be unreasonable; he or she may leave his or her property to whomsoever he or she chooses and is under

---

1298. *Re Park's Estate* [1953] 2 All E.R. 1411; *Burns v. Burns* [2017] EWCA Civ 37.
1299. *See supra* Part I, Ch. 7, para. 127.
1300. *Re Walker* [2014] EWHC 71 (Ch). On the relationship between the MCA 2005 and the common law, *see* Law Commission, *Making a Will*, Law Com. C.P. 231 (2017), paras. 2.43 et seq.
1301. (1870) L.R. 5 Q.B. 549, 565.
1302. *See*, e.g., *Wood v. Smith* [1993] Ch. 90.

no obligation to make provision for those who are closest to him or her.[1303] Nevertheless, the courts are inevitably influenced by the content of the will and by whether it complies with social expectations about the disposition of property in deciding whether the requirement of capacity is satisfied. It may therefore be easier to show that a testator lacks capacity if the will disinherits those for whom the testator might have been expected to make provision. In *Boughton v. Knight*, e.g., the court held that 'there is a limit beyond which one feels that it ceases to be a question of harsh unreasonable judgment of character and that the repulsion which a parent exhibits towards one or more of his children must proceed from some mental defect in himself'.[1304] Similarly, in *Sharp v. Adam*,[1305] the irrational failure of the testator – who suffered from severely debilitating progressive multiple sclerosis that affected his cognitive function – to make any provision for his daughters was a factor taken into account by the courts in deciding that he lacked capacity.[1306] By contrast, in *Barry v. Butlin*[1307] the court held that it was quite understandable that the testator had left his property to his butler and his attorney instead of his violent son, from whom he had been alienated for some time.[1308]

*514.* As this indicates, a variety of factors may deprive a person of capacity. The Law Commission, in its review of the law, noted that capacity may be impaired by 'medication, pain levels, altered biochemistry, infection, stress, hypoglycaemia … and other temporary conditions or states' as well as by 'a learning disability, a personality disorder or through mental illness'.[1309] As was pointed out in *Re Key (Deceased)*, there is now a better understanding of the circumstances that might deprive an individual 'of the power of rational decision-making',[1310] and it has been suggested that a new test might better reflect 'modern understandings of capacity'.[1311]

*515.* If the capacity of the testator is challenged, it must be shown that he or she lacked capacity at the time that the will was actually made. This means that if a person who, in general, lacks capacity, makes a will in a lucid interval, the resulting document will be valid. The converse is also true. A will made by a person who is generally capable of making a will but who is at that particular point incapacitated – e.g., by alcohol or drugs – will not be valid. With some gradual degenerative diseases it may be difficult to pinpoint the moment at which a person no longer has capacity: it has been acknowledged that the dividing line between having capacity

---

1303. *See*, e.g., *Gill v. RSPCA* [2010] EWCA Civ 1430; *The Vegetarian Society v. Scott* [2013] EWHC 4097 (Ch).
1304. (1873) L.R. 3 P. & D. 64, at 69.
1305. [2006] EWCA Civ 449.
1306. *See also Kostic v. Chaplin* [2007] EWHC 2298 (Ch); *Re Ritchie (Deceased)* [2009] EWHC 709 (Ch); *Re Ashkettle (Deceased)* [2013] EWHC 2125 (Ch); *Re Wilson (Deceased)* [2013] EWHC 499 (Ch).
1307. (1838) 12 E.R. 1089.
1308. *See also Carr v. Thomas* [2008] EWHC 2859 (Ch); *McCabe v. McCabe* [2015] EWHC 1591 (Ch).
1309. Law Commission, *Making a Will*, Law Com. C.P. 231 (2017), para. 2.15.
1310. [2010] EWHC 408 (Ch).
1311. Law Commission, *Making a Will*, Law Com. C.P. 231 (2017), para. 2.41.

and no longer having capacity is an imprecise one and all that is necessary is to establish on which side of the line the testator fell at the time the will was made.[1312]

*516.* There is one exception to the requirement that the testator must be capable at the time of the making of the will, known as the principle in *Parker v. Felgate*.[1313] If the person in question has given instructions to a solicitor for the drawing up of the will at a time when he or she has full capacity, the resulting will which is drawn up may be valid even though at the time that the will was actually executed the testator lacks such capacity. The requirements of this exception are, however, quite narrowly defined. The testator must still have some understanding of the process at the time that the will is executed. According to the court in *Parker v. Felgate*, he must have been able either to remember and understand the instructions given to the solicitor, or to be able to understand each clause if it had been put to him, or to understand that he is engaged in executing the will for which he had given instructions. The court will also take into account the way in which the testator's instructions were conveyed: more caution is needed if the instructions have been conveyed by a third party than if the testator gave his instructions directly, whether in writing or orally.[1314]

*517.* In determining whether a person lacks capacity, the burden of proof is initially on the person propounding the will. Assuming the will appears rational, the court will presume capacity; however, if the objector raises a 'real doubt' about capacity then the evidential burden shifts back to the person propounding the will to establish capacity.[1315]

*518.* If a court decides that an individual lacked testamentary capacity, then their will is invalid and their estate will pass under the rules of intestacy (or according to the terms of any prior will made at a time that the person did have capacity). As the Law Commission has pointed out, the law thus needs to ensure that the test of capacity is set at the right level to ensure that the will 'does in fact represent the autonomous decision of the testator and is a genuine exercise of his or her testamentary freedom'.[1316]

---

1312. *Sharp v. Adam* [2006] EWCA Civ 449. *See also Jeffery v. Jeffery* [2013] EWHC 1942 (Ch), para. 256, in which a woman who suffered from occasional anxiety and mild depression was held to have capacity, the judge noting tartly that '[i]f people suffering from such complaints were unable to make wills, a large percentage of the population would be so inhibited'.
1313. (1883) 8 P.D. 171, approved by *Perrins v. Holland* [2010] EWCA Civ 1430. For a case applying the same principles to *inter vivos* transactions *see Singellos v. Singellos* [2010] EWHC 2353 (Ch).
1314. *In the Estate of Wallace* [1952] 2 T.L.R. 925.
1315. *Re Key (Deceased)* [2010] EWHC 408 (Ch), para. 97. *See also Bateman v. Overy* [2014] EWHC 432 (Ch), para. 139.
1316. Law Commission, *Making a Will*, Law Com. C.P. 231 (2017), para. 2.12.

## II. Undue Influence

*519.* If the testator has been unduly influenced to make a will that does not reflect his or her true wishes, then it will be set aside as invalid. It must be shown both that the influence led to the making of the transaction in question and that the resulting transaction was not the result of the free exercise of an independent will. The burden of proving undue influence lies upon the person who alleges it.[1317]

*520.* Coercion need not take a physical form, but a high threshold is set in determining whether more subtle forms of influence are 'undue'.[1318] In *Hall v. Hall*, the court distinguished between those influences which were legitimate and those which would invalidate a will:

> Persuasion, appeals to the affections or ties of kindred, to a sentiment of gratitude for past services or pity for future destitution – these are all legitimate and may be fairly pressed on a testator. On the other hand ... [i]mportunity or threats, such as the testator has not the courage to resist, moral command asserted and yielded to for the sake of peace and quiet, these, if carried to a degree in which the free play of the testator's judgment or discretion's overborne, will constitute undue influence, though no force is either used or threatened.[1319]

*521.* The idea that the testator's judgment must have been overborne also means that whether or not conduct amounts to undue influence in any particular case will depend upon the ability of the testator to resist the pressure brought to bear upon him or her. The weaker he or she is, the more likely it is that pressure will overbear his or her judgment:[1320] in *Wingrove v. Wingrove*,[1321] it was suggested that even badgering a weak person to make a will might constitute undue influence. By contrast, the judge observed of the 'spirited' testatrix in *Abbott v. Richardson* that he did not believe that 'anyone ... would have been able to get her to do anything important which she did not want to do'.[1322]

### §3. Formalities for Making a Will

*522.* A will must be made in writing, and must be signed or acknowledged by the testator before witnesses who themselves sign the will.[1323] The same formalities

---

1317. *Craig v. Lamoureux* [1920] A.C. 349.
1318. *See*, e.g., *Parfitt v. Lawless* (1872) L.R. 2 P. & D. 462; Law Commission, *Making a Will*, Law Com. C.P. 231 (2017), para. 7.59.
1319. (1868) L.R. 1 P. & D. 481, at 482. *See*, e.g., *Ark v. Kaur* [2010] EWHC 2314 (Ch).
1320. *See*, e.g., *Hampson v. Guy* (1891) 64 L.T. 778; *Killick v. Pountney*, unreported, 31 Mar. 1999.
1321. (1886) 11 P.D. 81. *See also Schomberg v. Taylor* [2013] EWHC 2269 (Ch).
1322. [2006] EWHC 1291 (Ch), para. 199. *See also Re Good, Deceased* [2002] EWHC 640 (Ch); *Wharton v. Bancroft* [2011] EWHC (Ch) 3250; *Parker v. Litchfield* [2014] EWHC 1799 (Ch).
1323. *Wills Act 1837*, s. 9, as substituted by the *Administration of Justice Act 1982*, s. 17.

must be observed by persons making a joint will, and if any alterations are made to the original will. As the Court of Appeal has noted in *Barrett v. Bem*:

> there is no discretion on the part of the court to override compliance with these conditions in order to give effect to the putative testator's intentions or wishes [and] since the validity of a will necessarily arises after the principal actor is dead, there are powerful policy reasons for insisting on their fulfilment.[1324]

## I. Writing, Signatures and Witnesses

*523.* A will may be written – whether handwritten, typed or printed – on any substance.[1325] Presumably, it may also be written in any substance, although if it is written in a combination of pen and pencil the court may decide that the parts in pencil were not intended to form part of the final version.[1326]

*524.* The testator's signature may take the form of a mark that is intended to represent the testator's name:[1327] even a thumb mark or a cross will suffice.[1328] The will may even be signed by another person as long as this is done in the testator's presence and by his or her direction;[1329] this, however, requires some instruction to this effect by the testator rather than merely passive acquiescence:

> the court should not find that a will has been signed by a third party at the direction of the testator unless there is positive and discernible communication (which may be verbal or non-verbal) by the testator that he wishes the will to be signed on his behalf by the third party.[1330]

It is a further condition of validity that the testator should have 'intended by his signature to give effect to the will'.[1331] Prior to the amendments made by the Administration of Justice Act 1982 the law had required that the signature be placed at the foot or end of the will; now the signature may be placed at the head of the will as long as the 'the writing of the will and the appending of the signature are all one operation'.[1332]

*525.* At least two persons must witness the testator's signature.[1333] The witnesses to the will need not be present when the testator signs the will, but if they are not he or she must acknowledge his or her signature before them. The witnesses do

---

1324. [2012] EWCA Civ 52, para. 18.
1325. *See*, e.g., *Hodson v. Barnes* (1926) 43 T.L.R. 71 (an eggshell).
1326. *Re Adams* (1872) L.R. 2 P. & D. 367.
1327. *Re Chalcraft* [1948] P. 222. *See also Reynolds v. Reynolds* [2005] EWHC 6 (Ch) (initials sufficed).
1328. *Re Finn's Estate* (1935) 105 L.J.P. 36.
1329. *Wills Act* 1837, s. 9(a).
1330. *Barrett v. Bem* [2012] EWCA Civ 52, at para. 36.
1331. *Wills Act* 1837, s. 9(b).
1332. *Wood v. Smith* [1993] Ch. 90; followed in *Weatherhill v. Pearce* [1995] 1 W.L.R. 592.
1333. *Wills Act* 1837, s. 9(c).

not need to know that the document they are signing is a will,[1334] but must be able to see the testator's signature.[1335] Both witnesses must be present in the room at the same time that the testator is signing or acknowledging his or her signature,[1336] and must be both able to see[1337] and aware of what is going on.[1338] As the court noted in *Hudson v. Parker*[1339] 'the witnesses should see and be conscious of the act done, and be able to prove it by their own evidence: if the witnesses are not to be mentally, as well as bodily present, they might be asleep, or intoxicated, or of unsound mind'.

526. After the testator has signed the will (or acknowledged his or her signature), each witness must attest and sign the will or acknowledge his or her signature in the presence of the testator (but not necessarily in the presence of any other witness).[1340] All parties must sign the same physical document: it is not sufficient for the witnesses to sign a document containing a photocopy of the testator's signature.[1341]

527. In the absence of 'the strongest evidence' to the contrary, the inference that the will was validly executed will be drawn from the presence of the relevant signatures on the will.[1342]

528. If the testator has left instructions in other documents which have not been executed as wills, these may be regarded as incorporated into the will if three requirements are satisfied. First, the document must be in existence at the time when the will is executed (or republished).[1343] Second, it must be referred to as an existing document.[1344] And finally, the will must provide a sufficient description of the document to enable it to be identified.[1345]

---

1334. *Keigwin v. Keigwin* (1843) 163 E.R. 841.
1335. *Hudson v. Parker* (1844) 163 E.R. 948.
1336. *Re Groffman* [1969] 2 All E.R. 108; *Re Colling* [1972] 3 All E.R. 729; *Weatherhill v. Pearce* [1995] 1 W.L.R. 592; *see also Re Singh (Deceased)* [2011] EWHC 2097 (Ch), in which it was held that the deceased had visited each witness separately and that the will was therefore invalid; *Watts v. Watts* [2014] EWHC 668 (Ch).
1337. *See,* e.g., *Re Gibson* [1949] 2 All E.R. 90 (Blind Person Unable to be a Witness).
1338. *Brown v. Skirrow* [1902] P. 3.
1339. (1844) 163 E.R. 948.
1340. *Wills Act 1837,* s. 9(d). *See,* e.g., *Couser v. Couser* [1996] 3 All E.R. 256; *Re Whelan* [2015] EWHC 3301 (Ch) (home-made will invalid as the testatrix was not present when it was signed).
1341. *Lim v. Thompson* [2009] EWHC 3341 (Ch).
1342. *Sherrington v. Sherrington* [2005] EWCA Civ 326; *Kentfield v. Wright* [2010] EWHC 1607 (Ch).
1343. *Re Saxton* [1939] 2 All E.R. 418; *In the Goods of Lady Truro* (1866) L.R. 1 P. & D. 201.
1344. *Re Smart* [1902] P. 238.
1345. *Allen v. Maddock* (1858) 14 E.R. 757; cf. *The University College of North Wales v. Taylor* [1908] P. 140.

## II.  Joint Wills

*529.* Two or more persons may execute one document as the will of both of them.[1346] In this case, both (or all) must sign the will. Although the resulting document is known as a joint will, it is in effect treated as the separate will of each of the parties. Each is entitled to revoke or alter the will at any time,[1347] and when each dies, probate will be granted of the will as the will of that person. Joint wills should be distinguished from mutual wills, which operate as a restriction on freedom of testation and are considered further below.

## III.  Alterations

*530.* If changes have been made to a will after it was executed, the court will need to decide whether they should stand part of the will, and, if not, whether the original clauses can still be read.

*531.* It is presumed that any alterations to the will were made after the execution of the will and are accordingly not valid. This presumption is rebuttable by either intrinsic or extrinsic evidence. For example, if the alterations were written in the same ink as the rest of the will,[1348] this would suggest that they were made contemporaneously with the rest of the will; alternatively, there might be evidence from witnesses that the alterations had been made before the will was executed. If it can be shown that the alterations were made before the will was executed, the execution of the will obviously covers the alteration as well.

*532.* If a testator wishes to make alterations at a later date, he or she must comply with the same formalities as are required for making a will. The legislation provides that the signature of the testator and the subscription of the witnesses must 'be made in the margin or on some other part of the will opposite or near to such alteration, or at the foot or end of or opposite to a memorandum referring to such alteration, and written at the end or some other part of the will'.[1349]

*533.* If there is no evidence that the alterations were made before the execution of the will and the formalities required by section 21 have not been complied with, the alterations are not valid and the original unaltered version of the will be admitted to probate. If, however, the effect of the alterations has been to obliterate the words of the original will, then the part that is no longer 'apparent' will be revoked if this was the testator's intention. The result will be that the will is admitted to probate with blank spaces. So the court is faced with the choice between finding that

---

1346. *See*, e.g., *Re Govier (Deceased)* [1950] P. 237.
1347. *Hobson v. Blackburn and Blackburn* (1822) 1 Add. 274.
1348. *In the Goods of Hindmarsh* (1866) 1 P. & D. 307.
1349. *Wills Act* 1837, s. 21.

the original words are still apparent and admitting them to probate or admitting neither the original words nor the alterations to probate – i.e., a choice between carrying out what the testator has ceased to want and what he or she never contemplated. The courts have tended to lean in favour of the former option, holding in one case that the original words of the testator were still apparent on the basis that they could be deciphered by an expert in handwriting using a magnifying glass.[1350] The court does draw a distinction between cases where the words can be read by looking at the document itself – however sophisticated the devices used to assist the eye – and cases where the words can only be read by producing a new document.[1351] Physical interference with the original document – e.g., removing strips of paper pasted over the original clauses – is prohibited.

## §4. DIFFERENT TYPES OF WILL

*534.* Two different types of will should be considered: the first, privileged wills, may be made by soldiers and sailors without the formalities usually required for a valid will; the second, statutory wills, may be made on behalf of persons who lack capacity to make a will.

## I. Privileged Wills

*535.* Soldiers in military service, mariners or seamen at sea, and members of the naval or marine forces in actual military service, are all allowed to dispose of their property without complying with the usual formalities for making a will – or indeed any formalities at all.[1352] The wills of such persons may therefore consist simply of a handwritten letter or even an oral statement to another person. The one crucial requirement is that there must have been some testamentary act, defined in *In the Estate of Knibbs* as 'a statement of the deceased's wishes for the disposition of his property which is not merely imparted to his audience as a matter of information or interest, but is intended by him to convey to that audience a request explicit or implicit to see that his wishes are carried out'.[1353]

*536.* The definition of those entitled to the privilege has been interpreted very widely: 'soldier' includes doctors, nurses, and chaplains,[1354] and such a person will be on 'actual military service' if he or she is 'actually serving with the Armed Forces in connexion with military operations which are or have been taking place or are believed to be imminent'.[1355] Thus, periods of training prior to the actual military operation will count for this purpose, and the privilege is not confined to war but

---

1350. *In the Goods of Brasier* [1899] P. 36.
1351. *In the Goods of Itter* [1950] P. 130.
1352. *Wills Act* 1837, s. 11.
1353. [1962] 2 All E.R. 829, and *see Re Stable* [1919] P. 7.
1354. *Re Stanley* [1916] P. 192; *Re Wingham* [1949] P. 187.
1355. *Re Wingham* [1949] P. 187, per Denning L.J.

applies to any military operations.[1356] Similarly, the phrase 'mariner or seaman' has been held to include a barman on a liner,[1357] a ship's radio officer[1358] and even a typist,[1359] while a person may be deemed to be 'at sea' as soon as orders to join the ship have been received.[1360]

*537.* In addition to this exemption from the usual formalities, a soldier or sailor is entitled to make a will under the age of 18 years,[1361] and a gift to a witness will be valid.[1362] A privileged testator may revoke the will with the same ease.[1363] Another striking feature of the law is that a will made when the testator was privileged will govern the disposition of his or her property whether he or she dies in action or lives to a ripe old age, unless it is subsequently revoked.[1364]

## II. Statutory Wills

*538.* If an adult lacks the capacity to make a will, the Court of Protection may order that a will should be made on his or her behalf.[1365] The will must state that it is signed by the adult who lacks capacity acting by the authorized person; must be signed by the authorized person with both the name of the adult who lacks capacity and his or her own name, in the presence of two or more witnesses present at the same time; must be attested and subscribed by those witnesses in the presence of the authorized person, and must be sealed with the official seal of the court.[1366]

In deciding whether to make a will, and in what terms, the courts will follow the process laid down by the 2005 Act.[1367] The overarching principle is that the decision of the court must be in the person's best interests, and the weight to be attached to any particular factor will differ from case to case.[1368] The objective 'best interests' of an individual are of course not necessarily the same as his or her subjective wishes,[1369] and the Court of Protection has the power to order the execution of a statutory will even if a will already exists. This power may be particularly important where there are doubts as to whether the individual had capacity to make the earlier will. As one judge has noted:

---

1356. *Re Jones* [1981] 1 All E.R. 1.
1357. *In the Estate of Knibbs* [1962] 2 All E.R. 829.
1358. *Re Servoz-Gavin (Deceased)* [2009] EWHC 3168 (Ch).
1359. *Re Hale* (1915) 2 I.R. 362.
1360. *In the Goods of Newland* [1952] P. 71; contrast *Re Rapley's Estate* [1983] 3 All E.R. 248.
1361. *Wills (Soldiers and Sailors) Act* 1918, s. 1.
1362. *Re Limond* [1915] 2 Ch. 240.
1363. *Wood v. Gossage* [1921] P. 194.
1364. *Re Wardrop* [1917] P. 54; *Booth v. Booth* [1926] P. 118.
1365. *See Mental Capacity Act* 2005, s. 16 (On Appointment) and s. 18(1)(i) (On the Deputy's Power to Execute a Will).
1366. *Mental Capacity Act* 2005, Sch. 2, para. 3(2).
1367. *Re P* [2009] EWHC 163 (Ch), para. 38; *NT v. FS* [2013] EWHC 684 (COP).
1368. For the factors to be considered, *see Mental Capacity Act* 2005, s. 4.
1369. For criticism of this criterion in this context *see* R. Harding, 'The rise of statutory wills and the limits of best interests decision-making in inheritance' (2015) 78(6) M.L.R. 958.

Given the importance attached by the Court to the protected person being remembered for having done the 'right thing' by his will, it is open to the Court, in an appropriate case, to decide that the 'right thing' to do, in the protected person's best interests, is to order the execution of a statutory will, rather than to leave him to be remembered for having bequeathed a contentious probate dispute to his relatives and the beneficiaries named in a disputed will.[1370]

§5. REVOCATION OF A WILL

539. There are four ways of revoking a will. Three relate directly to the will itself: It is revoked if it is destroyed by the testator or replaced by another will, or if there is a duly attested document declaring the testator's intention to revoke.[1371] However, a revocation will be ineffective if the testator lacked capacity at the time, the test of capacity being the same as that for making a will.[1372] The fourth is based on the inferred intentions of a testator who enters into a marriage or civil partnership; on doing so any existing will is revoked.[1373]

I. Destruction

540. Legislation provides that a will may be revoked 'by the burning, tearing, or otherwise destroying the same by the testator, or by some person in his presence and by his direction, with the intention of revoking the same'.[1374] There are two elements to this, as the court noted in *Cheese v. Lovejoy*, 'all the destroying in the world without intention will not revoke a will, nor all the intention in the world without destroying, there must be the two'.[1375] One corollary of this is that the testator must be capable of exercising a free and competent choice at the time that the will was destroyed. The level of understanding required to revoke a will by destruction is the same as that required to make a new will or revoke a will by a formal declaration in writing, on the basis that the law should not require different standards of capacity for different types of revocation.[1376] The courts do recognize, however, that there may be no direct evidence of the testator's intentions other than the destruction of the will. If the will cannot be found, or is found in a mutilated form, the court will presume that the testator destroyed it with the intention of revoking it, provided that he or she was in possession of the will up to the time of his or her

---

1370. *Re D (Statutory Will)* [2010] EWHC 2159 (Ch), although *see also Re Jones* [2014] EWCOP 59 for the limits of this approach.
1371. *Wills Act* 1837, s. 20.
1372. *Hinton v. Leigh* [2009] EWHC 2658 (Ch).
1373. *Wills Act* 1837, s. 18, as amended by *Administration of Justice Act* 1982 and Marriage (Same Sex Couples) Act 2013 (marriage) and s. 18B, added by the *Civil Partnership Act* 2004 (civil partnership).
1374. *Wills Act* 1837, s. 20.
1375. (1877) 2 P.D. 251.
1376. *Re Sabatini* (1969) 114 S.J. 35; *Wickens v. Carnell* [2002] EWHC 2699 (Ch).

death.[1377] The courts have stressed that this presumption is not a rigid one and that the task of the court 'is to decide on the balance of probabilities having regard to all the evidence before the Court ... whether the testator destroyed the will with the intention of revoking it'.[1378] The strength of the presumption will depend on the care with which the will was kept during the testator's lifetime,[1379] and it may be rebutted by evidence that the testator did not intend to revoke the will.[1380]

541. It may also be the case that the intention of the testator in destroying the will was conditional upon some other event or assumption. If so, the will only be revoked if the condition is satisfied. Thus *In the Estate of Southerden*,[1381] the testator burnt his will in the mistaken belief that if he died intestate his wife would be entitled to the whole estate. The Court of Appeal held that his intention to revoke the will was conditional on this assumption being true; since it was not, the will remained valid. The fact that the testator intends to make a new will does not prevent the destruction of the old one from being unconditional: a desire to disinherit one person need not be conditional upon a desire to bequeath property to another.[1382]

542. Of course, without the physical act of destruction, the testator's intentions are irrelevant. The key question is what degree of destruction is necessary to revoke a will? While the legislation refers to 'burning' and 'tearing' it would be harsh if a slight tear or the singeing of the paper were to revoke the will. However, to accept as valid a will of which certain clauses are crossed out and on which is written 'this is revoked' – as in *Cheese v. Lovejoy*[1383] – might seem to disregard the testator's intentions. But the law of succession adopts the view that a testator manifests his or her intentions by complying with the legal requirements, and these stipulate that the destruction should be thorough.

It is, however, sufficient if the testator destroys an essential part of the will, such as his or her signature or that of the attesting witnesses. Since a will cannot exist without these formalities, their physical destruction entails the legal destruction of the whole. The signatures may be physically removed from the document,[1384] or rendered unreadable.[1385] If, by contrast, the part of the will destroyed by the testator was relatively unimportant, the court may hold that the remainder of the will is still valid,[1386] unless the testator had intended to substitute other pages at a later date.

---

1377. *Bell v. Fothergill* (1870) 2 P.D. 148.
1378. *Nicholls v. Hudson* [2006] EWHC 3006 (Ch), para. 36.
1379. *See*, e.g., *Rowe v. Clark* [2005] EWHC 3068 (Ch) (Will was not Carefully looked After); *Nicholls v. Hudson* [2006] EWHC 3006 (Ch) (Testator an Absent-minded Alcoholic); *Re Whelan* [2015] EWHC 3301 (other important documents had also been lost).
1380. *See*, e.g., *Wren v. Wren* [2006] EWHC 2243 (Ch) (Deceased made Statements Confirming the Existence of the Will Down to the Date of his Death).
1381. [1925] P. 177.
1382. *Re Jones* [1976] Ch. 200.
1383. (1877) 2 P.D. 251.
1384. *Hobbs v. Knight* (1838) 163 E.R. 267.
1385. *Re Adams* [1990] 1 Ch. 601.
1386. *In the Estate of Nunn* [1936] 1 All E.R. 555; *Re Everest* [1975] 1 All E.R. 672.

Such an intention would indicate that the testator did not intend the remaining part to govern the disposition of his or her property by itself, and the entire will would therefore be revoked.[1387]

*543.* The act of destruction need not be carried out by the testator himself or herself – since it is possible that he or she may be too weak to undertake the task – but if it is to be revoked, it must be destroyed in his or her presence and at his or her direction. Thus if the testator tells someone to destroy the will, and that person goes into the next room to carry out the task, the will remains valid. Similarly, the destruction of a will by another person without an express instruction from the testator will not revoke it, even if the testator subsequently acquiesces in the will's destruction.[1388]

## II. Another Will or Codicil

*544.* A valid will or codicil will, in general, revoke any earlier one, and wills that have been professionally drafted or written on a standard will form usually contain a clause by which the testator expressly revokes all previous wills and codicils. (An invalid will, of course, will be of no effect in revoking an earlier will).[1389]

*545.* It should however be noted that even a clear statement in the will that earlier wills are thereby revoked may not have this effect if the court is satisfied that this was not the testator's intention. For example, a general revocation clause may be followed by a statement suggesting that the impact of the new will was intended to be more limited – as in *In the Estate of Wayland*,[1390] in which a general revocation clause was followed by a statement that the new will was only intended to deal with the testator's property in England. The court held that the will did not revoke a separate will that had been made in Belgium and dealt with the testator's property in that country. Similarly, the court may decide that the revocation clause was included by mistake. This occurred in *Re Phelan*,[1391] where the testator was under the mistaken belief that stocks and shares had to be dealt with under separate wills and thus made three wills within minutes, each dealing with a different single investment in a unit trust and each containing a revocation clause. It was held that all the wills could be admitted to probate as they were not inconsistent. The omission of the revocation clauses would give effect to the true intention of the testator.

*546.* Even if the later will or codicil does not include a specific clause revoking an earlier will, this will be its effect, insofar as it is inconsistent with any earlier will. This means that it is possible to add a codicil providing for the disposition of an item of property not previously dealt with in the will without affecting the validity

---

1387. *Leonard v. Leonard* [1902] P. 243.
1388. *Gill v. Gill* [1909] P. 157.
1389. *See*, e.g., *Re Whelan* [2015] EWHC 3301.
1390. [1951] 2 All E.R. 1041.
1391. [1971] 3 W.L.R. 888.

of the entire will. By contrast, if the codicil provides that a certain item, previously left to A, is now to pass to B, that specific disposition in the original will is revoked, while a new will or codicil that is entirely inconsistent with the original document will revoke the old will in its entirety. Conversely, where the new will is not inconsistent with the earlier one, both may stand.[1392]

547. If the new will makes the same gift to the same person, the court may hold that the revocation of the first will was conditional upon the validity of the second. In *Re Finnemore*,[1393] the testator's first will left a house and three-quarters of the residue of the estate to the defendant. This was repeated in two subsequent wills, which varied the disposition of the remainder of the estate. Unfortunately, the later two wills were both witnessed by the defendant's husband and so the gift failed.[1394] The court held that the intention of the testator when he made his last will could not be said to be an intention to revoke the gifts in favour of the defendant. The testator was labouring under a mistake as to the effect of his last two wills and his revocation of the provisions of the first will was qualified and conditional on the will being a valid will for the purpose of disposing of his property in favour of the defendant.

## III. Writing Declaring an Intention to Revoke

548. It is also possible to revoke a will without making a new one. The legislation provides that writing declaring an intention to revoke, executed in the same manner as a will, will have the effect of revoking the will. Once again, *Cheese v. Lovejoy*[1395] provides an example of how not to revoke a will. The testator wrote 'this is revoked' the back of it and threw it into the wastepaper basket (from which it was later retrieved). Had he and two witnesses signed the statement, it would have had the desired effect; without complying with the necessary formalities, it was of no effect.

## IV. Marriage

549. A marriage or civil partnership is considered to be such a fundamental change in a person's life that any testamentary dispositions made while single must be reconsidered. Any existing will is therefore revoked on a person's marriage or civil partnership.[1396] The rule belongs to a time when marriage marked the beginning of a couple's life together, but now that premarital cohabitation is common it is possible that the parties will already have made wills before the wedding. If the premarital will left the estate solely to the future spouse or civil partner, and neither

---

1392. *Perdoni v. Curati* [2012] EWCA Civ 1381.
1393. [1992] 1 All E.R. 800.
1394. *Wills Act* 1837, s. 15.
1395. (1877) 2 P.D. 251.
1396. *Wills Act* 1837, s. 18(1), and s. 18B (as inserted by the *Civil Partnership Act* 2004, Sch. 4). However, the conversion of a civil partnership into a marriage will not revoke any will made during the currency of the relationship.

has any children, the same result will be achieved under the intestacy rules. More problematic is the situation where provision is made for those who would not stand to inherit under the intestacy rules – e.g., friends or charities – or where the division dictated by the intestacy rules is less generous than the testamentary provision. This is likely to be a particular problem for older couples with children from previous relationships.

*550.* The law does attempt to mitigate these problems by providing that a will made in contemplation of marriage – or a particular disposition in such a will – will not be revoked by the marriage unless this was the testator's intention.[1397] This is logical in view of the fact that the rationale behind automatic revocation is the need to ensure that adequate provision is made for the new spouse, but the exception has been strictly construed. An express statement in the will that it is made in contemplation of the testator's marriage to a particular person will suffice; an express statement that it is made in contemplation of marriage without the intended spouse being named will not.[1398] The same principle applies to specific dispositions in the will that are made in contemplation of marriage: such dispositions may be upheld even if the remainder of the will is revoked.[1399] The same rules now apply to civil partners.[1400]

*551.* There is a second exception in the statute, which provides that 'a disposition in a will in exercise of a power of appointment shall take effect notwithstanding the testator's subsequent marriage unless the property so appointed would in default of appointment pass to his personal representatives'.[1401] The result of this is that if the testator has made an appointment of property which would otherwise pass to his or her estate, then it will be revoked upon his or her marriage in order that the estate, and thus the family, may benefit. However, if he or she has made an appointment of property which would otherwise pass to someone completely different – e.g., a charity – then there is little point in such an appointment being revoked by marriage, as this will not benefit his or her family. Again, the same rules now apply to civil partners.[1402]

*552.* Finally, it should be noted that a void marriage or civil partnership will have no effect on the validity of either party's will, but a marriage or civil partnership that is merely voidable will revoke any wills that the parties have made, on the basis that such a union is valid until it has been annulled.[1403] Since a person's inability to consent – whether by reason of mental incapacity or other influences – renders a marriage voidable rather than void, this leads to the rather odd consequence that the only way for a mentally incapable person personally to revoke a will is to

---

1397. *Ibid.*, s. 18(3) and (4).
1398. *Sallis v. Jones* [1936] P. 43.
1399. *Wills Act* 1837, s. 18(4).
1400. *Ibid.*, s. 18B(3) and (4), although note the restrictive interpretation in *Court v. Despallieres* [2009] EWHC 3340 (Ch).
1401. *Wills Act* 1837, s. 18(2).
1402. *Ibid.*, s. 18B(2).
1403. *Re Roberts* [1978] 3 All E.R. 225.

subsequently marry or enter into a civil partnership. In order to address this anomaly, the Law Commission has provisionally proposed that a will should not be revoked by a marriage entered into at a time when one of the parties lacked testamentary capacity and is unlikely to recover that capacity.[1404]

§6. REVIVAL OF A WILL

*553.* The revocation of a will is not always the end of the story. It is possible for a revoked will to be revived if the testator changes his or her mind yet again and decides to stand by the original disposition of his or her estate. Legislation makes specific provision for this contingency. A will may be revived if it is re-executed or if the testator executes a codicil with the intention of reviving the will.[1405] Each method requires three elements to be satisfied: namely that the will still exists, that the testator intended to revive the will and that there was some formal act of revival. Once the will has been revived it is deemed to operate from the date of revival.

The former option is the more straightforward. If the testator chooses to re-execute the will, it is presumed that he or she intended to revive it, and as long as he or she complies with the usual formalities for the execution of the will the original will be revived.

*554.* The execution of a codicil with the intention of reviving the will is slightly more problematic. The court has held that the testator's intention to revive the will may be demonstrated:

> either by express words referring to a will as revoked and importing an intention to revive the same, or by a disposition of the testator's property inconsistent with any other intention, or by some other expressions conveying to the mind of the Court with reasonable certainty, the existence of the intention in question.[1406]

Merely attaching the codicil to the will that it is intended to revive is insufficient; it must make express reference to the earlier document.[1407] Repeating dispositions made in the revoked will also indicate that it was the testator's intention to revive the earlier document. The court may need less persuasion of the testator's intention to revive an earlier will where revocation was by marriage or civil partnership rather than deliberate intent. In the case of *In the Goods of Davis*,[1408] the testator was informed that his will had been revoked by his marriage. The will in question had left all his estate to the woman who subsequently became his wife but was not stated to have been made in contemplation of marriage. He wrote on the envelope of the

---

1404. Law Commission, *Making a Will*, Law Com. C.P. 231 (2017), para. 11.62.
1405. *Wills Act* 1932, s. 22. *See*, e.g., *Hoare Trustees v. Jacques* [2008] EWHC 2022 (Ch).
1406. *In the Goods of Steele* (1868) 1 P. & D. 575.
1407. *Marsh v. Marsh* (1860) 1 Sw. & Tr. 528.
1408. [1952] P. 279.

will that she was now his wife and this statement was signed and attested. The court upheld this as a valid codicil that therefore had the effect of reviving the will that had been revoked by marriage.

555. The above discussion has focused on the indecisive testator who reverts to his original will. A second possibility is that the testator simply revokes the revoking will or codicil. This does not have the effect of reviving the original will unless the testator has indicated that this is his intention. An example is provided by *In the Goods of Hodgkinson*.[1409] Here the first will left all of the testator's property to 'his dear friend Jane'. Three months later the testator made another will leaving his real property to his sister, thus implicitly revoking the gift of such property to Jane. Later still he revoked the second will. The Court of Appeal held that the gift of the real property was not revived by the cancellation of the second will and thus probate was only admitted of so much of the first will as dealt with the disposition of the testator's personal property.

§7. RESTRICTIONS

556. It is usually stated as axiomatic that there are no restrictions on a testator's freedom of testation; he or she can dispose of his or her property as he or she wishes. There is no requirement that a certain proportion of the estate should be left to a spouse or children, although certain persons are entitled to apply to the court for provision if the disposition of the estate does not make reasonable provision for them. Since this possibility exists whether or not the deceased left a will, it is given separate consideration:[1410] this section will focus on self-imposed restrictions on freedom of testation.

I. Contracts to Make a Will

557. A testator may have entered into a contract regarding the disposition of his or her property. If the will that is admitted to probate is inconsistent with the terms of the contract then the court is entitled to go outside the terms of the will to enforce the contract. The contract must of course comply with the usual legal requirements for the creation of a contract, i.e., offer and acceptance, consideration,[1411] certainty of terms and the intention to create legal relations. Contracts relating to land must additionally be made in writing incorporating all the terms of the contract and signed by both parties.[1412] If these requirements are not satisfied then there is no

---

1409. [1893] P. 339.
1410. *See* Part IV, Ch. 3.
1411. *See,* e.g., *Irani v. Irani* [2006] EWHC 1811 (Ch).
1412. *Law Reform (Miscellaneous Provisions) Act* 1989, s. 2.

contract to bind the freedom of the testator. Less formal promises regarding the disposition of the estate may, however, raise a claim based on proprietary estoppels in certain circumstances.[1413]

## II. Mutual Wills

*558.* If two persons enter into a legally binding agreement that both will make their wills in a particular form and both then execute a joint will (or separate wills) to give effect to that agreement, then, after the death of the first, the power of the survivor to alter the disposition of his or her estate will be restricted.[1414] The point is not that the survivor is unable to alter or revoke his or her will – since a will is by definition a revocable document – but that the survivor's property will be held on a constructive trust for the beneficiaries agreed with the first testator.[1415]

Since the doctrine of mutual wills imposes a restriction on freedom of testation, it has been closely confined by the courts. There must be clear and satisfactory evidence of an actual agreement between the parties that they will enter into mutual wills and that the surviving party will be bound by the arrangement.[1416] Such evidence may be provided by an express declaration in the parties' wills or by extrinsic evidence.[1417] The court will not infer such an agreement from the mere fact that the wills are executed simultaneously and in identical terms.[1418] If the agreement involves the disposition of land then it must also comply with prescribed formalities.[1419] However, this requirement does not apply where the land is included in a gift of the residue, a distinction which has recently been described as 'rather capricious, even unprincipled'.[1420] The suggested solution in that case was to rely on the doctrine of proprietary estoppel rather than the establishment of a contract.[1421]

---

1413. *See further* Part IV, Ch. 4, paras 590–593.
1414. *Dufour v. Pereira* (1769) 21 E.R. 332; and *see* most recently *Legg v. Burton* [2017] EWHC 2088 (Ch).
1415. *Re Hagger* [1930] 2 Ch. 190; *Re Green* [1951] Ch. 148; *Re Cleaver* [1981] 2 All E.R. 1018; *Re Dale* [1994] Ch. 31; *Walters v. Olins* [2008] EWCA Civ 782. On the powers of the beneficiary, *see Thomas and Agnes Carvel Foundation v. Carvel* [2007] EWHC 1314 (Ch). For criticism of the resulting lack of flexibility *see* S Hudson and B Sloan, 'Testamentary Freedom: Mutual Wills Might Let You Down' in *Modern Studies in Property Law* (2015).
1416. *Re Dale* [1994] Ch. 31; *Re Goodchild, deceased* [1997] 1 W.L.R. 1216; *Birch v. Curtis* [2002] EWHC 1158.
1417. *Charles v. Fraser* [2010] EWHC 2154 (Ch); *Fry v. Densham-Smith* [2010] EWCA Civ 1410; *Legg v. Burton* [2017] EWHC 2088 (Ch).
1418. *Re Oldham* [1925] Ch. 75; *Gray v. Perpetual Trustee Co Ltd* [1928] A.C. 391; *Re Goodchild, Deceased* [1997] 1 W.L.R. 1216; *Davies v. Revenue and Customs Commissioners* [2009] UKFTT 138 (TC); *Charles v. Fraser* [2010] EWHC 2154 (Ch).
1419. *Law Reform (Miscellaneous Provisions) Act* 1989, s. 2, and *see Healey v. Brown* [2002] W.T.L.R. 849.
1420. *Legg v. Burton* [2017] EWHC 2088 (Ch), at para. 23.
1421. *Ibid.,* at para. 24.

It should also be noted that before the death of the first testator, either or both parties may revoke their will(s); similarly, if it transpires that the first of the testators to die had altered his or her will before his or her death, the survivor will be relieved from the obligation to dispose of the estate in the terms agreed.[1422]

## §8. INTERPRETATION OF A WILL

*559.* Three situations are considered in this section: first, that the testator did not know or approve of the contents of the will; second, that a mistake was made in transcribing the intentions of the testator, thereby requiring rectification of the will; and, third, that the testator's intentions are unclear from the face of the will.

## I. Knowledge and Approval of the Contents of the Will

*560.* It is necessary for the court to be satisfied that the testator knew and approved of the contents of the will. This will normally be assumed from the fact that the will was executed by a capable testator but in cases of challenge the burden lies on the person propounding the will. Certain circumstances also require the issue of knowledge and approval to be specifically considered, for example if the will was signed 'by a blind or illiterate testator or by another person at the direction of the testator'.[1423]

*561.* In *Gill v. RSPCA* the Court of Appeal held that the role of the court is to:

> consider all the relevant evidence available and then, drawing such inferences as it can from the totality of that material … come to a conclusion whether or not those propounding the will have discharged the burden of establishing that the testatrix knew and approved the contents of the document which is put forward as a valid testamentary disposition.[1424]

Applying this, the Court of Appeal held that the testatrix did not know and approve of the terms of a will leaving her entire estate to the Royal Society for the Prevention of Cruelty to Animals (RSPCA) – a charity of which she had spoken disparagingly in the past – rather than to her only daughter, to whom she was very close. The evidence was that the drafting of the will had been instigated by her domineering husband, who made a will in similar terms, and that the testatrix, who suffered from severe agoraphobia and anxiety, would have been unlikely to have taken in the terms of the will when she attended the solicitor's office to sign it.

---

1422. *Re Hobley* (1997) *The Times*, 16 Jun. 1997.
1423. Non-Contentious Probate Rules 1987/2024, r. 13.
1424. *Gill v. RSPCA* [2010] EWCA Civ 1430, at para. 22, quoting the unreported case of *Crerar v. Crerar*. The test was also applied in *Re Whelan* [2015] EWHC 3301 (Ch).

In rare cases the court may also find that there was only a partial knowledge and approval of the contents of the will.[1425] In this case the particular clause of which the testator did not know or approve can be notionally excised by the court.[1426]

## II. Rectification

562. There may be evidence to show that certain words or clauses in the will were included by mistake and that the will therefore fails to carry out the testator's intentions. If the court is satisfied that the mistake was due either to a clerical error,[1427] or a failure on the part of the person drawing up the will to understand the testator's instructions,[1428] then the court has the power to rectify the will,[1429] and may direct that words that were included by mistake be omitted and new words substituted. The scope for rectification has been enhanced by the recent decision of the Supreme Court in *Marley v. Rawlings*,[1430] in which it was held that a 'clerical error' was not confined to mistakes involved in copying or writing out a document but could encompass those 'arising out of office work of a relatively routine nature, such as preparing, filing, sending [and], organizing the execution of, a document'.[1431] It was accordingly decided that the fact that a husband and wife had each signed the other's will by mistake could be classified as a clerical error and could be rectified by importing the intended clauses into the document that had been signed.

## III. Construction

563. In the past, the courts have tended to assert that their role is to interpret the language used by the testator in making his or her will, not to try to guess what his or her intentions were.[1432] However, in *Marley v. Rawlings* the Supreme Court signalled that the same approach should be taken to the interpretation of a will as to any other legal document. As Lord Neuberger stated:

> the court is concerned to find the intention of the party or parties, and it does this by identifying the meaning of the relevant words, (a) in the light of (i) the natural and ordinary meaning of those words, (ii) the overall purpose of the document, (iii) any other provisions of the document, (iv) the facts known or

---

1425. *Paynter v. Hinch* [2013] EWHC 13 (Ch).
1426. *Marley v. Rawlings and another* [2014] UKSC 2, para. 46.
1427. *See*, e.g., *Re Williams* [1985] 1 W.L.R. 905; *Wordingham v. Royal Exchange Trust Co Ltd* [1992] Ch. 412; *Re Segelman* [1995] 3 All E.R. 676; *Pengelly v. Pengelly* [2007] EWHC 3227 (Ch).
1428. *See*, e.g., *Sprackling v. Sprackling* [2008] EWHC 2696 (Ch).
1429. *Administration of Justice Act* 1982, s. 20(1).
1430. *Marley v. Rawlings and another* [2014] UKSC 2.
1431. *Ibid.*, para. 75. *See*, e.g., *Gledhill v. Arnold* [2015] EWHC 2939 (Ch) (failure to record the testator's instructions correctly deemed to be a clerical error).
1432. *Perrin v. Morgan* [1943] A.C. 399; *Re Jones* (1997) 94(18) L.S.G. 31.

assumed by the parties at the time that the document was executed, and (v) common sense, but (b) ignoring subjective evidence of any party's intentions.[1433]

In addition, under section 21 of the Administration of Justice Act 1982, if the terms of the will are meaningless or ambiguous, extrinsic evidence is admissible to ascertain what the testator's intentions were.[1434] The court may, e.g., hear evidence of the testator's use of language: if he or she ascribed a particular meaning to a disputed word, then the court will follow.[1435] Technical words used by a layman will generally be construed as bearing the meaning that they would have for a professional,[1436] unless it is clear that a different meaning was intended.[1437] Direct evidence of the testator's intentions may also be admissible, for example, 'what he told the drafter of the will, or another person, or by what was in any notes he made or earlier drafts of the will which he may have approved or caused to be prepared'.[1438] A will may also be interpreted so as to correct a mistake made by the testator, as in *Guthrie v. Morel*[1439] where the reference in the will to No. 87 (which the testator did not own) was interpreted to mean No. 81 (which he did) or in *Slattery v. Jago*[1440] where the name of the intended beneficiary was omitted by mistake. As this indicates, there may be some overlap between interpretation and rectification, and the precise boundary between the two remains a matter of debate.[1441]

§9. Losing the Right to Benefit under a Will

*564.* In certain situations, beneficiaries may lose the right to benefit under the will: where they have witnessed it, or have subsequently been divorced from the testator, or have killed the testator.

## I. Witnesses

*565.* Neither witnesses nor the spouses or civil partners of witnesses are entitled to benefit under a will.[1442] The fact that a beneficiary has witnessed a will does not mean that the will is not valid, merely that the beneficiary is not entitled to benefit

---

1433. *Ibid.*, para. 19.
1434. *Administration of Justice Act* 1982, s. 21; *Re Williams* [1985] 1 W.L.R. 905; *Parkinson v. Fawdon* [2009] EWHC 1953 (Ch); *Re Huntley (Deceased)* [2014] EWHC 547 (Ch); *Re Burnard (Deceased)* [2014] EWHC 340 (Ch); *Re Harte (Deceased)* [2015] EWHC 2351 (Ch).
1435. *In Re Davidson* [1949] Ch. 670.
1436. *Re Cook* [1948] Ch. 212.
1437. *Re Bailey* [1945] Ch. 191; *Reading v. Reading* [2015] EWHC 946 (Ch) ('issue' interpreted to include stepchildren in the context of this specific will).
1438. *Marley v. Rawlings and another* [2014] UKSC 2, para. 26.
1439. [2015] EWHC 3172 (Ch).
1440. [2015] EWHC 3976 (Ch).
1441. *See*, e.g., B Häcker, 'What's in a Will?' in B Häcker and C Mitchell (eds) *Current Issues in Succession Law* (2016).
1442. *Wills Act* 1837, s. 15; *Civil Partnership Act* 2004, Sch. 4, para. 3.

under the will. If, however, the will would have been valid without the beneficiary acting as a witness – i.e., if there are at least two witnesses who do not stand to benefit from the will – then the fact that the beneficiary has done so will be disregarded.[1443]

## II. Divorce, Dissolution or Annulment

*566.* The effect of a decree dissolving or annulling a marriage or civil partnership is that any gift to the former spouse or civil partner will take effect as if that person had died on the date of dissolution or annulment.[1444] A similar provision applies to any appointment of the former spouse as an executor or trustee of the will.[1445] Both rules may be excluded if the testator has expressed a contrary intention. There is also the possibility of the surviving party applying for financial provision from the other's estate.[1446]

## III. Forfeiture

*567.* The same rules apply to the forfeiture of an interest under a will as upon intestacy, and have already been considered.[1447]

## IV. Lapse and ademption

*568.* The basic rule is that a gift will lapse if it was made to a person who dies before the testator, and will therefore form part of the testator's residuary estate unless the testator has specifically provided for the contingency. If a gift of the residue lapses, the share of the deceased beneficiary will be distributed under the intestacy rules.

As under the intestacy rules, if the order of deaths is uncertain the court will presume that they occurred in order of seniority.[1448] Similarly, gifts to the testator's children or other issue will not fail if the intended beneficiary has children or other issue who are living at the date of the testator's death.[1449]

A gift of specific property will also fail (or 'adeem') if the testator no longer owns that property at the date of his or her death.

---

1443. *Wills Act* 1968, s. 1(1).
1444. *Wills Act* 1837, s. 18A(1)(b), as substituted by the *Law Reform (Succession) Act* 1995; *Wills Act* 1837, s. 18C(2)(b), as inserted by the *Civil Partnership Act* 2004.
1445. *Wills Act* 1837, s. 18A(1)(a), as substituted by the *Law Reform (Succession) Act* 1995; *Wills Act* 1837, s. 18C(2)(a), as inserted by the *Civil Partnership Act* 2004.
1446. *See* Part IV, Ch. 3, para. 563.
1447. *See* Part IV, Ch. 1, paras 484–486.
1448. *Law of Property Act* 1925, s. 184. For a recent application of this *see Jump v. Lister* [2016] EWHC 2160 (Ch).
1449. *Wills Act* 1837, s. 33, as amended by the *Administration of Justice Act* 1982.

# Chapter 3. Provision for Family and Dependants

## §1. INTRODUCTION

*569.* Wills, it has been noted, 'frequently give rise to feelings of disappointment or worse on the part of relatives and other would be beneficiaries'.[1450] Although a testator is under no obligation to make provision for his or her family and dependants, the court has the power to order provision out of the estate for certain specified family members and dependants if the provision made by the disposition of the estate was unreasonable. These powers may also be exercised where the deceased died intestate, whether or not the person applying for provision received anything under the intestacy rules.

## §2. ELIGIBILITY TO APPLY

*570.* The Inheritance (Provision for Family and Dependants) Act 1975 sets out a list of persons who are entitled to apply to the court. This includes the spouse or civil partner of the deceased,[1451] as well as a former spouse or civil partner who has not formalized another relationship.[1452] A child of the deceased – of whatever age – may bring a claim,[1453] as may a person who was treated as a child of the family.[1454] A cohabitant – whether of the same or opposite sex – may claim if he or she had been living with the deceased in the same household,[1455] as if they were the spouse[1456] or civil partner[1457] of the deceased, immediately[1458] before the date of the death, and for at least two years before that date.[1459] Finally, a person who 'immediately before the death of the deceased was being maintained, either wholly or partly,[1460] by the deceased' is also entitled to bring a claim.[1461]

---

1450. *Gill v. RSPCA* [2010] EWCA Civ 1430, at para. 16.
1451. *Inheritance (Provision for Family and Dependants) Act* 1975, s. 1(1)(a).
1452. *Ibid.*, s. 1(1)(b).
1453. *Ibid.*, s. 1(1)(c).
1454. *Ibid.*, s. 1(1)(d), as amended by *Inheritance and Trustees' Powers Act* 2014, Sch. 2, para. 2(2).
1455. *Churchill v. Roach* [2002] EWHC 3230; *Gully v. Dix* [2004] EWCA Civ 139.
1456. *See*, e.g., *Re Watson (deceased)* [1999] 1 F.L.R. 878. *See also Chekov v. Fryer* [2015] EWHC 1642 (Ch) in which the claimant was the former spouse of the deceased.
1457. *See*, e.g., *Baynes v. Hedger* [2008] EWHC 1587 (Ch).
1458. *Gully v. Dix* [2004] EWCA Civ 139.
1459. *Inheritance (Provision for Family and Dependants) Act* 1975, s. 1(1A), as inserted by the *Law Reform (Succession) Act* 1995; and s. 1(1B), as inserted by the *Civil Partnership Act* 2004.
1460. *See*, e.g., *Churchill v. Roach* [2002] EWHC 3230; *Lindop v. Agus, Bass and Hedley* [2010] 1 F.L.R. 631.
1461. *Inheritance (Provision for Family and Dependants) Act* 1975, s. 1(e), and *see further* s. 1(3). Changes made by the *Inheritance and Trustees' Powers Act* 2014 make it clear that a claim is no longer precluded where the "dependant" was contributing more to the needs of the deceased than vice versa.

§3.  POWERS OF THE COURT TO MAKE ORDERS

*571.*  The applicant must establish that the 'disposition of the deceased's estate effected by his will or the law relating to intestacy' is 'not such as to make reasonable financial provision' for him or her.[1462] The court will take all relevant circumstances into account in deciding whether or not this is the case, and is specifically directed to consider the financial resources and financial needs of the applicant(s) and of any beneficiary of the estate; any obligations and responsibilities that the deceased had towards any applicant or beneficiary; the size and nature of the net estate of the deceased;[1463] any physical or mental disability of any applicant or beneficiary; and the conduct of the applicant or any other person.[1464] If the application is brought by a current or former spouse or civil partner, the court is additionally directed to consider the applicant's age and contribution to the welfare of the deceased's family, and the duration of the marriage or civil partnership;[1465] similar considerations are also taken into account if the applicant was cohabiting with the deceased.[1466]

*572.*  Although the legislation makes reference to the 'needs' of the applicant, the neediness of a particular applicant is not sufficient justification for the court to make an order unless it was also unreasonable for the deceased not to make provision for the applicant.[1467] Adult children have experienced particular difficulty in establishing that their parents have not made reasonable financial provision for them.[1468]

§4.  THE BASIS FOR THE COURT'S AWARD

*573.*  Once the court is satisfied that the deceased failed to make reasonable financial provision for the applicant, it may – in the case of applicants other than a surviving spouse or civil partner – order such provision as is required for the applicant's maintenance.[1469] The Supreme Court has recently confirmed in *Ilott v. The Blue Cross* that maintenance is intended to meet the 'everyday expenses of living'.[1470] Even so, maintenance is not limited to periodical payments but may include the provision of a home.[1471] In the case of a surviving spouse or civil partner (unless

---

1462. *Inheritance (Provision for Family and Dependants) Act* 1975, s. 2(1).
1463. This is to be determined at the date of the hearing: *See Dingmar v. Dingmar* [2006] EWHC 1940 (Ch).
1464. *Inheritance (Provision for Family and Dependants) Act* 1975, s. 3(1).
1465. *Ibid.*, s. 3(2).
1466. *Ibid.*, s. 3(2A).
1467. *See*, e.g., *Barass v. Harding* [2001] 1 F.L.R. 138 (claim by former wife, the parties having divorced over thirty years earlier); *Garland v. Morris* [2007] EWHC 2 (Ch) (adult daughter who had not spoken to her father for the past fifteen years); *Ilott v. The Blue Cross* [2017] UKSC 17, at para. 19.
1468. *Re Jennings (dec'd)* [1994] Ch. D 286; *Garland v. Morris* [2007] EWHC 2 (Ch); cf. *Ilott v. The Blue Cross* [2017] UKSC 17.
1469. *Inheritance (Provision for Family and Dependants) Act* 1975, s. 1(2)(b).
1470. [2017] UKSC 17, at para. 14.
1471. *See*, e.g., *Churchill v. Roach* [2002] EWHC 3230; *Cattle v. Evans* [2011] EWHC 945 (Ch).

the parties were legally separated), the court may order such provision as it would be reasonable in all the circumstances for that person to receive, regardless of whether that provision is required for his or her maintenance.[1472]

574. In deciding what provision would be reasonable, the court is directed to the same list of factors that are taken into account in deciding whether the provision made was unreasonable and indeed in *Ilott v. The Blue Cross*, the Supreme Court suggested that the established two-stage process of asking whether there has been a failure to make reasonable financial provision and then what order should be made is in fact one single enquiry, in that the same conclusions will usually answer both questions.[1473] In the case of a surviving spouse or civil partner, the court is also required to consider the provision that the survivor might reasonably have expected to receive had the relationship had been terminated by divorce or dissolution rather than by death.[1474] This does not mean that the award will be the same as if the relationship had ended while both parties were still alive: as the courts have emphasized, the contexts of these different claims is very different and the awards made on the death of a partner will usually be more generous.[1475]

---

1472. *Inheritance (Provision for Family and Dependants) Act* 1975, s. 1(2)(a) and (aa).
1473. [2017] UKSC 17, at para. 24.
1474. *Inheritance (Provision for Family and Dependants) Act* 1975, s. 3(2).
1475. *P. v. G, P. and P. (Family Provision: Relevance of Divorce Provision)* [2004] EWHC 2944 (Fam); *Fielden v. Cunliffe* [2005] EWCA Civ 1508; *Lilleyman v. Lilleyman* [2012] EWHC 821 (Ch).

# Chapter 4. Acts *Inter Vivos* Related to the Estate

## §1. INTRODUCTION

*575.* A number of arrangements may be put in place by a person in contemplation of their death. Some – e.g., the making of gifts and establishment of trusts – may be motivated by the desire to minimize the amount of inheritance tax that is payable (at the time of writing 40% on any transfers over the value of GBP 325,000, although the threshold is regularly updated). Others – such as the joint tenancy – may be intended to ensure the smooth transmission of property, while nominations and insurance contracts are intended to secure payments by a third party to a nominated person. There is also the problem that the deceased may not have formalized his or her intentions. The circumstances in which a person may have a claim against the estate by virtue of proprietary estoppel also need to be considered.

## §2. GIFTS

*576.* The scope for an individual to escape liability for inheritance tax is restricted by the fact that gifts made less than seven years before a person's death may themselves be subject to inheritance tax. In such cases, the effective rate of tax payable on a gift will vary according to the lapse of time between the gift being made and the donor's death, as a reduction termed 'taper relief' is applied to the value of gifts made between three and seven years before the donor's death.[1476]

*577.* Certain gifts are exempt from inheritance tax, whenever made. These include a gift to a spouse or civil partner,[1477] gifts of GBP 250 or less to any one individual in any given tax year,[1478] and gifts to charities or registered clubs.[1479] Gifts given to a couple upon their marriage or civil partnership are also exempt from inheritance tax, although the amount that can be given free of tax depends on the relationship between the donor and the couple (up to GBP 5,000 in the case of parents, GBP 2,500 in the case of grandparents and remoter ascendants, and a maximum of GBP 1,000 from any other person).[1480] There is an annual exemption totalling GBP 3,000 in any tax year (which may be carried forward for one year, so that a maximum of GBP 6,000 may be given tax free).[1481] Finally, any transfers made out of the donor's income as part of his or her normal expenditure are also exempt.[1482]

*578.* A gift that does not fall within any of the above categories may still be free from inheritance tax if it is made more than seven years before the death of the

---

1476. *Inheritance Tax Act* 1984, s. 7(4).
1477. *Ibid.*, s. 18.
1478. *Ibid.*, s. 20.
1479. *Ibid.*, s. 23(1), as amended by *Corporation Tax Act* 2010, Sch. 1, para. 189.
1480. *Ibid.*, s. 22.
1481. *Ibid.*, s 19.
1482. *Ibid.*, s. 21(1).

donor. This is not automatic, however: for transfers taking effect after 22 March 2006, the only lifetime gifts that fall within this class are outright gifts, gifts into trusts for the disabled and gifts into bereaved minors' trusts whereby a person who received an interest in possession following the death of the person who set up the trust gives up that interest to be held on trust for the bereaved minor.

579. Even if a gift is made more than seven years before the death of the donor, it will not be exempt if the donor has retained a benefit in it. A person who retains a benefit in property that he or she has ostensibly given to another will be treated as the owner of that property for the purposes of inheritance tax.[1483] Minor benefits – e.g., an invitation to stay on a temporary basis in the property that was the subject of the gift – can, however, be disregarded. In addition, continued residence in the property – or the continued use of a chattel – will be disregarded if the donor provides full consideration (in money or money's worth) for the benefits received.[1484]

§3. TRUSTS

580. An individual may divest himself or herself of property in advance of death by directing that such property should be held on trust for another person. It is possible to declare oneself a trustee, and thereby pass beneficial ownership of the property in question to another person, but if the reason for declaring the trust is the settlor's impending death it would be more useful to convey the property to trustees with a direction that they hold it on trust. It should be noted, however, that the tax advantages of creating a trust are now much reduced, particularly since the Finance Act 2006.

581. In general, no special formalities are required for the creation of a trust. Indeed, in one case it was held that the words 'this money is as much yours as mine' was sufficient to create a trust over a bank account, this generous interpretation being encouraged by the fact that the parties were thought to be 'simple people, not understanding the subtleties of equity but understanding very well their domestic situation'.[1485] Depending on the property that forms the subject matter of the trust, further formalities may be required. For example, a declaration of trust of land must be evidenced in writing,[1486] while a declaration of trust over a subsisting equitable interest must be made in writing.[1487] Similarly, if property is to be transferred to trustees to hold on trust for specified beneficiaries, then the formalities appropriate

---

1483. *Finance Act* 1986, s. 102. *See*, e.g., *Buzzoni v. Revenue and Customs Commissioners* [2011] UKFTT 267 (TC), affirmed by *Buzzoni v. Revenue and Customs Commissioners* [2013] EWCA Civ 1684; *Matthews v. Revenue and Customs Commissioners* [2012] UKFTT 658 (TC).
1484. *Finance Act* 1986, Sch. 20, para. 6(1)(a).
1485. *Paul v. Constance* [1977] 1 All E.R. 195.
1486. *Law of Property Act* 1925, s. 53(1)(b).
1487. *Ibid.*, s. 53(1)(c).

for the transfer of that form of property must be complied with. A transfer will be effective as long as the transferor has transferred everything necessary for the transferee to perfect the title.[1488]

It is of course possible to create a trust that will only take effect upon the death of the settlor. Such a trust, however, is regarded as testamentary, and must comply with the formalities required for a valid will under the Wills Act 1837.

## I. Fixed Trusts

582.    Under a fixed trust the amount, or share, that each of the beneficiaries is to receive is fixed in advance by the settlor.

## II. Discretionary Trusts

583.    There are two types of discretionary trust: in the first, the trustees are required to distribute the property among all of the beneficiaries but have a discretion as to the shares each beneficiary is to receive, while in the second, the trustees have a discretion as to which persons within a specified class should benefit from the trust. In the first case, it must be possible to draw up a complete list of beneficiaries. By contrast, in the second it is generally sufficient if the class of potential beneficiaries is conceptually certain: the test is whether it is possible to say with certainty whether any given person is or is not a member of the class.[1489] A discretionary trust may, however, be struck down on the basis of administrative unworkability or capriciousness.[1490]

## III. Secret Trusts

584.    It is possible that an individual may wish to make provision for certain persons without their identity becoming known.[1491] The option of making a 'secret trust' has been used largely by men wishing to make provision for unacknowledged mistresses or children.[1492] Such a trust operates both through and outside a will. The secret trustee receives the property by means of the settlor's will, but the trust is imposed outside of the will and is therefore said to operate dehors the will. It must however be clear that the settlor intended to impose a legally enforceable obligation on the trustee; a mere expression of wishes will not suffice.

585.    A secret trust may be either fully secret or half-secret. The former occurs where the settlor leaves property to the secret trustee by will, apparently absolutely;

---

1488. *Re Rose* [1952] Ch. 499; *Zeital v. Kaye* [2010] EWCA Civ 159.
1489. *McPhail v. Doulton* [1971] A.C. 424.
1490. *Brown v. Burdett* (1882) 21 Ch. 667.
1491. *See*, e.g., *Rawstron v. Freud* [2014] EWHC 2577 (Ch), in which the identity of the beneficiaries was not disclosed.
1492. *See*, e.g., *Johnson v. Ball* (1851) 64 E.R. 1019; *Blackwell v. Blackwell* [1929] A.C. 318.

the latter is where it is clear from the will itself that the property is given on trust but the objects of that trust are not stated in the will itself. In both cases, the settlor must communicate the objects of the trust, or at least provide his or her instructions, even if in a sealed envelope,[1493] to the secret trustee during his or her lifetime,[1494] and the secret trustee must accept the trust (either expressly or by actions that will give the settlor the impression that he or she has accepted the trust).[1495] In the case of a half-secret trust, there is an additional requirement that the trust must have been declared before the execution of the will, so it can be regarded as incorporated into the will by the reference made to it in the will itself.[1496] A reference in the will to a future document will not be sufficient.[1497] Similarly, if the words in the will could be construed as including instructions given after making the will, any existing instructions will not have effect.[1498] The strictness with which the rules are applied shows how wary courts are of allowing testators to evade the requirements of the Wills Act 1837 by making dispositions of this kind.

## IV. Purpose Trusts

*586.* The law of England and Wales takes the view that a trust cannot be established for a private (i.e., non-charitable) purpose, since in such a case there is no person to enforce the trust.[1499] There are, however, a number of exceptions that are of particular relevance to a person contemplating death: a trust for the care and maintenance of specific animals will be valid, so provision may be made for the settlor's pets;[1500] leaving money for the erection or maintenance of a tomb, grave or monument is also accepted as a valid purpose trust,[1501] as is a trust for the saying of Roman Catholic masses in private.[1502] Ongoing purposes – as opposed to one-off events – must, however, be limited to take effect within the perpetuity period, which may be either a specified period of less than eighty years,[1503] the lifespan of someone connected with the trust (or of a specified person not connected with the trust) plus twenty-one years, or twenty-one years after the death of all statutory 'lives in being'.[1504] Thus in *Re Hooper*,[1505] in which there was a trust for the upkeep of certain graves and monuments 'so long as they can legally do so', the trust was held to be valid for twenty-one years, there being no relevant lives in being.

---

1493. *See*, e.g., *Re Boyes* (1884) L.R. 26 Ch. D. 531.
1494. *Re Cooper* [1939] Ch. 811; *In re Boyes* (1884) 26 Ch. D. 531.
1495. *McCormick v. Grogan* (1869) L.R. 4 H.L. 82.
1496. *Blackwell v. Blackwell* [1929] A.C. 318.
1497. *See*, e.g., *Re Bateman* [1970] 1 W.L.R. 1463.
1498. *Re Keen* [1937] Ch. 236.
1499. For discussion *see* M. Pawlowski and J. Brown, *Testamentary Trusts and the Rule against Capricious Purposes: an underlying Rationale?* 3 Tru. Law Int. 101. (2012).
1500. *Pettingall v. Pettingall* (1842) 11 L.J. Ch. 176; *Re Dean* (1889) 41 Ch. 552.
1501. *Trimmer v. Danby* (1856) 25 L.J. Ch. 424; *Mussett v. Bingle* [1876] W.N. 170.
1502. *Bourne v. Keane* [1919] A.C. 815.
1503. *Perpetuity and Accumulations Act* 1964, s. 1.
1504. *Ibid.*, s. 3.
1505. [1932] 1 Ch. 38.

§4. *DONATIO MORTIS CAUSA*

*587.* A *donatio mortis causa* is a gift made in contemplation of death and does not have to comply with the formalities required either for wills or for the transfer of property during the donor's lifetime. It does, however, have characteristics of both types of transactions, and has been described as 'amphibious', being 'a gift which is neither entirely *inter vivos* nor testamentary. It is an act *inter vivos* by which the donee is to have the absolute title to the subject of the gift not at once but if the donor dies'.[1506] The rationale is to allow persons on their deathbed to dispose of their property as they wish; however, as the Court of Appeal has noted, it also 'paves the way for all the abuses' that the statutes setting out the formal requirements were intended to prevent.[1507]

*588.* The three essential requirements of a valid *donatio mortis causa* were stated in *Sen v. Headley*:[1508]

First, the gift ... must have been made in contemplation, though not necessarily in expectation, of impending death. Secondly, the gift must have been made upon the condition that it is to be absolute and perfected only on the donor's death, being revocable until that event occurs and ineffective if it does not. Thirdly, there must be a delivery of the subject matter of the gift or the essential indicia of title thereto, which amounts to a parting with dominion and not mere physical possession over the subject matter of the gift.

*589.* In determining whether or not the gift was made in contemplation of death, the Court of Appeal held in *King v. Dubrey* that the donor 'should be contemplating death in the near future for a specific reason'.[1509] In that case the decision was that the donor was not contemplating her impending death at the time she gave the deeds of her property to her nephew. Earlier cases in which there had been a gap of some months between the gift being made and the donor's eventual death were similarly deemed not to have satisfied this requirement and to have been wrongly decided.[1510]

*590.* An absolute gift must comply with the appropriate formalities for the transfer of that form of property. The key characteristic of a *donatio mortis causa* is that it is conditional upon the death of the donor, and does not become absolute until that event occurs. Of course, if the donor believes that his or her condition is fatal then he or she may not stipulate what is to happen should he or she recover: in a number of cases the courts have been willing to infer an intention on the part of the donor that the property should be returned to him or her if he or she recovered.[1511] If the donor does recover, then the donee holds the property on trust for him or her.

---

1506. *Re Beaumont* [1902] 1 Ch. 889.
1507. *King v. Dubrey* [2015] EWCA Civ 581, para. 51.
1508. [1991] Ch. 425. *See also King v. Dubrey* [2015] EWCA Civ 581, para. 50.
1509. *King v. Dubrey* [2015] EWCA Civ 581, para. 55.
1510. *See*, e.g. *Vallee v. Birchwood* [2013] EWHC 1449 (Ch) (five months between gift and death).
1511. *Wilkes v. Allington*; *Re Lillingston* [1952] 2 All E.R. 184.

*591.* Perhaps most importantly, some act of transfer is required to pass 'dominion' over the property to the donee.[1512] This requirement is intended to avoid the dangers inherent in relying on the word of the intended donee alone.[1513] If the gift consists of chattels, there must either be delivery of the subject matter of the gift or a transfer of the means of getting at the property, e.g., a key.[1514] If it consists of land or intangible property, such as a chose in action, there must be delivery of the essential indicia of title.[1515] Such delivery may be indirect, as in *Sen v. Headley*.[1516] In this case, the donor told the donee that the house and all its contents were hers, that the deeds to the house were to be found in a steel box, and that the keys were in her bag. Since the donor had given her the keys to the box in which the deeds were kept, this was sufficient. It is more doubtful whether it is possible to create a *donatio mortis causa* if the property in question consists of registered land, since in registered land there is no bundle of title deeds and the land certificate is merely a record of the entries on the register. It is the entry on the register which constitutes the title, and this is not capable of transfer between individuals. It is unlikely that the transfer of a key to the house would suffice by itself: it is not the essential indicia of title to the property as there are many practical reasons why a key may be transferred to another person.

*592.* If the donor continues to deal with the property as if he or she owned it, then the courts will hold that there is no valid *donatio mortis causa*, or that the gift has been revoked. By contrast, the fact that the donor retains the actual item in question does not matter if he or she has relinquished control – e.g., if the donee has been given the key that provides access to it. The fact that the donor also retains a key will not matter if he or she is not in a position to make use of it. In *Sen v. Headley*[1517] and *Woodward v. Woodward*,[1518] the fact that the donor was in hospital effectively meant that he was unable to exercise any control over the property in question.

### §5. Joint Tenancies and Tenancies in Common

*593.* The decision to hold the beneficial title to property as either joint tenants or tenants in common merits consideration as an act *inter vivos* relating to the estate, since it will have important implications when one of the parties dies. Each tenant in common owns a share of the beneficial interest, and this share can be disposed of in the same way as any other form of property, or will form part of the estate of the deceased for the purpose of the intestacy rules. By contrast, joint tenants do not own distinct shares, and if one of them dies the doctrine of survivorship will apply, with

---

1512. *See* the summary in *King v. Dubrey* [2015] EWCA Civ 581, para. 59.
1513. *Re Wassenberg* [1915] 1 Ch. 195.
1514. *Ibid., Re Lillington* [1952]; *Woodward v. Woodward* [1995] 3 All E.R. 980 (car keys).
1515. *Birch v. Treasury Solicitor* [1951] 2 All E.R. 1198 (bank books); *Vallee v. Birchwood* [2013] EWHC 1449 (Ch) (deeds and key to the house).
1516. [1991] Ch. 425.
1517. *Ibid.*
1518. [1995] 3 All E.R. 980.

the result that the surviving joint tenant will be entitled to the entire beneficial interest. Even if the deceased joint tenant made a will dictating that the property should pass to another person, this will be of no effect. However, a joint tenancy has no advantages over a tenancy in common in terms of inheritance tax: the Inland Revenue ignores the central premise that a joint tenant owns no distinct share and will assess the estate of the deceased to inheritance tax as if the equity had been divided equally between all the joint tenants at the time of the death of the deceased.

*594.* The parties can, however, change their mind as to how they wish to hold the beneficial interest; a beneficial joint tenancy may be severed to become a tenancy in common in equal shares.[1519] This may be achieved by a number of different methods. Statute prescribes that severance may be brought about by a written notice indicating the writer's intention to bring about severance immediately.[1520] Notice of severance will be effective as soon as it is delivered.[1521] The legislation also preserved the common law methods of severance, which – as set out in *Williams v. Hensman*[1522] – are as follows: an act by any one of the joint tenants operating on his or her own share (e.g., a sale, mortgage or lease of that person's interest in the property, or that person's bankruptcy);[1523] mutual agreement among all of the joint tenants;[1524] or any course of dealing (such as the execution of mutual wills) that indicates that all of the joint tenants mutually treat their interests as constituting a tenancy in common.[1525]

*595.* It should also be noted that if the legal title to land is held by more than one person, it must be held under a joint tenancy, which cannot be severed.[1526] If one of the joint tenants dies, the doctrine of survivorship operates in exactly the same way, and the surviving joint tenant becomes the sole legal owner. This does not necessarily have any impact on the beneficial ownership of the property: if the deceased had severed the beneficial joint tenancy he or she would have been free to dispose of it, and the survivor will hold the property on trust for the estate of the deceased.

## §6. Nominations

*596.* A member of a pension scheme is usually entitled to nominate another person to benefit in the case of his or her death. Such nominations are regarded as contractual arrangements rather than testamentary dispositions and do not need to

---

1519. *Harris v. Goddard* [1983] 1 W.L.R. 1203.
1520. *Law of Property Act* 1925, s. 36(2), s. 196; *see*, e.g., *Quigley v. Masterson* [2011] EWHC 2529 (Ch).
1521. *Ibid.*, s. 196(4); *Kinch v. Bullard* [1999] 1 F.L.R. 66.
1522. (1861) 70 E.R. 862.
1523. *Re Dennis* [1995] 2 W.L.R. 367.
1524. *See*, e.g., *Burgess v. Rawnsley* [1975] Ch. 429; *Gore and Snell v. Carpenter* (1990) 60 P. & C.R. 456; *Perkins v. Borden* [2002] W.T.L.R. 595; *Heath v. Heath* [2009] EWHC 1908 (Ch).
1525. *See*, e.g., *Hunter v. Babbage* [1994] 2 F.L.R. 806.
1526. *Law of Property Act* 1925, s. 1(6), s. 34(2), s. 36(2).

comply with the requirements of the Wills Act.[1527] An added complication may arise if the person nominated was not intended to benefit personally from the nomination. This was the case in *Gold v. Hill*,[1528] in which Mr Gilbert, the person making the nomination, had informed Mr Gold, the nominee, that he wished him to look after Gilbert's cohabitant and children. The court drew an analogy with the secret trust and held that the nomination was valid and that Gold held the money as constructive trustee for the cohabitant.

### §7. INSURANCE POLICIES

*597.* Any person may take out a policy of insurance on his or her own life for the benefit of his or her children; a married person may also take out such a policy for the benefit of his or her spouse (and equally a civil partner may take out a policy for the other civil partner).[1529] Any moneys payable under such a policy do not form part of the estate of the insured. In addition, spouses and civil partners are presumed to have an insurable interest (for an unlimited amount) in each other's lives for the purposes of the Life Assurance Act 1774.[1530]

### §8. PROPRIETARY ESTOPPEL

*598.* All of the examples considered above involve a person taking deliberate steps to create legal arrangements in contemplation of their own death. Proprietary estoppel has a rather different role to play; an estoppel may arise where a person has made a promise to another that the latter has relied upon to his or her detriment and it would be unconscionable not to enforce that promise.[1531] The doctrine is of wide application, but this section will focus on one specific example – where a person has promised to leave property to another by will (or has been understood as making such a promise) and then fails to do so.

*599.* The first element that needs to be satisfied is that the owner had led or allowed the claimant to believe that the claimant will inherit property on the former's death. An assurance that is unambiguous, repeated on several occasions,

---

1527. *Re Danish Bacon Co Ltd Staff Pension Fund Trusts* [1971] 1 W.L.R. 248.
1528. [1999] 1 F.L.R. 54.
1529. *Married Women's Property Act* 1882, s. 11; *Civil Partnership Act* 2004, s. 70.
1530. *Reed v. Royal Exchange Insurance Co* (1795) 170 E.R. 198; *Griffiths v. Fleming* [1909] 1 KB 805; *Civil Partnership Act* 2004, s. 253.
1531. *Thorner v. Major* [2009] UKHL 18. For recent discussions of the doctrine *see*, e.g., *Rawlings v. Chapman* [2015] EWHC 3160 (Ch).

and known to others will clearly satisfy this requirement.[1532] Even less direct statements may, in certain cases, be regarded as tantamount to an assurance.[1533] However, vague promises of financial security do not suffice.[1534] It is also necessary that
the assurances should relate to identified property owned or about to be owned by
the person making the promise.[1535]

600. Of course, a will is a revocable document, and a promise that a gift will be
made in a will is not legally binding on the promisor.[1536] But if the promisee relies
on the assurance to his or her detriment, the assurance may become irrevocable.[1537]
The courts have adopted a broad concept of detrimental reliance in this context,
holding in *Gillett v. Holt* that it need not consist of the expenditure of money or any
quantifiable financial detriment 'so long as it is something substantial. The requirement must be approached as part of a broad inquiry as to whether repudiation of an
assurance is or is not unconscionable in all the circumstances'.[1538] In that case, Mr
Gillett and his family had completely subordinated their wishes to those of Mr Holt:
Mr Gillett had worked for him since he was 16, had deprived himself of the opportunity to better himself and devoted the best years of his life to him in the expectation that he would one day inherit Mr Holt's farming business. The Court of
Appeal held that Mr Gillett had shown that he had relied to his detriment on this
expectation, which had been encouraged by Mr Holt. Thus lifestyle choices, as well
as direct financial expenditure, may be held to constitute detrimental reliance, as
long as they can be linked to the expectation of an interest in the property.[1539]

Whether particular actions do constitute detrimental reliance may depend on the
person performing them. In *Campbell v. Griffin*,[1540] e.g., Mr Campbell had lodged
with an elderly couple for many years, although he ceased to pay rent in 1992, after
he had been living there for fourteen years. Over the years he helped out around the
house and gradually took on the role of carer for the increasingly frail couple. At
first instance, it was held that he had not acted to his detriment in the expectation of
being left the house, but had rather acted out of friendship and a sense of responsibility. The Court of Appeal disagreed, noting that 'a lodger does not normally cook
his landlords' evening meals, or delay going to work or go short of sleep to look
after them, or clean up after incontinence', while adding that a carer would generally expect to be well-paid for the sort of services Mr Campbell had provided. It is
significant, however, that emphasis was placed on Mr Campbell's status as a lodger:
it is possible that if these services had been performed by someone more closely

---

1532. *Gillett v. Holt* [2000] 3 W.L.R. 815; cf. *Murphy v. Burrows* [2004] EWHC 1900 (Ch).
1533. *Thorner v. Major* [2009] UKHL 18; *Suggitt v. Suggitt* [2011] EWHC 903 (Ch).
1534. *Layton v. Martin* [1986] 2 F.L.R. 227; *Murphy v. Rayner* [2011] EWHC 1 (Ch).
1535. *Thorner v. Major* [2009] UKHL 18.
1536. *See*, e.g., *MacDonald v. Frost* [2009] EWHC 2276 (Ch).
1537. *Gillett v. Holt* [2000] 3 W.L.R. 815; *Jiggins v. Brisley* [2003] EWHC 841.
1538. *Gillett v. Holt* [2000] Ch. 210 at 232.
1539. *See also Evans v. HSBC Trust Co (UK) Ltd* [2005] W.T.L.R. 1289; *Davies v. Davies* [2015] EWHC
      1384 (Ch).
1540. [2001] EWCA Civ 990.

related to the couple then the court would indeed have held that they were attributable to friendship – or love and affection – rather than the expectation of an interest.

It should however be noted that, in the absence of some assurance, actions of this kind will not give rise to a claim.[1541]

601. Even if all the elements of an estoppel have been established, this does not necessarily mean that the promisee will receive exactly what was promised. In estoppel cases, the remedy awarded by the court will be the minimum equity to do justice and the courts have stressed that the remedy awarded should be proportionate both to the expectation and to the detriment suffered.[1542]

---

1541. _Cook v. Thomas_ [2010] EWCA Civ 227.
1542. _See_, e.g., _Jennings v. Rice_ [2002] EWCA Civ 159 (monetary award based on the commercial cost of the services provided); _Davies v. Davies_ [2015] EWHC 1384 (Ch) (award of the family farm to the son who had worked on it since his teens).

# Chapter 5. Acquisition and Administration of the Estate

## §1. Determining Who Is to Administer the Estate

*602.* The persons responsible for administering the estate of a deceased person are known as his or her personal representatives. This term covers both executors and administrators.[1543]

A testator may have appointed a person or persons to act as executors of his or her will, although the nominated persons are free to accept or renounce the office before taking probate or performing any other acts that indicate an intention to assume the role of executor. The executor has the power to apply for a grant of probate, which should be obtained within six months of the testator's death. If the executor dies before completing the tasks demanded by his or her office, those tasks will devolve upon the executor of the executor's own will.[1544]

If no executor was appointed in the will, the court will grant letters of administration with the will annexed. In order of priority, the persons to whom such a grant will be made comprise a trustee of the residuary personal or real estate, a residuary legatee or devisee, the personal representative of any residuary legatee or devisee, any other legatee or devisee, a creditor, or, finally, the personal representative of a legatee, devisee, or creditor.[1545]

If the deceased died intestate, then the court will grant letters of administration to (in order of priority) the deceased's surviving spouse or civil partner, children (and the issue of any children who died before the deceased), parents, siblings of the whole blood, siblings of the half-blood, grandparents, uncles and aunts of the whole blood, and uncles and aunts of the half-blood. The issue of children, siblings, and aunts and uncles who died before the deceased stand in the same degree as their parents would have done.[1546]

## §2. Acquisition of the Estate

*603.* It is the duty of the personal representative(s) to 'collect and get in the real and personal estate of the deceased and administer it according to law'.[1547] The entire real and personal estate of the deceased will devolve on to the personal representative(s),[1548] but action may be needed to ensure payment of debts owed to the deceased or to carry on any cause of action vested in the deceased at the time of his or her death.[1549]

---

1543. For full details, *see* R. Kerridge & A.H.R. Brierley, *Parry and Kerridge: The Law of Succession* Ch. 17 (12th ed., Sweet & Maxwell 2009).
1544. *Administration of Estates Act* 1925, s. 7(1).
1545. For the details *see Non-contentious Probate Rules* 1987, S.I. 1987/2024, r. 20.
1546. *Non-contentious Probate Rules* 1987, S.I. 1987/2024, r. 22.
1547. *Administration of Estates Act* 1925, s. 25(a), as amended by the *Administration of Estates Act* 1971.
1548. *Ibid.*, s. 1(1).
1549. *See* the *Law Reform (Miscellaneous Provisions) Act* 1934, s. 1(1).

It may be necessary for the personal representatives to realize the assets of the deceased in order to carry out the administration of the estate. Personal representatives accordingly have extensive powers to sell, mortgage or lease both real and personal property.[1550]

§3.  ADMINISTRATION OF THE ESTATE

*604.*  Funeral and testamentary expenses are payable out of the estate of the deceased (assuming it to be solvent), as are any debts owed by the deceased.[1551] Special rules apply to insolvent estates.[1552]

The personal representatives are required to distribute the estate to the persons entitled under the will of the deceased or under the intestacy rules, as applicable.

---

1550. *Administration of Estates Act* 1925, s. 39.
1551. *Ibid.*, s. 34(3). The order in which the assets of the deceased should be applied to meet such expenses is set out in *Administration of Estates Act* 1925, Sch. 1, Part II.
1552. *See* the *Administration of Insolvent Estates of Deceased Persons Order* 1986 S.I. 1986/1999, as amended by the *Administration of Insolvent Estates of Deceased Persons (Amendment) Order* 2002, S.I. 2002/1309.

# Selected Bibliography

§1. Books

Bainham, A. & S. Gilmore. *Children: The Modern Law*. 4th ed. Bristol: Jordan Publishing, 2013.

Bainham, A., et al. (eds). *Children and Their Families: Contact, Rights and Welfare*. Oxford: Hart, 2003.

Bridgeman, J., H. Keating & C. Lind (eds). *Regulating Family Responsibilities*. Farnham: Ashgate, 2011.

Bridgeman, J., H. Keating & C. Lind (eds). *Taking Responsibility, Law and the Changing Family*. Farnham: Ashgate, 2010.

Choudhry, S. & J. Herring. *European Human Rights and Family Law*. Oxford: Hart, 2010.

Clarkson, C.M.V. & J. Hill. *The Conflict of Laws*. 4th ed. Oxford: Oxford University Press, 2011.

Cretney, S. *Family Law in the Twentieth Century: A History*. Oxford: Oxford University Press, 2003.

Cretney, S. *Same Sex Relationships: From 'Odious Crime' to 'Gay Marriage'*. Oxford: Oxford University Press, 2006.

Diduck, A. *Law's Families*. London: Butterworths, 2003.

Douglas, G. *An Introduction to Family Law*. 2nd ed. Oxford: Oxford University Press, 2004.

Douglas, G. & N. Lowe. *The Continuing Evolution of Family Law*. Bristol: Family Law, 2009.

Eekelaar, J. *Family Law and Personal Life*. Oxford: Oxford University Press, 2006.

Eekelaar, J., M. Maclean & S. Beinart. *Family Lawyers: The Divorce Work of Solicitors*. Oxford: Hart, 2003.

Eekelaar, J. & M. Maclean, *Family Justice: The Work of Family Judges in Uncertain Times*. Oxford: Hart, 2013.

Ebtehaj, F., B. Lindley & M. Richards (eds). *Kinship Matters*. Oxford: Hart, 2006.

Fortin, J. *Children's Rights and the Developing Law*. 3rd ed. Cambridge: Cambridge University Press, 2009.

George, R. *Ideas and Debates in Family Law*. Oxford: Hart, 2012.

Gilmore, S. & L. Glennon. *Hayes and Williams' Family Law*. 4th ed. Oxford: Oxford University Press, 2014.

Gilmore, S., J. Herring & R. Probert (eds). *Landmark Cases in Family Law*. 2nd ed. Oxford: Hart, 2015.

## Selected Bibliography

Graveson, R.H. & F.R. Crane. *A Century of Family Law*. London: Sweet & Maxwell, 1957.

Harris-Short, S., J. Miles and R. George. *Family Law: Text, Cases and Materials*. 3rd ed. Oxford: Oxford University Press, 2015.

Herring, J. *Family Law*. 7th ed. Harlow: Pearson Education Limited, 2015.

Kerridge, R. & A.H.R. Brierley. *Parry and Kerridge: The Law of Succession*. 12th ed. London: Sweet & Maxwell, 2009.

Lowe, N. & G. Douglas. *Bromley's Family Law*. 11th ed. Oxford: Oxford University Press, 2015.

Maclean, M. & Eekelaar J. *Managing Family Justice in Diverse Societies*. Oxford: Hart, 2013.

Maclean, M & J. Kurczewski. *Making Family Law: A Socio Legal Account of Legislative Process in England and Wales, 1985 to 2010*. Oxford: Hart, 2011.

Masson, J., R. Bailey-Harris & R. Probert. *Cretney's Principles of Family Law*. 8th ed. London: Sweet & Maxwell, 2008.

Miles, J. & R. Probert (eds). *Sharing Lives, Dividing Assets*. Oxford: Hart, 2009.

Miles, J., P. Mody and R. Probert (eds). *Marriage Rites and Rights*. Oxford: Hart, 2015.

Murphy, J. *International Dimensions in Family Law*. Manchester: Manchester University Press, 2005.

Probert, R. (eds). *Family Life and the Law: Under One Roof*. Aldershot: Ashgate, 2007.

Probert, R. & C. Barton (eds). *Fifty Years in Family Law: Essays for Stephen Cretney*. Antwerp/Cambridge: Intersentia, 2012.

Probert, R. & M. Harding, *Cretney and Probert's Family Law*. 9th ed. London: Sweet & Maxwell, 2015.

Probert, R., S. Gilmore & J. Herring (eds). *Responsible Parents and Parental Responsibility*. Oxford: Hart, 2009.

Sawyer, C. & M. Spero. *Succession, Wills and Probate*. 3rd ed. Abingdon: Routledge, 2015.

Wood, H., et al. *Cohabitation: Law, Practice and Precedents*. 6th ed. Bristol: Family Law, 2015.

## §2. ARTICLES

Bailey-Harris, R. 'The Paradoxes of Principle and Pragmatism: Ancillary Relief in England and Wales'. *International Journal of Law Policy and the Family* 19, no. 2 (December 2005): 229.

Barlow, A. 'Is Modern Marriage a Bargain? Exploring Perceptions of Prenuptial Agreements in England and Wales'. *Child and Family Law Quarterly* 24, no. 3 (2012): 304.

Bendall, C. 'Some Are More "Equal" than Others: Heteronormativity in the Post-*White* Era of Financial Remedies'. *Journal of Social Welfare and Family Law* 36, no. 3 (2014): 260.

Challinor, E. 'Debunking the Myth of Secret Trusts'. *Conveyancer and Property Lawyer* (November/December 2005): 492.

Chan, W. 'Cohabitation, Civil Partnership, Marriage and the Equal Sharing Principle'. *Legal Studies* 33, no. 1 (2013): 46.

Chau, P.L. & J. Herring. 'Defining, Assigning and Designing Sex'. *International Journal of Law Policy and the Family* 16, no. 3 (December 2002): 327.

Choudhry, S. & H. Fenwick. 'Taking the Rights of Parents and Children Seriously: Confronting the Welfare Principle under the Human Rights Act'. *Oxford Journal of Legal Studies* 25, no. 3 (2005): 453.

Cooke, E. 'Children and Real Property – Trusts, Interests and Considerations'. *Family Law* (June 1998): 349.

Cooke, E. 'Wives, Widows and Wicked Step-Mothers: A Brief Examination of Spousal Entitlement on Intestacy'. *Child and Family Law Quarterly* 21, no. 4 (2009): 423.

Cownie, F. & A. Bradney. 'Divided Justice, Different Voices: Inheritance and Family Provision'. *Legal Studies* 23, no. 4 (November 2003): 566.

Cretney, S. 'Community of Property Imposed By Judicial Decision'. *Law Quarterly Review* 119 (July 2003): 349.

Cretney, S. 'The Family and The Law – Status or Contract?'. *Child and Family Law Quarterly* 15, no. 4 (2003): 403.

Cretney, S. 'The Forfeiture Act 1982: The Private Member's Bill as an Instrument of Law Reform'. *Oxford Journal of Legal Studies* 10, no. 3 (Autumn 1990): 289.

Diduck, A. 'Ancillary Relief: Complicating the Search for Principle'. *Journal of Law and Society* 38, no. 2 (2011): 272.

Douglas, G. *'Re J (Leave to Issue Application for Residence Order)* – Recognising Grandparents' Concern or Controlling their Interference?' *Child and Family Law Quarterly* 15, no. 1 (2003): 103.

Douglas, G. & A. Perry. 'How Parents Cope Financially on Separation and Divorce – Implications for the Future of Ancillary Relief'. *Child and Family Law Quarterly* 13, no. 1 (2001): 51.

Douglas, G., J. Pearce & H. Woodward. 'Cohabitants, Property and the Law: A Study of Injustice'. *Modern Law Review* 72, no. 1 (2009): 24.

Eekelaar, J. 'Beyond the Welfare Principle'. *Child and Family Law Quarterly* 14, no. 3 (2002): 237.

Eekelaar, J. 'Parental Responsibility: State of Nature or Nature of the State'. *Journal of Social Welfare and Family Law* 1 (1991): 37.

Eekelaar, J. 'Property and Financial Settlements on Divorce: Sharing and Compensating'. *Family Law* 36 (September 2006): 754.

Fenwick, H. 'Clashing Rights, the Welfare of the Child and the Human Rights Act'. *Modern Law Review* 67, no. 6 (November 2004): 889.

Fox, L. 'Reforming Family Property – Comparisons, Compromises and Common Dimensions'. *Child and Family Law Quarterly* 15, no. 1 (2003).

Freeman, M. 'The Best Interests of the Child? Is the Best Interests of the Child in the Best Interests of Children?'. *International Journal of Law Policy and the Family* 11, no. 3 (1997): 360.

Gaffney-Rhys, R. 'Same-Sex Marriage but Not Mixed-Sex Partnerships: Should the Civil Partnership Act 2004 Be Extended to Opposite Sex Couples?'. *Child and Family Law Quarterly* 26, no. 2 (2014).

## Selected Bibliography

Gaffney-Rhys, R. 'The Law Relating to Affinity after *B and L v. UK*'. *Family Law* 35 (2005): 955.

George, R. 'Practitioners' Views on Children's Welfare in Relocation Disputes: Comparing Approaches in England and New Zealand'. *Child and Family Law Quarterly* 23, no. 2 (2011): 178.

Gill, K. & A. Van Engeland, 'Criminalization or 'Multiculturalism without Culture'? Comparing British and French approaches to tackling forced marriage'. *Journal of Social Welfare and Family Law* 36, no. 3 (2014): 241.

Gilmore, S. 'Court Decision Making in Shared Residence Order Cases: A Critical Examination'. *Child and Family Law Quarterly* 18, no. 4 (2006): 478.

Gilmore, S. 'Parental Responsibility and the Unmarried Father – A New Dimension to the Debate'. *Child and Family Law Quarterly* 15, no. 1 (2003): 21.

Glennon, L. 'Obligations between Adult Partners: Moving from Form to Function?'. *International Journal of Law Policy and the Family* 22, no. 1 (April 2008): 22.

Glister, J. 'Section 199 of the Equality Act 2010: How Not to Abolish the Presumption of Advancement'. *Modern Law Review* 73 (2010): 807.

Guest, A.G. 'Family Provision and the Legitima Portio'. *Law Quarterly Review* 73, no. 1 (January 1957): 74.

Hale, B. 'Equality and Autonomy in Family Law'. *Journal of Social Welfare and Family Law* 33, no. 1 (2011): 3.

Hale, B. 'Families and the Law: The Forgotten International Dimension'. *Child and Family Law Quarterly* 21, no. 4 (2009): 413.

Harding, M. 'The Harmonisation of Private International Law in Europe: Taking the Character Out of Family Law?'. *Journal of Private International Law* 7, no. 1 (2011): 203.

Harris, P.G. & R.H. George. 'Parental Responsibility and Shared Residence Orders: Parliamentary Intentions and Judicial Interpretations'. *Child and Family Law Quarterly* 22, no. 2 (2010): 151.

Harris-Short, S. 'Family Law and The Human Rights Act: Judicial Restraint or Revolution?'. *Child and Family Law Quarterly* 17, no. 3 (2005): 329.

Haskey, J. 'Cohabitation in Great Britain: Past, Present and Future Trends – And Attitudes'. *Population Trends* 103 (Spring 2001): 4.

Haskey, J. 'Trends in Marriage and Divorce in England and Wales: 1837–1987'. *Population Trends* 48 (Summer 1987): 11.

Hasson, E. 'Wedded to "Fault": The Legal Regulation of Divorce and Relationship Breakdown'. *Legal Studies* 26, no. 2 (June 2006): 267.

Hayes, M. 'Relocation Cases: Is The Court of Appeal Applying the Correct Principles?' *Child and Family Law Quarterly* 18, no. 3 (2006): 351.

Herring, J. 'Farewell Welfare?'. *Journal of Social Welfare and Family Law* 27, no. 2 (July 2005): 159.

Herring, J. & R. Taylor. 'Relocating Relocation'. *Child and Family Law Quarterly* 18, no. 4 (2006): 517.

Kaganas, F. 'Grandparents' Rights and Grandparents' Campaigns'. *Child and Family Law Quarterly* 19, no. 1 (2007): 17.

Kaganas, F. 'Regulating Emotion: Judging Contact Disputes'. *Child and Family Law Quarterly* 23, no. 1 (2011): 63.

Kiernan, K. & K. Smith. 'Unmarried Parenthood: New Insights from the Millennium Cohort Study'. *Population Trends* 114 (Winter 2003): 26.

Lowe, N. 'The Allocation of Parental Rights and Responsibilities – The Position in England and Wales'. *Family Law Quarterly* 39, no. 2 (Summer 2005) 267.

McGlynn, C. 'The Europeanization of Family Law'. *Child and Family Law Quarterly* 13, no. 1 (2001): 35.

Mee, J. 'Proprietary Estoppel and Inheritance: "Enough Is Enough?"' *Conveyancer and Property Lawyer*, no. 4 (2013): 280.

Miles, J. '*Charman v. Charman* (No. 4) – Making Sense of Need, Compensation and Equal Sharing after Miller/McFarlane'. *Child and Family Law Quarterly* 20, no. 3 (2008): 378.

Miles, J. 'Marriage and Divorce in the Supreme Court and the Law Commission: For Love or Money?'. *Modern Law Review* 74, no. 1 (2011): 430.

Miller, G. 'Dependants, Cohabitants and Family Provision'. *Private Client Business* 5 (2000): 305.

Miller, G. 'Provision for Adult Children under the Inheritance (Provision for Family and Dependants) Act 1975'. *Conveyancer and Property Lawyer* (January/February 1995): 22.

Miller, G. 'Provision for a Surviving Spouse'. *Private Client Business* 2 (2007): 144.

Morgan, J. 'The Child As Tenant: Rights and Responsibilities'. In *Studies in Property Law Vol II*, edited by E. Cooke. Oxford: Hart, 2003.

Munby, J. 'Families Old and New – The Family and Article 8'. *Child and Family Law Quarterly* 17, no. 4 (2005): 487.

Newnham, A. 'Shared Residence: Lessons from Sweden'. *Child and Family Law Quarterly* 23, no. 2 (2011): 251.

Northover, A. & G. Dennison. 'Genetic Testing and the Impact on the Family'. *Family Law* 32 (October 2002): 752.

Potter, G. & C. Williams. 'Parental Responsibility and the Duty to Consult – The Public's View'. *Child and Family Law Quarterly* 17, no. 2 (2005): 207.

Probert, R. '*Sutton v. Mishcon de Reya and Gawor & Co: Cohabitation Contracts and Swedish Sex Slaves*'. *Child and Family Law Quarterly* 16, no. 4 (2004): 453.

Probert, R. 'Common Law Marriage: Myths and Misunderstandings'. *Child and Family Law Quarterly* 20, no. 1 (2008): 1.

Probert, R. 'The Evolving Concept of "Non-marriage"'. *Child and Family Law Quarterly* 25, no. 3 (2013): 314.

Reece, H. '"Bright Line Rules May Be Appropriate in Some Cases, but Not Where the Object Is to Promote the Welfare of the Child": Barring in the Best Interests of the Child?'. *Child and Family Law Quarterly* 22, no. 4 (2010): 422.

Reece, H. 'The Paramountcy Principle: Consensus or Conflict'. *Current Legal Problems* 49, no. 2 (1996): 267.

Sawyer, C. 'The Child Is Not a Person: Family Law and Other Legal Cultures'. *Journal of Social Welfare and Family Law* 28, no. 1 (March 2006): 1.

Scherpe, J. 'A Comparative Overview of the Treatment of Non-matrimonial Assets, Indexation and Value Increases'. *Child and Family Law Quarterly* 25, no. 1 (2013): 61.

## Selected Bibliography

Sheldon, S. 'From "Absent Objects of Blame" to "Fathers Who Want to Take Responsibility": Reforming Birth Registration Law'. *Journal of Social Welfare and Family Law* 31, no. 4 (2009): 373.

Smith, L. 'Clashing Symbols? Reconciling Support for Fathers and Fatherless Families After the Human Fertilisation and Embryology Act 2008'. *Child and Family Law Quarterly* 22, no. 1 (2010): 46.

Trinder, L. 'Shared Residence: A Review of Recent Research Evidence'. *Child and Family Law Quarterly* 22, no. 4 (2010): 475.

Wasoff, F. 'Public Attitudes and Law Reform: Extending the Legal Framework for Child Contact to Unmarried Fathers, Grandparents and Step-Parents?'. *Journal of Social Welfare and Family Law* 31, no. 2 (2009): 159.

Williams, J. 'Effective Government Structures for Children? The UK's Four Children's Commissioners'. *Child and Family Law Quarterly* 17, no. 1 (2005): 37.

# Index

# Index

# Index

**Index**

Lightning Source UK Ltd.
Milton Keynes UK
UKHW022026231121
394455UK00005B/336